READING THE BIBLE AFTER
CHRISTENDOM

Dedicated to Steve and Nettie Matthews

READING THE BIBLE AFTER CHRISTENDOM

Lloyd Pietersen

Paternoster:
thinking faith

Copyright © 2011

17 16 15 14 13 12 11   7 6 5 4 3 2 1

First published in 2011 by Paternoster
Paternoster is an imprint of Authentic Media Limited
Presley Way, Crownhill, Milton Keynes, MK8 0ES
www.authenticmedia.co.uk

British Library Cataloguing in Publication Data

A catalogue record for this book is available from
the British Library

ISBN 978-1-84227-735-5

Cover design by Philip Miles
Printed and bound in Great Britain by Bell and Bain, Glasgow

Contents

Contents

Series Preface

Many Christians have focused on the challenges of postmodernity in recent years, but most have neglected the seismic shifts that have taken place with the disintegration of a nominally Christian society. *After Christendom* is an exciting new series of books exploring the implications of the demise of Christendom and the challenges facing a church now living on the margins of Western society.

Post-Christendom, the first volume in the series, investigated the Christendom legacy and raised issues that are further explored in the books that follow. The authors of this series, who write from within the Anabaptist tradition, see the current challenges facing the church not as the loss of a golden age but as opportunities to recover a more biblical and more Christian way of being God's people in God's world. The series addresses a wide range of issues, such as social and political engagement, how we read Scripture, peace and violence, mission, worship, and the shape and ethos of church after Christendom.

These books are not intended to be the last word on the subjects they address, but an invitation to discussion and further exploration. One way to engage in this discussion is via the After Christendom Forum hosted by the Anabaptist Network: {www.postchristendom.com}

Acknowledgements

This book could not have been written without the input and support of many people. First, I must thank my friends and colleagues in the Anabaptist Network Steering Group in whose company the idea for this book was first conceived and who have patiently listened to my explanations of the various potential configurations of the book. I must single out Stuart Murray who has read the whole manuscript and offered numerous helpful suggestions and is responsible for the vast majority of the material in Chapter 4. Special thanks are due too to Alan and Eleanor Kreider who also read most of the manuscript and whose wisdom and friendship have always been highly valued.

My colleagues at the Research Centre for the Bible and Spirituality at the University of Gloucestershire have been very supportive and some of them have heard and commented on portions of Chapter 13. A big thank you to Dee Carter, Andrew Lincoln, Gordon McConville, Melissa Raphael-Levine, Shelley Saguaro and Hilary Weeks.

Grateful thanks are due to everyone at Paternoster, particularly Robin Parry, for the professional way in which they have brought the manuscript to successful completion and for their patience in waiting for the inevitably missed deadlines.

Grateful thanks too to Noel Moules for his friendship over the years and for the opportunity to teach on Workshop and to lead Advanced Workshop. Teaching Workshop students over many years has undoubtedly contributed to Part 2 of this book. I am also very grateful to two cohorts of Advanced Workshop students who have stretched me with their articulate, intelligent questions in hermeneutics classes. Many thanks too to my team:

Linda Csernus, Sue Haslehurst, and Cherryl Hunt; without their love and support Advanced Workshop would not have happened. My family and friends have sustained me many times when I thought I would never finish. The love and support of my wife, Sheila, is more precious to me than words could ever convey. She too read portions of the manuscript and commented carefully and with great insight. My children, Beth, Keren, Kez, and Jed, have grown up with Dad's endless hours in the study and I love them dearly. Jed has also read most of the manuscript and commented astutely with a historian's eye. Claire Lacey, Jill Ogilvy, Simon Scott, and Steve Webster-Green, as well as Sheila, my fellow members of Bristol Peace Church, have been a constant source of wonderful, playful, and agonizing communal engagement with the biblical texts. Jane and Roger Griffiths have provided fantastic hospitality and great holidays away from it all. A huge debt of gratitude is due in particular to four very special friends whose love and support have meant so much to me over a difficult period: Helen Bond, Tierney Fox, Kath Gardner-Graham, and Bridget Gilfillan Upton. Finally, Steve and Nettie Matthews have been a constant source of love, encouragement and support. They have truly proved themselves again and again to be faithful friends over the years and to them this book is gratefully dedicated.

Foreword

Lloyd Pietersen has written an important and challenging book to which sustained attention must be paid. He begins with a recognition that biblical interpreters in the West (and the whole church) now occupy a new cultural situation that requires a renovation of many assumptions and practices, not least the way in which Scripture is read and interpreted. His use of the term "Christendom" points both to the challenge and to the seductions to which the church, over time, has succumbed. The book begins with a stunning historical summary of the establishment of Christendom that was to enthrall the imagination of the church for many centuries . . . until now. Pietersen can see that decisions made by Constantine within the scope of six quick days settled the creedal, canonical, and political matrix of the church for all time to come . . . until now. The outcome was to make the church the handmaid of imperial power and to hand interpretation over to the sociopolitical elites. While the matter of political influence and entitlement is abundantly clear, what matters for this book is the doctrinal Gestalt of creation-sin-redemption that came to dominate and control the church's interpretation of Scripture. That grid, with its accent on "the fall," lined out human persons and human community as powerless, and handed authority over the forgiveness of sin to the imperial church. Pietersen marks the way in which this theological grid has been everywhere accepted without serious critical reservation.

It is a welcome breath of fresh air that Pietersen invites the reader to inhale when he moves to the interpretive practice of the sixteenth century. While the appeal to authority shifted in the interpretation of Scripture in the sixteenth century, in fact the "magisterial" reformation of Luther and Calvin did not challenge the theological grid or the controlling political alliance that came with it, even if Calvin moved toward the new, emerging mercantile class.

It was, so Pietersen sees clearly, the daring and defiant Anabaptist tradition of the sixteenth century that moved outside the accepted elites' assumptions and proposed the reading of Scripture outside the dominant doctrinal pattern. This was, already in the sixteenth century, a reading from the margin, even though there was at the time very little room outside the church-state hegemony. Pietersen advances the conviction that this marginal reading, outside the assumptions of Constantinian control, is the wave of the future.

Of course others have said that much. But Pietersen has done astonishing homework in order to walk the reader, book by book, through the Bible, noticing what can be seen from the margin, much of which is missed in hegemonic reading. This reading recognizes that the Bible itself is complex, thick, and multivoiced in a way that resists theological reductionism, the kind nurtured by the administration of Constantine.

Pietersen shows that when one steps outside the doctrinal consensus and its political spin-offs one sees that the Bible cannot be managed as it has been in Christendom. Thus the contrast between Constantinian reading and reading from the margin issues in important outcomes for the contemporary practice of the Bible. Pietersen shows how this latter reading is characteristically practical and pragmatic, vigorously bent toward the ethical, and summoning to missional urgency and daring.

It is axiomatic that within Western Christianity there is no real energy or need for mission . . . beyond benighted Africa! The lack of such need is enacted in infant baptism that permits everyone to be born into faith. But when the Bible is seen to be a critical alternative to every hegemonic arrangement, then the recovery of missional reading and missional energy outside the framework of the established West becomes urgent and viable.

In this shrewd book many lines of critical freshness converge. The reader will come to see that we have very raw rereading to do, based on intense unlearning of the world formed in those six imperial days. While Pietersen does not say so, it is worth considering the contrast between the six days' work of Constantine and the six-day job of the Creator in Genesis 1. Constantine's six days had the effect of squelching newness and controlling the administration of well-being. By contrast the "original" six-day deal was for limitless fruitfulness.

Pietersen's book is a pedagogical project and I have learned much from it. At the same time, it is a passionate pastoral summons to the church to recover the world bespoken in the text and entrusted to us. Given the highly visible and unmistakable failure of the Constantinian system, this fresh reading may be just what is required, not simply to revive the church but to mediate the moral energy needed for a new society. Much of this has long been known among faithful Mennonites, the circle from which this book arises. But beyond Mennonites, this book is an important invitation to critique old categories of power and truth, and to read again, and so to be empowered for a different life in the world.

Walter Brueggemann
Columbia Theological Seminary
December 1, 2009

1

Introduction

A quote

> In the Bullshit Department, a businessman can't hold a candle to a
> clergyman. 'Cause I gotta tell you the truth, folks. When it comes
> to bullshit, big-time, major league bullshit, you have to stand in
> awe of the all-time champion of false promises and exaggerated
> claims: religion. No contest. No contest. Religion. Religion easily
> has the greatest bullshit story ever told.
> Think about it. Religion has actually convinced people that
> there's an invisible man – living in the sky – who watches every-
> thing you do, every minute of every day. And the invisible man
> has a special list of ten things he does not want you to do. And if
> you do any of these ten things, he has a special place, full of fire
> and smoke and burning and torture and anguish, where he will
> send you to live and suffer and burn and choke and scream and
> cry forever and ever 'til the end of time!
> But he loves you.
> He loves you, and he needs money.[1]

A scenario

A young, feminist woman is persuaded by her friends, after
many hours of conversation, to attend their local church session.
The reading for that service is taken from 1 Timothy 2:8–15.

> I desire, then, that in every place the men should pray, lifting up
> holy hands without anger or argument; also that the women

should dress themselves modestly and decently in suitable clothing, not with their hair braided, or with gold, pearls, or expensive
clothes, but with good works, as is proper for women who profess
reverence for God. Let a woman learn in silence with full submission. I permit no woman to teach or to have authority over a man;
she is to keep silent. For Adam was formed first, then Eve; and
Adam was not deceived, but the woman was deceived and
became a transgressor. Yet she will be saved through childbearing,
provided they continue in faith and love and holiness, with mod-
esty.[2]

After being reassured by her friends that this was really in the
Bible, she storms out of the church reinforced in her view that the
teaching of the church is responsible for the whole history of
misogyny in the West.

The Bible and Christendom

In the quote, taken from a well-known social networking website,
we have in a nutshell the problems inherent in attempting to read
the Bible after Christendom. This is clearly a problem affecting the
West, which has inherited the legacy of Christendom. In this environment clergy are the greatest purveyors of "bullshit" (more so
than business people!) and Christianity (which is equated with
"religion") tells the story of an invisible (male) God who issues ten
commandments concerning inappropriate behavior and punishes
with eternal, conscious torment those who engage in such behavior. However, somehow this God loves us, yet needs our money!
The writer knows something about the Bible (the notion of an
invisible God, the Ten Commandments, apparent references in the
New Testament to eternal damnation and that God is love), yet is
unable to relate these accounts into any coherent story, preferring
instead to label the whole thing as simply "bullshit". The final
comment is particularly telling – Christianity is perceived as
inevitably associated with wealth.

In the scenario, which although fictitious is easily imagined,
the young feminist instinctively associates the Bible with misogyny and this is borne out for her first-hand when she actually

encounters a biblical text for the first time. After Christendom, the Bible still retains some of its cultural power but it is rarely read and the understandings of the Bible that emerge outside the church are inevitably filtered through the inheritance of centuries of Christendom.

There has been a plethora of books about reading the Bible in recent years.[3] I have learned much from these books as will be apparent in what follows. However, the thesis of this book is that the alliance between church and state from the second half of the fourth century onwards has resulted in ways of reading the Bible fundamentally alien to that of the earliest church.[4] The current situation in the West, in which that alliance is increasingly questioned and the church is correspondingly progressively more marginalized, suggests that fresh ways of reading the Bible in the contemporary context may surprisingly have deep resonances with the early church.

Christendom defined

Christians have a complex relationship with the Bible. All Christians regard the Bible as somehow significant for faith and conduct but exactly what that significance is remains disputed. For some Protestants, especially those of a conservative persuasion, the Bible is central and authoritative whereas the Roman Catholic and Orthodox Churches emphasize the authority of church tradition as well as scripture. However, common to the main traditions of Christianity in the West is the fact that the Bible has been read for centuries in the context of Christendom. Craig Carter defines Christendom in the following way:

> Christendom is the concept of Western civilization as having a religious arm (the church) and a secular arm (civil government), both of which are united in their adherence to Christian faith, which is seen as the so-called soul of Europe or the West. The essence of the idea is the assertion that Western civilization is Christian. Within this Christian civilization, the state and the church have different roles to play, but, since membership in both is coterminous, both can be seen as aspects of one unified reality – Christendom.[5]

Stuart Murray defines the shift to Christendom as follows:[6]

- The adoption of Christianity as the official religion of city, state or Empire.
- Movement of the church from the margins to the centre of society.
- The creation and progressive development of a Christian culture or civilisation.
- The assumption that all citizens (except Jews) were Christian by birth.
- The development of a "sacral society", *corpus Christianum*, where there was no freedom of religion and political power was divinely authenticated.
- The definition of "orthodoxy" as the belief all shared, determined by powerful church leaders with state support.
- Imposition, by legislation and custom, of a supposedly Christian morality on the entire society (though normally Old Testament morality was applied).
- Infant baptism as the symbol of obligatory incorporation into Christian society.
- The defence of Christianity by legal sanctions to restrain heresy, immorality and schism.
- A hierarchical ecclesiastical system based on a diocesan and parish arrangement, analogous to the state hierarchy and buttressed by state support.
- A generic distinction between clergy and laity, and relegation of laity to a largely passive role.
- Two-tier ethics, with higher standards of discipleship ("evangelical counsels") expected of clergy and those in religious orders.
- Sunday as an official holiday and obligatory church attendance, with penalties for non-compliance.
- The requirement of oaths of allegiance and oaths in law courts to encourage truth telling.
- The construction of massive and ornate church buildings and the formation of huge congregations.
- Increased wealth for the church and obligatory tithes to fund the system.
- Division of the globe into "Christendom" and "heathendom" and wars waged in the name of Christ and the church.

- Use of political and military force to impose Christianity, regardless of personal conviction.
- Reliance on the Old Testament, rather than the New, to justify these changes.

In this context whenever the Bible was appealed to by those in authority it was in order to reinforce these fundamental tenets of Christendom and support the status quo. As noted above, often it was the Old Testament that was particularly given precedence.[7] Of course, throughout the history of Christendom, there have been other voices outside the mainstream who have appealed to the Bible in order to critique Christendom. However, these dissenting traditions have always been marginalized and at times persecuted by those with a vested interest in maintaining the status quo.[8]

Post-Christendom

Murray's seminal work documents the shift taking place in the West from Christendom to post-Christendom. He notes the following transitions in this shift:

- The Christian story and churches have moved from the center to the margins.
- Christians are now a minority.
- Christians therefore no longer feel at home in the dominant culture.
- Christians no longer enjoy automatic privileges but find themselves as one community among many in a plural society.
- The church no longer exercises control over society but instead Christians can exercise influence only through faithful witness to the Christian story and its implications.
- The emphasis is now no longer on maintaining the status quo but on mission in a contested environment.
- Churches can no longer operate mainly in institutional mode but must learn to operate once again as part of a movement.

In this changing context it can no longer be assumed that ordinary people know the contents of the Bible or even the basic outline of the Christian story. Christians reading the Bible after Christendom will need to operate with a very different mindset both to sustain the church and to engage with culture. Murray suggests that there are three primary moves that need to be made in reading the Bible in this fresh environment. The first is that Christendom hermeneutics needs to be disavowed. This involves employing a hermeneutic of suspicion which critically scrutinizes long-established readings of Scripture. The second is to employ fresh angles of vision with which to approach biblical texts. Finally, a hermeneutic of retrieval is employed so that biblical texts can be read in ways which resonate with our changing context.[10]

In this book I seek to follow Murray's suggestion. The first part, which provides a historical overview, critically examines the Christendom model by providing a summary of biblical interpretation before Christendom (Chapter 2), an analysis of the effect Constantine had on subsequent reading of the Bible (Chapter 3), and a detailed examination of an alternative approach which sought to subvert Christendom in both its Catholic and Protestant forms – namely that of the sixteenth-century Anabaptists (Chapter 4).

I then turn in Part 2 to reading the whole Bible. In Chapter 5 I suggest that Jesus should be central to any *Christian* biblical interpretation. In this chapter I suggest fresh angles of vision with which to approach biblical texts – Jesus as prophet, pastor, and poet – rather than the traditional "offices" of prophet, priest, and king. This leads to a summary of the whole Bible in the rest of Part 2 in Chapters 6 to 12 focusing on an introduction to the overall script (6); the Pentateuch (7); the Historical Books (8); Wisdom literature (9); the Prophets (10); the Gospels and Acts (11); and the Letters and Revelation (12).

In Part 3 I employ a hermeneutics of retrieval to suggest two areas in which the Bible can profitably be read in our contemporary context: spirituality (Chapter 13) and mission (Chapter 14). In the concluding chapter I summarize what has gone before by suggesting that reading the Bible after Christendom is inevitably a reading from the margins and should be done in community in ways that engage with the Bible as prophetic, subversive and sustaining for the Christian journey.

I write as a biblical scholar with a passionate concern for authentic discipleship. As a biblical scholar I am profoundly aware of the shortcomings of this book. At so many points I wanted to explore further and nuance the discussion with even more footnotes than this work already has! I trust that colleagues in the academic world will still find the book useful. On the other hand, as a biblical scholar, I am also conscious that this work will be viewed as too academic by some. At many points I have left the reader to make connections between what I outline in this introduction and in the first part of the book concerning post-Christendom, and the readings of Parts 2 and 3 without making those connections explicit. I hope that in this way readers will be encouraged to use this book together and thereby help one another to make connections as they seek to read the Bible in community. I also recognise that a persistent feature of our post-Christendom context is a degree of biblical illiteracy. I have, therefore, gone into some detail, particularly in the sections on the New Testament, to give some general biblical background as well as specific tools for reading post-Christendom.

I realise that my emphasis on reading the Bible in community can ironically be undermined by my apparent sole authorship of this book! However, as will be apparent from the detailed footnotes, I am indebted to a host of others who have thought considerably about aspects of biblical interpretation. In particular, and in keeping with my conviction that post-Christendom Bible reading should be open to a variety of voices, my debt to Walter Brueggemann is apparent throughout. Brueggemann combines biblical scholarship with a passionate concern for the church and a clear respect for the biblical text as it stands. He comes from a very different tradition from mine but I readily and gratefully acknowledge this debt. Furthermore, Chapter 4 is almost entirely written by Stuart Murray, an expert on Anabaptist hermeneutics, with only some slight editing by me. So in many ways this book is anything but sole-authored!

Part 1

Historical overview

2

Reading the Bible Before Christendom

Introduction

Craig Carter chastises the fourth-century bishops for allowing the emperor to intervene in church affairs. He notes that they had more than adequate resources with which to resist this. In particular, "[t]hey had the life and teachings of Jesus, the Holy Scriptures, and the guidance of the Holy Spirit in understanding how to follow Jesus in these new circumstances."[1] Carter's criticism assumes, therefore, that the Bible was read in a very different way in the first three centuries from how it was read subsequently within Christendom. This chapter consequently summarizes the ways in which the Bible was read by Christians prior to the fourth century.

The New Testament

The New Testament writers themselves reread the Jewish Scriptures in the light of Jesus and, therefore, produce thoroughly christocentric readings.[2] For John, Jesus is the Messiah (1:41) and the one about whom the Law and the Prophets wrote (1:45). John begins with a deliberate echo of the opening of Genesis, but instead of "[i]n the beginning . . . God", John has "[i]n the beginning . . . Word" and Jesus is identified as "the Word became flesh". Furthermore, John concludes with a reference to the Parousia: "until I come" (21:23). Thus John "matches the span of the whole canon".[3] In Matthew, Jesus is the fulfilment of the Law and the Prophets (5:17–20). Matthew presents Jesus as a new Moses with five discourses corresponding to the Pentateuch (5:1 – 7:27; 9:36 – 10:42; 13:1–52; 17:22 – 18:35; 23:1 – 25:46). Matthew's genealogy serves as a bridge between the two Testaments and recapitulates the whole Old Testament story from Abraham onwards. Like John, Matthew closes with a reference to "the end of the age" (28:20). Luke has the risen Jesus demonstrating to the two disciples on the way to Emmaus that all the Scriptures point to him (24:27) and that he is the fulfilment of the Law, the Prophets, and the Psalms (24:44). Luke's genealogy recapitulates the whole Old Testament story. Mark has no equivalent mention of either the Law or the Prophets. However, as Roth has demonstrated, Mark's narrative strategy is to extend the story line of the Law and the Prophets by continuing where the Prophets end with the anticipation of Elijah in Malachi 4:5–6 (cf. Mark 9:11–13).[4]

Paul makes it clear that, for him, the primary advantage of being a Jew is that "Jews were entrusted with the oracles of God" (Rom. 3:1–2). For him, the gospel was "promised beforehand through his prophets in the holy scriptures" (Rom. 1:2) and his understanding of "the righteousness of God" is "attested by the law and the prophets" (Rom. 3:21).

Hebrews recognizes that God spoke in the past through the prophets but has now spoken definitively through Christ (1:1–2); while 1 and 2 Peter speak of the prophets prophesying about salvation in Christ (1 Pet. 1:10–12; 2 Pet. 1:16–19). Finally, Revelation is saturated with allusions to the Jewish Scriptures.

What Francis Watson says of Paul, therefore, is true of the New Testament as a whole: "Paul has no independent interest in the meaning of scripture as such: the meaning of scripture is identical to its significance, and both are to be found in its manifold, direct and indirect testimony to God's saving action in Christ."[5]

First-century Jewish exegesis

The New Testament writers thus creatively meditate on their recent experience of Jesus and reread the Old Testament in the light of this experience. The ways in which the Old Testament is interpreted are in line with standard Jewish interpretation of the time. According to Longenecker Jewish exegesis in the first century can "be classified under four headings: literalist, midrashic, pesher, and allegorical."[6]

(1) *Literalist.* This is where texts were read according to their plain sense. Texts would be quoted or alluded to in a straightforward way. This was particularly true of legal texts. In the New Testament we see this, for example, in Romans 13:9; 1 Corinthians 6:16; Galatians 5:14.

(2) *Midrash.* Various rules of midrashic interpretation sought to examine the text from all angles and thus derive interpretations that are not immediately obvious. Hillel, whose teaching predates the New Testament, had seven rules which were subsequently developed in the second century AD into thirteen and, even later, into thirty-two. Paul, in particular, appears to use all seven of Hillel's rules at different times. Most characteristic is the stringing together of verses on the basis of analogous words or phrases, which corresponds to Hillel's second rule.[7]

(3) *Pesher.* This form of interpretation is found in the Dead Sea Scrolls and is based on the revelation of a mystery along the lines of Daniel 9:24–27. In this way Old Testament texts are actualized for the benefit of the contemporary readers. In the New Testament this can be found particularly in the "this is that" fulfilment motif, for example, Luke 4:16–21; Acts 2:14–21.

(4) *Allegory.* Philo was the primary Jewish allegorist of the first century. This was in keeping with his apologetic concern to vindicate the Jewish Scriptures in the context of Greek philosophy. Allegorical methods of interpretation were popular among philosophically inclined readers of Homer who highlighted the absurdity of reading him at a literal level. Allegory assigns a "spiritual" meaning to the text beyond its literal meaning and various details in the text are given this transferred meaning. In the New Testament, allegory is employed in some of the parables (e.g. Matt. 13:1–23) and by Paul (1 Cor. 9:9–10; Gal. 4:21–31).

To the above the New Testament adds typology, a method which sees parallels between persons and/or events in the Old Testament and their analogous fulfilment in the New Testament, for example, creation and new creation; Adam and Christ (Rom. 5:14); exodus and salvation (1 Cor. 10:6–11). All these approaches serve to place the story of Jesus firmly within biblical salvation history. As Ellis states: "for the New Testament writers faith in Jesus means faith in the story of Jesus, the story of God's redemptive activity in the history of Israel that finds its high-point and fulfilment in Jesus."[8]

However, the New Testament does not offer a monolithic interpretation of the significance of the Jesus story. There is room for differing perspectives in dialogue with one another. The Gospels each tell the story in their own way and John, of course, is quite different from the Synoptic Gospels. Paul and James construe the relationship between faith and works differently and the tension between Paul and the leaders of the church in Jerusalem is never far from the surface – both in Acts and in Paul's letters.

Second and third centuries

Apostolic Fathers

The writings of the Apostolic Fathers are closest in time to the New Testament. It is instructive, therefore, to see how a sample of them read the Bible.[9]

1 Clement

Written around AD 95–97 from Rome to Corinth, 1 Clement is probably the earliest extant Christian document outside the New Testament, although the *Didache*, probably to be dated to early in the second century in its final form, is widely believed to contain much older elements. The book of 1 Clement is full of biblical quotations and allusions. In particular, Clement urges the Corinthian congregation to embrace humility based on the example of Jesus (16.1–17). In the prayer of 59 – 61 many Old Testament references occur and in 12.7 the scarlet cord of Rahab (Josh. 2:18) is seen as a type of Christ's redemption.

Ignatius

Ignatius, bishop of Antioch in Syria, wrote seven letters on his way from Antioch to martyrdom in Rome. The vast majority of scholars date them to the second half of Trajan's reign (AD 110–117). In a significant passage Ignatius refers to those who only regard the Old Testament as Scripture – they refer to the Old Testament as "the archives". Ignatius responds: "for me, the 'archives' are Jesus Christ, the inviolable archives are his cross and death and his resurrection and the faith which comes through him."[10] Just prior to this he appeals to the teaching of Christ. For Ignatius, therefore, the life, death, and resurrection of Jesus clearly form the heart of the Scriptures. In another passage he urges his readers to pay attention to the prophets – the Old Testament is important – but they must pay particular attention to the gospel.[11] As Greer explains: "[w]hat he must mean is that the Hebrew Scriptures have authority only when read in the light of the Christian faith."[12] The early Christians clearly understood Jesus to be the interpretive key to the Bible.

Barnabas

This polemical essay, cast in the form of a letter, is usually dated to the first quarter of the second century. For Barnabas, although the covenant was originally given to Jews, it was immediately taken away from them when Moses broke the stone tablets because of their idolatry. Consequently, everything in the law points forward to Jesus and is not meant to be understood literally. Barnabas, therefore, employs extensive use of midrash and allegory to demonstrate that Christians are the true heirs of God's covenant. Allegory is particularly used to provide Christian interpretations of Old Testament texts. For example, *Barnabas* 9.7–9 states:

> Learn abundantly, therefore, children of love, about everything: Abraham, who first instituted circumcision, looked forward in the spirit to Jesus when he circumcised, having received the teaching of the three letters. For it says: "And Abraham circumcised ten and eight and three hundred men of his household."[13] What, then, is the knowledge that was given to him? Observe that it mentions

the "ten and eight" first, and then after an interval the "three hundred". As for the "ten and eight", the I is ten and the H is eight;[14]
thus you have "Jesus". And because the cross, which is shaped like
the T, was destined to convey grace, it mentions also the "three
hundred". So he reveals Jesus in the two letters, and the cross in
the other one. He who placed within us the implanted gift of his
covenant understands. No one has ever learned from me a more
reliable word, but I know that you are worthy of it.

As well as the apostolic fathers, a number of key figures in the
second and third centuries also make significant statements
about the Bible. Four are particularly worthy of mention: Justin
Martyr, Irenaeus, Tertullian, and Origen.

Justin Martyr

For Justin (ca. 110–65) the incarnation of Christ is the key to unlock-
ing the real meaning of the Old Testament (*Dial.* 100.2). He regards
Old Testament persons and events as types of Christ and the church
but, unlike Barnabas, does not employ allegory to make this point.
He regularly reads the Old Testament christologically and, in dialogue with Trypho (a Jew), he attributes the latter's lack of understanding of these texts to spiritual blindness. Justin regards the
church as the true spiritual Israel (*Dial.* 11). His treatment of Old
Testament law is quite sophisticated and anticipates later Christian
thought on the subject. Justin divides the law into two categories:
the moral law (although he does not use this term) which involves
worship and holy living – this he regards as continuing to be valid
– and the ritual or ceremonial law. He divides the latter into two
parts. One he considers to be prophetic and, by the use of typology,
points to Christ; the other was given to the Jews precisely because
of their hardness of heart and consists of such things as literal cir-
cumcision, special days, sacrifices, and the various food and purity
laws. These are no longer binding for Christians.

Irenaeus

For Irenaeus (ca. 135 – ca. 202), "[t]he Bible contains the complete
stock and in addition the reliable standard of the truth."[15] It is

important to know the whole Bible to avoid error. "'You may freely eat of every tree of the garden,' that is, eat from every Scripture of the Lord; but you shall not eat with an uplifted mind, nor touch any heretical discord."[16] Irenaeus clearly teaches the perspicuity of Scripture: "Since, therefore, the entire Scriptures, the prophets, and the Gospels, can be clearly, unambiguously, and harmoniously understood by all, although all do not believe them."[17] He articulates this view of the unity between the Old and New Testaments in the face of the considerable gnostic threat of his day. In the light of this threat he is the first to advocate a "rule of faith": the truth is safeguarded by authentic apostolic tradition preserved and handed down by authorized leaders of the church.[18]

Tertullian

Tertullian (ca. 155/160 – ca. 225) famously rejected the influence of Greek philosophy on biblical interpretation: "What has Jerusalem to do with Athens, the Church with the Academy, the Christian with the heretic?"[19] In support of this statement he specifically cites Colossians 2:8 "[s]ee to it that no one takes you captive through philosophy and empty deceit." He generally rejects allegory while accepting traditional typology. However, he does recognize that Jesus himself made use of allegory. At the end of the day Tertullian, like Irenaeus, resorts to the rule of faith and the principle of authority.

Origen

Origen (ca. 185–253) was raised in a wealthy Christian family and his father was martyred during the reign of Septimus Severus (193–211), leaving the family destitute. He is famous both for his allegorical interpretation of Scripture and for advocating the notion of *apokatastasis* – God's universal reconciliation of all, including Satan, to himself. As a result he has often been dismissed in the past. However, he passionately believed in the divine inspiration of all Scripture and this led him to the view that every text has both a literal and spiritual meaning. In fact he developed a hermeneutical theory of the threefold sense of

Scripture. He was concerned to establish the literal sense and thus concentrated on philology. He produced the "Hexapla" in which the Hebrew text, a transliteration of the Hebrew into Greek and the translations of Aquila, Symmachus, the Septuagint, and Theodosius were arranged in six adjacent columns. However, Origen recognized that many texts raised problems at the literal level, as both the gnostics and Marcion had pointed out. Far from rejecting the God of the Old Testament or treating him as inferior to the God of the New Testament, Origen suggested that these difficulties were deliberately placed in the text to lead readers to a deeper, spiritual meaning. For Origen the three senses of Scripture correspond to body, soul, and spirit. The literal sense provides clarity in areas that all Christians need to understand. The second sense is open to Christians who have obtained wisdom and knowledge, whereas the third sense is only available to those who are mature (1 Cor. 2:6–7).

The rule of faith

As stated above, Irenaeus was the first to explicitly articulate a rule of faith to combat the claims of those he considered heretical. He insisted that this rule of faith could be traced back from his own time to the original apostles through a clear succession of bishops.

> It is within the power of all, therefore, in every Church, who may wish to see the truth, to contemplate clearly the tradition of the apostles manifested throughout the whole world; and we are in a position to reckon up those who were by the apostles instituted bishops in the Churches, and [to demonstrate] the succession of these men to our own times; those who neither taught nor knew of anything like what these [heretics] rave about. For if the apostles had known hidden mysteries, which they were in the habit of imparting to "the perfect" apart and privily from the rest, they would have delivered them especially to those to whom they were also committing the Churches themselves.[20]

The rule of faith, although expressing the fundamental beliefs of the church, was essentially narrative in form, running from creation to the prophets (Old Testament) to the story of Jesus through to consummation.

> The Church, though dispersed throughout the whole world, even to the ends of the earth, has received from the apostles and their disciples this faith: [She believes] in one God, the Father Almighty, Maker of heaven, and earth, and the sea, and all things that are in them; and in one Christ Jesus, the Son of God, who became incarnate for our salvation; and in the Holy Spirit, who proclaimed through the prophets the dispensations of God, and the advents, and the birth from a virgin, and the passion, and the resurrection from the dead, and the ascension into heaven in the flesh of the beloved Christ Jesus, our Lord, and His [future] manifestation from heaven in the glory of the Father "to gather all things in one," and to raise up anew all flesh of the whole human race, in order that to Christ Jesus, our Lord, and God, and Saviour, and King, according to the will of the invisible Father, "every knee should bow, of things in heaven, and things in earth, and things under the earth, and that every tongue should confess" to Him, and that He should execute just judgment towards all; that He may send "spiritual wickednesses," and the angels who transgressed and became apostates, together with the ungodly, and unrighteous, and wicked, and profane among men, into everlasting fire; but may, in the exercise of His grace, confer immortality on the righteous, and holy, and those who have kept His commandments, and have persevered in His love, some from the beginning [of their Christian course], and others from [the date of] their repentance, and may surround them with everlasting glory.[21]

A shorter version can be found in Book 3 of *Against Heresies*:

> To which course many nations of those barbarians who believe in Christ do assent, having salvation written in their hearts by the Spirit, without paper or ink, and, carefully preserving the ancient tradition, believing in one God, the Creator of heaven and earth, and all things therein, by means of Christ Jesus, the Son of God; who, because of His surpassing love towards His creation, condescended to be born of the virgin, He Himself uniting man through Himself to God, and having suffered under Pontius Pilate, and

rising again, and having been received up in splendour, shall come in glory, the Saviour of those who are saved, and the Judge of those who are judged, and sending into eternal fire those who transform the truth, and despise His Father and His advent.[22]

Although these examples fail to mention the life of Jesus, Irenaeus specifically mentions the Gospels when talking about the perspicuity of Scripture, as highlighted above. Tertullian's rule of faith, however, is explicit concerning Jesus' life:

Now, with regard to this rule of faith – that we may from this point acknowledge what it is which we defend – it is, you must know, that which prescribes the belief that there is one only God, and that He is none other than the Creator of the world, who produced all things out of nothing through His own Word, first of all sent forth; that this Word is called His Son, *and*, under the name of God, was seen "in diverse manners" by the patriarchs, heard at all times in the prophets, at last brought down by the Spirit and Power of the Father into the Virgin Mary, was made flesh in her womb, and, being born of her, went forth as Jesus Christ; thenceforth He preached the new law and the new promise of the kingdom of heaven, worked miracles; having been crucified, He rose again the third day; (then) having ascended into the heavens, He sat at the right hand of the Father; sent instead of Himself the Power of the Holy Ghost to lead such as believe; will come with glory to take the saints to the enjoyment of everlasting life and of the heavenly promises, and to condemn the wicked to everlasting fire, after the resurrection of both these classes shall have happened, together with the restoration of their flesh. This rule, as it will be proved, was taught by Christ, and raises amongst ourselves no other questions than those which heresies introduce, and which make men heretics.[23]

This longer narrative though can also be condensed by Tertullian into one which does not mention the life of Jesus:

The rule of faith, indeed, is altogether one, alone immoveable and irreformable; the rule, to wit, of believing in one only God omnipotent, the Creator of the universe, and His Son Jesus Christ,

born of the Virgin Mary, crucified under Pontius Pilate, raised
again the third day from the dead, received in the heavens, sitting
now at the right (hand) of the Father, destined to come to judge
quick and dead through the resurrection of the flesh as well (as of
the spirit).[24]

The rule of faith, in its shortened form, formed the basis for the
subsequent creeds. As both Irenaeus and Tertullian omit explicit
mention of the life of Jesus in some articulations of their rule of
faith, yet clearly are very interested in his life, it is important not
to read too much into this lack of reference in the creeds.
However, as I shall argue below, the combination of creed and
Christendom effectively served to marginalize Jesus' deeds and
actions over time. Jesus is subsequently seen primarily as Savior
and Conquering King.

Summary

The earliest Christians were concerned to read all Scripture in the
light of Christ. Many thus employed typology to see various persons and events in the Old Testament as foreshadowing Christ.
However, a number went further than this to read Christ into the
Old Testament texts themselves by means of allegory. Origen represents the most sustained and sophisticated use of allegory
before Christendom emerged. Whatever we may think of these
allegorical methods, they do represent a sustained attempt both
to treat the whole Bible seriously and to see Christ at the center of
all biblical interpretation. The rule of faith, particularly as articulated by Irenaeus and Tertullian, presupposed the entire biblical
narrative with the Gospels occupying a central place in that narrative.

I will leave the last words of this chapter to some of these early
church fathers:

> If any one, therefore, reads the Scriptures with attention, he will
> find in them an account of Christ, and a foreshadowing of the new
> calling. For Christ is the treasure which was hid in the field, that
> is, in this world (for "the field is the world"); but the treasure hid

in the Scriptures is Christ, since He was pointed out by means of types and parables.[25]

Every part of Holy Writ announces through words the coming of Our Lord Jesus Christ, reveals it through facts and establishes it through examples. . . . For it is our Lord who during all the present age, through true and manifest adumbrations, generates, cleanses, sanctifies, chooses, separates, or redeems the Church in the Patriarchs, through Adam's slumber, Noah's flood, Melchizedek's blessing, Abraham's justification, Isaac's birth, and Jacob's bondage.[26]

3

Christendom and the Bible

Introduction

Gregory of Nazianzus (ca. 329–90) stepped down from his position as bishop of Constantinople in 381, uttering the following words:

> No one told me I was to contend with consuls and prefects and the most illustrious generals, who hardly know how to relieve themselves of their abundance of possessions. No one told me I was expected to put the treasuries of the church to the service of gluttony, and the poor-boxes to the services of luxury. No one told me I must be equipped with superb horses and mounted on an ornamental chariot, and there would be a great hush during my solemn progresses, and everyone must make way for the Patriarch as though he were some kind of wild beast, with the people opening out in great avenues to let me pass, as I came like a banner from afar. If these things offended you, then I say they all belong to the past. Forgive me.[1]

This eloquently sums up the position in Constantine's city less than sixty years after the Council of Nicaea of 325 (see below). The church was home to the powerful in society, used its newfound wealth to enhance the status quo and expected its leaders to conduct themselves with due pomp and circumstance. Profoundly countercultural texts such as Luke 22:24–27 must inevitably have been marginalized as the church adopted precisely the same role as that criticized in such texts. For example, Damasus became bishop of Rome in 366 following a conflict with his rival Ursinus in which 137 lost their lives. After being accused of responsibility for homicide by the city prefect, he was rescued by the intervention of wealthy friends. Damasus' subsequent entertainments were said to surpass even imperial hospitality. Praetextatus, a rich aristocrat, is consequently credited with saying, "Make me bishop of Rome and I will become a Christian."[2] Although the church was gaining in influence throughout the third century,[3] this accelerated after Constantine.

> After Constantine the social status of high clergy quickly advanced. It became less common for an emancipated slave like Callistus of Rome to become bishop, less uncommon for a man like Cyprian, of (probably) senatorial rank, to find his way into holy orders. Constantine invested bishops with magistrates' powers of proving wills and arbitrating in disputes. As early as 313 he may have conferred the exalted secular rank of Illustrious on high clergy. The Council of Arles in 314 addressed the bishop of Rome by the title "most glorious" which in secular usage was enjoyed by very distinguished persons with precedence second only to the imperial family. As bishops acquired a social rank, so they also acquired the corresponding insignia.[4]

The Constantinian effect

The effect of Constantine on the subsequent development of Christianity cannot be overstated. It is not, of course, that Christendom, as defined in Chapter 1, emerged full-fledged during Constantine's reign, nor even that the shift to Christendom began with him. Carter rightly notes that Christendom emerged as a result of a "275-year-long process lasting from the middle of the third century to 528, when Emperor Justinian made it illegal for citizens not to be Christians."[5] Nevertheless, specific events associated with Constantine had a dramatic effect. In this chapter I will consider four such events: the Edict of Milan in 313, the Council of Nicaea in 325, the Edict against the Heretics shortly after this and, crucially for the argument of this book, the decisive step towards defining the New Testament canon when, around 331, Constantine ordered the church historian Eusebius, bishop of Caesarea, to produce fifty new Bibles for his new churches in Constantinople.

The Edict of Milan

Diocletian (284–305) ruled the Roman Empire with the assistance of three subordinate co-regents: Maximian, Galerius, and Constantius Chlorus (the father of Constantine). In the first twenty years of his reign Diocletian practiced toleration towards Christians, and indeed a number of his close associates, including his wife Prisca and daughter Valeria, were either Christians or favorable to Christianity. Diocletian himself, however, was never converted. In the final years of his reign Galerius, who was also his son-in-law and fiercely anti-Christian, persuaded him to take action against the Christians. In 303 Diocletian issued three edicts against Christians, each more severe than its predecessor.

Maximian issued the fourth, and worst of all, in April 304 as a result of which churches were burned, Bibles destroyed, Christians were deprived of public office and civil rights, and all were obliged, on pain of death, to sacrifice to the gods. This series of persecutions began on February 23, 303 with the destruction of the church in Nicomedia and soon spread over the whole Roman Empire with the exception of Britain, Gaul, and Spain, areas ruled by Constantius who did as much as he could to spare the Christians – he destroyed some churches but no one was executed. Constantius died in July 306 and his soldiers proclaimed his son Constantine as emperor. In the East, Diocletian abdicated in 305 and persecution intensified under Galerius who instituted a two-year reign of terror against the Christians from 308 to 310 during which they had no alternatives but to renounce their faith or starve to death. In 311 Galerius suffered a terrible disease and eventually brought an end to the persecution by issuing an edict on April 30 while dying in great pain. This edict allowed Christians to assemble provided they did not disturb the order of the state and, significantly, instructed Christians to pray to their God for the welfare of the emperor. Galerius was succeeded by Maximin Daia who was defeated in a civil war by Licinius.

Meanwhile, in the West, Maximian was succeeded by his son Maxentius. In 312 Constantine crossed the Alps and, fatefully, under the banner of the cross and invoking the aid of the Christian God, he defeated Maxentius against the odds on October 27. This left Constantine supreme in the West and Licinius in the East. The two met at Milan in February 313 and issued a joint edict which announced religious freedom for all and the restoration, at the expense of the imperial treasury, to Christians of all property which had been confiscated. This freedom proved short-lived in the East where Licinius, after falling out with Constantine, renewed persecution for a short period until his defeat by Constantine in 324. At this point Constantine became sole emperor and the church enjoyed increasingly the privileges of power.

The Edict of Milan in itself is to be welcomed as it enshrined the principle of religious freedom and toleration. However, the church should have embraced this without uncritically accepting Constantine's subsequent favor. For example, not only did Constantine return confiscated property but he lavished huge sums on erecting basilicas in Rome, Bethlehem, and Jerusalem as well as two magnificent churches in Constantinople. Twelve years after the edict, and less than one year after Constantine became sole emperor, favor turned to direct influence.

The Council of Nicea

The church of the first three centuries had been used to disputes. The pages of the New Testament bear eloquent testimony to disputes and factions from its earliest years. However, until Constantine, these disputes were not subject to political interference and the only weapons at the church's disposal were those of rhetorical persuasion by appeal to the Scriptures and the ultimate sanction of excommunication. This all changed with Constantine. As early as 314 Constantine convened a council at Arles to hear the appeal of Donatus against Caecilian, the bishop of Carthage, who was considered by Donatus and his followers to be unworthy of office as he had cooperated with the authorities during the earlier persecutions. Although Constantine did not preside over this council he was a clear supporter of Caecilian and so, unsurprisingly, the Council found in the latter's favor. This decision marked a turning point in the subsequent Donatist controversy which dominated African church life for the next century. From this point on the Donatists were "determined to keep the purity of the church unstained by any communion with the compromised and compromising Catholics."[6]

After Constantine had moved to the East he found the Greek churches in dispute over what had begun as a local quarrel between Alexander, bishop of Alexandria, and his presbyter Arius. Arius argued that God the Father was alone without beginning and that, therefore, God the Son must have had a beginning and came into existence at some point before the times and the ages. The Arian slogan was, therefore, "there was [a time] when he [Christ] was not." Arius was profoundly concerned to preserve monotheism and he regarded any notion of Christ's eternal existence as a threat to that monotheism. Furthermore, Arius had influential supporters in Eusebius of Caesarea and Eusebius, bishop of Nicomedia. Constantine, hearing of the dispute, sent his adviser Hosius, bishop of Cordova, to investigate and convened a council of bishops at Ancyra to meet after Easter 325. Hosius sided with Alexander and, at a council at Antioch at which he presided, also had Eusebius of Caesarea excommunicated subject to confirmation by the Council of Ancyra. Constantine responded by transferring the council from Ancyra to Nicea so that he could personally control the proceedings.

The Council of Nicea, opened on May 20, 325, was the first ecumenical church council, made possible by imperial decree and attended by some 220 bishops, mainly from the East. Constantine immediately assumed direct control of the conference. After an initial speech in Latin, urging the bishops to achieve unity and peace, business began. Several petitions were handed to Constantine with complaints against various parties. He burned each of them without saying a word. Then the debate proper ensued and, as this heated up, Constantine intervened and led the discussion himself, speaking in Greek.[7] At one point Eusebius was asked to give his confession of faith and responded with the creed used in his church at Caesarea:

> We believe in one God the Father Almighty, maker of all things visible and invisible; and in one Lord Jesus Christ, the Word of God, God of God, Light of Light, Life of Life, the only-begotten

Son, the first-born of every creature, begotten of God the Father before all ages, by whom also all things were made; who for our salvation was made flesh and made his home among men; and suffered; and rose on the third day; and ascended to the Father; and will come again in glory, to judge the quick and the dead. [We believe] also in one Holy Ghost.[8]

This creed, with its reference to Jesus as "first-born," crucially dropped from the eventual Nicene Creed, could be construed as Arian. Constantine immediately indicated his approval, thus ending all question of excommunication, but then asked Eusebius whether he was prepared to accept the term *homoousios* ('of one substance') to explain the relationship between the Father and the Son. Put on the spot by Constantine, Eusebius agreed and the Arian position consequently collapsed. At the end of the conference, about one month later, the bishops were asked to sign a new creedal formulation – the Nicene Creed – which included the term *homoousios*. Two bishops who were close friends of Arius refused to sign and were immediately sent into exile. The Creed ended with the following anathema: "But those who say: 'There was a time when he was not;' and 'He was not before he was made;' and 'He was made out of nothing,' or 'He is of another substance' or 'essence,' or 'The Son of God is created,' or 'changeable,' or 'alterable' – they are condemned by the holy catholic and apostolic Church."[9]

At the end of the conference the attending bishops sent letters to all other bishops throughout the empire conveying the council's decisions. Constantine also sent a letter to the same recipients making the decisions the law of the realm. In addition to the Nicene Creed, the Council of Nicea issued twenty canons dealing with church order and regulating promotions through the church hierarchy.

Constantine's direct involvement now meant that church decisions carried the full weight of imperial law and the final sanction, previously limited to excommunication from the church, was now exile or worse. Eusebius tellingly refers to Constantine as a "general" or "universal" bishop:

But he [Constantine] exercised a peculiar care over the church of God: and whereas, in the several provinces there were some who differed from each other in judgment, he, *like some general bishop constituted by God*, convened synods of his ministers. Nor did he disdain to be present and sit with them in their assembly, but bore a share in their deliberations, ministering to all that pertained to the peace of God.[10]

The Edict against the Heretics

Constantine's Edict against the Heretics, as reported by Eusebius below, was issued shortly after the Council of Nicea. Whereas in previous persecutions Christian property had been confiscated and Bibles had been burned, now the property of those considered heretics is to be handed over to the orthodox church and their books are to be burned. Furthermore, Eusebius, a bishop, reports this with glee. For Eusebius the church is now "one harmonious whole" directly as the result of imperial coercion. This is a far cry from the church wrestling with issues by debate and exercising its own discipline in the spirit of Jesus. Orthodoxy is now no longer defined simply by appeal to apostolic succession and the received tradition of biblical interpretation, as with Irenaeus' "rule of faith." Instead orthodoxy is deeply implicated in the power politics of imperial decree. Instead of the Pauline hope that the church will grow into "the unity of the faith" (Eph. 4:13), unity is imposed by force from above.

Victor Constantinus, Maximus Augustus, to the heretics.

"Understand now, by this present statute, you Novatians, Valentinians, Marcionites, Paulians, you who are called Cataphrygians, and all you who devise and support heresies by means of your private assemblies, with what a tissue of falsehood and vanity, with what destructive and venomous errors, your doctrines are inseparably interwoven; so that through you the healthy soul is stricken with disease, and the living becomes the prey of everlasting death . . . Why then do I still bear with such abounding evil; especially since this protracted clemency is the cause that some who were sound are become tainted with this pestilent disease? Why not at once strike, as it were, at the root of so great a mischief by a public manifestation of displeasure?

"Forasmuch, then, as it is no longer possible to bear with your pernicious errors, we give warning by this present statute that none of you henceforth presume to assemble yourselves together. We have directed, accordingly, that you be deprived of all the houses in which you are accustomed to hold your assemblies: and our care in this respect extends so far as to forbid the holding of your superstitious and senseless meetings, not in public merely, but in any private house or place whatsoever . . . And in order that this remedy may be applied with effectual power, we have commanded, as before said, that you be positively deprived of every gathering point for your superstitious meetings, I mean all the houses of prayer, if such be worthy of the name, which belong to heretics, and that these be made over without delay to the catholic Church; that any other places be confiscated to the public service, and no facility whatever be left for any future gathering; in order that from this day forward none of your unlawful assemblies may presume to appear in any public or private place. Let this edict be made public."

Thus were the lurking-places of the heretics broken up by the emperor's command, and the savage beasts they harboured (I mean the chief authors of their impious doctrines) driven to flight. Of those whom they had deceived, some, intimidated by the emperor's threats, disguising their real sentiments, crept secretly into the Church. For since the law directed that *search should be made for their books*, those of them who practised evil and forbidden arts were detected, and, these were ready to secure their own safety by dissimulation of every kind. Others, however, there were, who voluntarily and with real sincerity embraced a better hope. Meantime the prelates of the several churches continued to make strict inquiry, utterly rejecting those who attempted an entrance under the specious disguise of false pretences, while those who came with sincerity of purpose were proved for a time, and after sufficient trial numbered with the congregation. Such was the treatment of those who stood charged with rank heresy: those, however, who maintained no impious doctrine, but had been separated from the one body through the influence of schismatic advisers, were received without difficulty or delay. Accordingly, numbers thus revisited, as it were, their own country after an absence in a foreign land, and acknowledged the Church as a mother from whom they had wandered long, and to whom they now returned with joy and gladness. *Thus the members of the entire body became united, and compacted in one harmonious whole; and the one catholic Church, at unity with itself, shone with full lustre, while no heretical or schismatic body anywhere continued to exist.* And the credit of having achieved this mighty work our Heaven-protected emperor alone, of all who had gone before him, was able to attribute to himself.[11]

Constantine and the canon

Prior to Constantine, Christians, and those who considered themselves Christians, certainly had a collection of sacred texts but these varied according to the type of Christianity on offer. For the church at this point was not "one harmonious whole", but consisted of various factions, each with its own Scriptures and truth claims. In this period there gradually emerged a large international network of Christians who liked to refer to themselves as the "Catholic Church". But at this stage this group, although large, did not command universal assent. For example, Jewish Christians had their preferred gospels and anti-Trinitarian Christology; Marcionites were probably the largest group in Asia Minor and northern Syria in the late second century and their scriptures consisted of a severely truncated Gospel of Luke and Paul's letters (excluding the Pastoral Epistles); gnostics had their own distinctive gospels, and so on. Even the Scriptures of the "Catholic Church" were not fixed. Eusebius, in his *Ecclesiastical History*, spells out the criteria used by the Catholics to evaluate and select Scripture: "As I proceed in my history, I shall carefully show with the succession of the apostles what ecclesiastical writers in their times respectively made use of any of the *disputed* writings and what opinions they have expressed, both respecting the *incorporated* and *acknowledged* writings and also what respecting those that were not of this description."[12]

The criteria that Eusebius spells out here are:

- Apostolic succession. Bishops of churches where a chain of apostolic succession could be demonstrated were responsible for deciding what were appropriate Scriptures.
- Use by previous ecclesiastical writers. For Eusebius this means those belonging to the Catholic Church. Eusebius would never

use this term of Marcionites, gnostics or Montanists, for example.

• The opinions of these writers on acknowledged and disputed texts.

Using these criteria Eusebius arrives at three categories of sacred text.[13] First, there are the writings acknowledged as genuine. By this he means that there has been historic, unanimous consensus. In this category he places the four Gospels, Acts, all thirteen letters of Paul, Hebrews (probably), 1 John, 1 Peter, and "if proper" Revelation. Second, there are those which are disputed but known and approved by many (but not all). These are: James, Jude, 2 Peter, and 2 and 3 John. Third, there are those which are both disputed and "spurious" (i.e. not known or approved by many). These are: *Acts of Paul, Shepherd of Hermas, Revelation of Peter, Epistle of Barnabas, Institutions of the Apostles, the Gospel according to the Hebrews* and, "if it should appear right," Revelation. Revelation appears in both Eusebius' first and third categories. This is probably due to its widespread acceptance by the earliest ecclesiastical writers on the one hand and increasing skepticism in Eusebius' day of its apostolic authorship on the other.[14]

So until the time of Eusebius the Catholic Church operated with a relatively open-ended collection of Scriptures at the core of which was a small collection universally acknowledged as genuine.

> For our part, we may note especially the "open-ended" nature of his results: a small number of universally acknowledged, *genuine* writings, followed by another short list of *disputed* writings awaiting further consideration, and finally a large number of *spurious*, rejected writings. Like the good philosopher he was, Eusebius left the question of *disputed* writings at that – open to the ongoing deliberations of fellow scholars and the providence of God.[15]

However, around 331 Constantine ordered Eusebius to produce fifty new Bibles for his new churches in Constantinople. The key issue after this edict was which of the disputed books would those Bibles contain? For now another new phenomenon has emerged under Constantine – imperially authorized Bibles. It is only a short time later, in 367, that we have our current listing of twenty-seven New Testament books in Athanasius' Festal Letter, together with the first description of them as "canon". Significantly, other listings from around this time contain twenty-six books (they exclude Revelation – the one book in our current New Testament that appears in Eusebius' "disputed and spurious" list).[16] From then on the old terminology of "authentic," "disputed," and "spurious" is replaced by the legal terminology of "canonical" and "non-canonical." The first council to endorse the present canon of twenty-seven books was the Synod of Hippo Regius in North Africa in 393. The imperially authorized Bibles of 331 thus marked the decisive step towards canonical closure of the New Testament. As David Dungan so eloquently puts it: "After Constantine's Bible had been produced, and in the tense atmosphere that followed the Council of Nicaea, what bishop would dare use a Bible in his cathedral that differed in content from one used by the bishops in Constantinople? He would likely be informed upon and investigated. He could lose his office or worse!"[17]

Disavowing Constantinian readings of Scripture

Inevitably the emergence of Christendom under Constantine had a significant effect on the way in which the Bible was read. Simonetti states:

> The new policy towards the Church begun by Constantine affected the development of exegetical literature, between the 4th and 5th centuries, as of every other type of literature. The great expansion of Christian religion, accompanied, generally speaking, by a lower level of preparation and conviction on the part of the new initiates brought about the need to encourage greater familiarity with Scripture, both at the popular and at a more intellectual level, by means of both the homily and the commentary.[18]

This "great expansion of Christian religion" was a direct result of the church's newfound status. As increasingly people were perceived as being born into the church the inevitable result was general biblical illiteracy and a consequent reliance on the biblical knowledge of the ecclesiastical hierarchy. This served to accentuate the division between clergy and laity.

Whereas the church of the second and third centuries had to contend on the one hand with the relationship between the two Testaments posed by Marcion and the gnostics and, on the other hand, with questions of authority and charismatic enthusiasm posed by the Montanists, the next two centuries witnessed enormous theological controversy over Christology and the doctrine of the Trinity. However now, as stated above, with imperial sanction, victory in the debate could have major political implications. Increasingly the Bible was being read from the perspective of those in power, resulting in readings that reinforced the church's increasing wealth, sanctified a priesthood-laity divide and consequently established a patriarchal hierarchy within the church. Any reading of the Bible from an explicitly post-Christendom perspective will, therefore, need to disavow such readings.

Disavowing readings from the perspective of the powerful

As the church came to power, the radical teachings of the New Testament concerning attitudes to wealth and status were increasingly ignored and the Old Testament, especially texts concerning the period of the monarchy, became prominent. The church could far more easily identify with the wealth and status of Solomon than the relative poverty of Jesus!

Luke 19:11–27

A graphic example of the way biblical interpretation has been affected by status is Luke's parable of the ten minas. The traditional interpretation, which goes back to at least the third century, is that this parable concerns how disciples should behave in the period from Jesus' ascension to his parousia.[19] Jesus exhorts his disciples to use the gifts they have been given in order to increase his kingdom. Some commentators assume that Jesus is literally commending some form of capitalist economics in which wealth is used to generate further wealth. Alex Singleton, for example, commenting in the *Daily Telegraph* online on July 28, 2008 concerning a demonstration by 600 Anglican bishops against poverty states:

> What a pity . . . that these bishops seemed completely confused about the causes of global poverty. Holding signs demanding that leaders of rich countries keep their (politically-driven) promises to halve global poverty by 2015, they fell into the trap of believing that countries like Chad and Ethiopia are poor because of the actions of rich countries. Instead of quoting Micah 6:8, which calls believers "to do justice, and love kindness," they should have been quoting the parable of the talents, which criticises the servant who is only given one talent but who does nothing with it.[20]

The irony of the above comment is that a secular commentator uses the traditional interpretation of the church, which has been compromised by its alliance with wealth and status throughout Christendom, against contemporary clergy who, in the midst of Christendom's decline, have become sensitized to real issues of poverty!

Interestingly, those deeply affected by poverty and coming to this parable with fresh eyes see a completely different meaning. In Luke's Gospel discipleship means giving up everything to follow Jesus (12:32–34; 14:33; 16:13; 18:18–30; 19:8–9). Luke begins with the announcement of status reversal in the words of the Magnificat (1:46–55) and has Jesus declare that he has come to bring good news to the poor (4:18). In this context it is very unlikely that Luke would use a parable about wealth to encourage wealth creation or even a metaphorical application such as using our God-given gifts to extend the kingdom. Furthermore, the parable comes not long after the story of the rich ruler in 18:18–25 and is immediately preceded by the story of Zacchaeus for whom salvation comes when he declares that he will give half of his possessions to the poor and use the remaining half to recompense those he has defrauded fourfold (19:8–9). This would have left Zacchaeus with nothing, prec-isely the Lukan requirement for discipleship, as Tannehill rightly recognizes.

It may seem surprising that Jesus approves of Zacchaeus's plan to give half of his goods to the poor, while he told the rich ruler to sell all and distribute it to the poor (18:22). Although some interpreters understand verse 8 as Luke's effort to arrive at a more reasonable (but still quite demanding) standard for rich people in the Lukan communities, I take the total statement in verse 8 as an indication that Zacchaeus recognizes two requirements for his money – care for the poor and fourfold compensation of those defrauded in his previous dealings – and simply divide his wealth between these two requirements. There is, of course, no accounting of how much Zacchaeus owes to those defrauded. Such details would not fit a pronouncement story. Nevertheless, the supposition is that such compensation will take all or most of the wealth not given away, leaving Zacchaeus pretty much in the same position as the rich ruler, had he chosen to follow Jesus.[21]

Given these contextual indicators, a parable in Luke about wealth is likely to be critical of its acquisition. Furthermore, Luke situates this parable near to Jerusalem, the seat of power, in the midst of expectation "that the kingdom of God was to appear immediately" (19:11). The parable goes on to illustrate that the kingdom has very different values from the power structures of the world. Jesus begins the parable by echoing the position of Archelaus, Herod's son, immediately after the death of Herod. The question as to whether Archelaus should succeed Herod was contested due to his violence and a delegation was sent to Rome to oppose his appointment. Rome responded by dividing Herod's kingdom between three sons. Archelaus received half, but only with the title of ethnarch (and the promise of future kingship). On his return from Rome he treated both Jews and Samaritans "barbarously" so that, after ten years, he was deposed by Rome and direct rule was imposed. Hearers of the parable would thus have immediately recognized Archelaus in the description of the nobleman in 19:12–15a, 21, 27. In this context Jesus demonstrates how different the values of the kingdom are. The powerful of this world expect their servants to use wealth to gain more wealth for them and they are rewarded accordingly (19:17–18). But those in the kingdom refuse to play the wealth game and refuse even to put the money on deposit in a bank to earn interest (19:20–23). In the world those who have receive more and those who have nothing have everything taken from them (19:26) – an apt description of how wealth works to serve the interests of the rich and powerful at the expense of the poor. This is in complete contrast to the Lukan view of discipleship articulated in 18:28–30 where giving up everything results in rich reward.[22]

I have spent some time on this parable just to demonstrate that readings from the margins completely subvert the natural Christendom reading which is still favored by commentators.

Priesthood-laity divide

Although the church became increasingly hierarchical as early as the second century, with the beginnings of monarchical episcopacy already found in Ignatius, it was imperial influence on episcopal appointments that served to accelerate the division between clergy and laity. Prior to Constantine bishops were freely elected by the local congregations, although there also had to be recognition of the appointment by bishops of neighboring churches. However, by 381 the power of appointment in the East was concentrated in the hands of the patriarchs of Alexandria, Antioch, and Constantinople with the latter being specifically appointed by the emperor. In the West too a regular system of imperial nomination of bishops gradually emerged.[23] As bishops became more and more divorced from their congregations so responsibility for ecclesiastical functions became concentrated in the priestly hierarchy. The reading and exposition of Scripture consequently became the preserve of the clergy. Biblical interpretation became professionalized. This is a far cry from the Pauline ideal of every member of the congregation having something vital to contribute to the life of the community as a whole (1 Cor. 12 – 14).

Patriarchy

Furthermore, this priestly hierarchy was exclusively male. This meant that biblical interpretation throughout the period of Christendom was in the hands of a male elite. Patriarchal readings of Scripture were therefore inevitable in which women were at best marginalized and more often rendered invisible. This has had profound consequences for the life of the church with texts such as 1 Corinthians 14:34 and 1 Timothy 2:11–15 being taken out of context and given more prominence than they deserve. Post-Christendom readings will consequently be suspicious of all marginalizing interpretations.

Conclusion

Within the space of some six years, three significant events had occurred. First, without precedent in the history of the church to this date, a doctrinal dispute was settled through the convening of an ecumenical council under imperial direction. Second, far more was now at stake for the theological "losers" than simply being branded as heretics. Imperial disfavor meant the possibility of banishment or even death. Whereas before theological disputes were the matter of debate, albeit heated at times, now those considered "orthodox" could enforce their position with the full weight of imperial authority. Thus the Arians, the losers at Nicea, were anathematized and books written by Arius were ordered to be burned with the death penalty for disobedience. Third, an oft-neglected aspect of Constantine's legacy, under his direction the New Testament canon as an authorized list of authoritative books appeared. The origins of orthodox, creedal Christianity with its canon of Scripture are thus inextricably bound up with issues of coercion, power politics, and violence.

The official, imperially authorized, canon of Scripture "closed down what had been a thriving, sometimes heated, and fundamentally beneficial controversy over the authentic writings of the apostles and the correct interpretation of them."[24] It was not that crucial decisions were not made prior to Constantine. The Catholic Church of the second and third centuries was well able to reject Marcionism, Gnosticism, and Montanism, for example, without the threat of violent sanctions against those considered heretical.

Rejecting biblical interpretation from a Christendom mindset, however, cannot mean reopening the canon – we have to acknowledge as a historical given the Bibles we now have.[25] But the recognition that the content of our current Bibles was, at the end of the day, decided by imperial politics should fundamentally challenge naive notions of biblical inspiration and inerrancy. Nevertheless, such a disavowal should result in hermeneutical openness and a willingness to listen closely to, and engage with, those with whom we disagree without anathematizing them. For example, in direct comparison with the fateful events of Nicea and following, Arian perspectives on the nature of Jesus are very much alive today. In a similar way to my comments about the canon above, we also have to acknowledge as a historical given the profound effects of the Nicene Creed on subsequent Christianity. However, it will not do, from a post-Christendom perspective, to brand contemporary Arians as heretics on the basis of the Nicene Creed, precisely because of the coercive elements involved in that creed's origins.[26] Instead those who hold to some form of Arian or adoptionist Christology or those who are unwilling to accept "orthodox" views on the Trinity should receive a fair hearing and be engaged with on the basis of debate over the relevant New Testament texts.

In the next chapter I will focus on a movement that sought within Christendom to break free from the dominant biblical interpretation of the powerful elite within the church – both Catholic and Protestant.

4

The Bible and the Subversion of Christendom: The Anabaptists

The sixteenth-century ecclesiastical context

Introduction

Stuart Murray, in a series of four appendices in *Post-Christendom*, highlights four radical movements that sought a different way from the prevailing Christendom mindset. These were: the Donatists of the fourth century; the Waldensians of the twelfth to the sixteenth century; the Lollards of the fifteenth century and the Anabaptists of the sixteenth century.[1] The Anabaptists, in particular, have proved to be a fruitful resource for contemporary thinking in our post-Christendom context. In this chapter, therefore, I will examine the Anabaptists' approach to reading the Bible.[2]

Sixteenth-century options

In this section I will attempt to indicate some of the ecclesiastical issues that were current in the early sixteenth century and some of the options available. Anabaptism was one of these options. For some, it was the option to which they committed themselves permanently and for which they were prepared to suffer and die; for others, it was an option they explored and committed themselves to for a period before moving on into another option; for many others, it was an attractive but dangerous option, with which they sympathized without expressing a commitment.

In the early sixteenth century, the monopoly of the Catholic Church was being destroyed and there were many views of what should replace this, many options competing for the allegiance of those who were disillusioned with medieval Catholicism. It is difficult for us to comprehend the magnitude of such a change, the paradigm shift that was involved, where individuals were becoming free to choose in matters of faith. There was, without doubt, still much pressure to conform but there were now viable options to consider.

The main options were as follows.

Catholicism

Despite the persistent and widespread criticism of the Catholic Church by discontented theologians, philosophers, clergy, and lay people throughout the later Middle Ages, the thought of leaving the "mother church" was abhorrent to very many of its sternest critics. The unity of the church and of the sacral society which was Christendom were regarded as sacrosanct and schism was perceived as a great evil. Among these critics were John Wyclif in England, Jan Hus in Bohemia and, of course, the great humanist Erasmus. Despite their trenchant criticisms, these men were concerned to reform the corrupt church rather than opting out of it. Their anticlericalism was not a rejection of the church but a call for reform and renewal. Their followers and those they influenced frequently moved beyond them and started sectarian movements (the Lollards in England, the Czech Brethren in Bohemia, the humanists Conrad Grebel and Felix Mantz in Zurich), but this was not an option that others were prepared to countenance. For vast numbers, both the spiritually minded but loyal and the unconcerned nominal church members, there was no real likelihood of leaving the Catholic Church – at least, not unless they found themselves living in newly Reformed territories.

The Protestant Reformation

Here the emphasis was on the recovery of true doctrine, the removal of ecclesiastical corruption, the provision of effective preaching and pastoral ministry. Despite initial uncertainty, the Reformers accepted gratefully the support of certain political authorities and committed themselves to maintaining the existing state-church amalgam. Their goal was the gradual reformation of the whole of society, moving at a speed that would not unduly disturb the social status quo, relying on a combination of preaching reform and state-enforced changes of practice. Different branches of this reform movement emerged – Lutheran, Zwinglian, Calvinist, Anglican – and there were significant areas of disagreement between these. But the fundamental approach to reform was the same and the result was the emergence of various political/religious entities in which some version of Protestantism achieved recognition as the new state religion. The phrase *cuius regio eius religio* described this arrangement – the religious choice of the political leadership of a city or region determined the religious commitment of those who lived under this authority. Freedom of choice in matters of faith was determined politically rather than individually in what were, in effect, mini-Christendoms. Individuals could and did choose to move from one place to another in order to find freedom to practice their form of religion.

The Anabaptists

Here the emphasis was on the separation of the church from the state, the recovery of what was perceived as a New Testament ecclesiology, ethical renewal that resulted in discipleship and mission in a society regarded as non-Christian. Although on many theological issues the Anabaptists agreed with the Reformers, especially with Ulrich Zwingli and some of the more radical Lutherans, their program of reform was very different. Indeed, it is better described as a program of restoration or restitution, rather than an attempt to reform existing institutions. Christendom was to be rejected rather than transmuted. Though there were occasional attempts to gain political influence or attract political support for an Anabaptist program, it soon became apparent that this was not a viable option and that Anabaptism would not find territories within which they could practice their faith without fear of persecution. They were tolerated in certain cities or regions for a while but often faced a choice of conforming, migrating, imprisonment, or execution.

The Spiritualists

Here the emphasis was on personal spirituality as the core of true faith, relegating outward forms and ceremonies to a nonessential status or seeing them as positive hindrances, both to spiritual growth and to unity. The reform of the church was not of great significance, if by this was meant a concern with ceremonial and structural issues. There is no doubt that this was an attractive option in an age of bitter disputes over ceremonies and structures. Spiritualists might conform outwardly to whatever form of religion was required locally, since such conformity was irrelevant to spiritual life, but continue to hold their own beliefs. Unguarded statements might result in trouble, but this option did not represent the same kind of challenge as the Reformation did to the Catholic authorities or as Anabaptism did to both the Catholic and Reformed authorities.

These options are sometimes presented on a continuum – with Catholics on the far right, followed by Lutherans, Calvinists, Zwinglians, Radical Reformers, Anabaptists, other radical groups, and Spiritualists on the far left. However, as might be expected, this continuum is only moderately helpful. On different issues these groups occupied different positions on the continuum.

Furthermore, many people moved from one option to another or went through several stages. Some became Protestants, then Anabaptists and then returned to the Reformed churches. Some became Anabaptists and then became Spiritualists. Anabaptism was for some a stage on their spiritual journey rather than their final destination. So Anabaptism was fluid, with fuzzy edges. Some important figures within the Anabaptist movement were people in transition, who contributed significantly to the growth and thinking of the movement but who did not ultimately find a home within it. Among these were Hans Denck, Hans Bünderlin, Jakob Kautz, Christian Entfelder, and Obbe Philips.

Anabaptists and the Bible

Biblical study

Anabaptists were recognized, by friends and enemies alike, as a "biblical people", in an age when the rediscovery and dissemination of the Bible was effecting major changes in the social, religious, and intellectual life of Europe. It is difficult to assess how many were able to read the Bible for themselves, or the extent to which reading the Bible motivated people to embrace principles taught by the Reformers. But historians of the period agree that the introduction of printing fifty years earlier and the distribution of the Bible in the vernacular were significant factors in the way in which the Reformation spread and took root among lay people. Those who could not read the Bible themselves were able to listen to others reading it in a language they could understand.

Anabaptists were not the only ones reading the Bible with enthusiasm and fascination; but they were distinguished by an unusual passion for it. The Bible was read, studied, memorized, recited, discussed, and applied, by individuals, in the home, in church meetings, and in informal discussion groups. Preaching and teaching played a major part in their gatherings, as it did in Reformed churches, but they also expected many members of the congregation to contribute questions and insights, rather than listening passively to their leaders.

A favorite passage among Swiss Anabaptists was 1 Corinthians 14:26–33. They expected a multiplicity of differing contributions from congregational members. Consequently, ordinary Swiss Anabaptists were much more involved than their counterparts in the Reformed churches – who were used to listening to the ordained minister expounding the sermon – in exploring and interpreting Scripture. They searched the Bible for themselves and participated in the congregational process of discerning its meaning and application. They were, even in an age of widespread biblical rediscovery, a peculiarly biblical   people.

The significance of Anabaptist approaches to the Bible

There are several reasons for investigating long-ignored Anabaptist principles of biblical interpretation (hermeneutics).

Text-based interpretation

Anabaptist hermeneutics developed contemporaneously with the Reformers' hermeneutics, the approach from which the prevailing historical-critical method of biblical interpretation derived. Anabaptists, though indebted to the Reformers' methodology, recognized limitations and advocated different approaches. Reappraisal of this sixteenth-century alternative provides historical support for attempts to address limitations of the historical-critical method, revealing weaknesses in its Reformation roots and offering perspectives similar to those advocated by recent critics. The current critique of methods which focus on examining the historical context of the original authors and audiences as the primary locus of meaning yields fresh approaches that focus far more on the text itself as we shall see in subsequent chapters.

Key hermeneutical issues

Significant issues of interpretation emerged from debates between Anabaptists and Reformers, Spiritualists and other Anabaptist leaders: the relationship between the Testaments, the Spirit's role in interpretation, the hermeneutical significance of the congregation, the epistemological significance of obedience, and the extent to which Scripture is perspicuous. The Reformers' triumph and suppression of Anabaptism ensured that their hermeneutical views were embraced by subsequent generations. But these issues remain contentious. If the tradition that developed from the Reformers' hermeneutics has failed to provide adequate resolution, it is worth re-examining the Anabaptist tradition.

The role of the Spirit in interpretation

Many recent ecclesial developments resonate with ways Anabaptists dealt with similar issues. Examples include the challenge of liberation theologies to the traditional relationship between understanding and application, and the challenge of charismatic movements to persistent marginalization of the Spirit in hermeneutics. Anabaptists rejected many prevailing ideological commitments and developed a hermeneutic appropriate for a movement of the poor, powerless, and oppressed. This provides a sixteenth-century vantage point from which to assess liberationist developments. As a movement within which the relationship between word and Spirit was extensively explored, Anabaptism offers resources for developing a hermeneutic for charismatic churches, and insights into strained relationships between such churches and those whose emphasis is on the word.

Congregational hermeneutics

Anabaptist practices were developed in congregations rather than seminaries. They represent an alternative historical paradigm and a heritage as long as that of the scholarly approach. Studying this approach and appreciating its value can contribute towards closing the widely acknowledged gap between scholars and churches.

Interpretation from the perspective of the poor and persecuted

Anabaptists, unlike Reformers and most scholarly interpreters, were mainly poor, uneducated, and persecuted. This gave them insights into Scripture that were less accessible to their more comfortable contemporaries, but analogous to the experience of the early churches and many Christian communities today. At the start of the third millennium – for the first time since early in the first millennium – most Christians are poor. Furthermore, persecution is the experience of a surprising number. Anabaptist perspectives are pertinent in many parts of the church today.

Interpretation from outside the mainstream

Anabaptist hermeneutics is significant as one expression of an interpretative approach that has characterized numerous fringe groups throughout church history. Studying these groups reveals diversity but also areas of fundamental agreement that distinguish them from their mainstream contemporaries. The persistence of this alternative approach suggests it may contain valuable elements neglected by others.

Rejection of the alliance of church and state

Anabaptists' rejection of the Constantinian synthesis of church and state affected their biblical interpretation, just as its acceptance by Catholics and Protestants influenced their hermeneutics. Anabaptists rejected Christendom assumptions and adopted a hermeneutic that reflected this in its presuppositions, methods, and conclusions. This offers us an approach with historical roots as deep as the Reformers' that is more appropriate for interpreting Scripture in our post-Christendom context.

Discerning Anabaptist hermeneutics

To understand Anabaptist hermeneutics, merely examining significant leaders' writings is inadequate. The contribution of leaders, especially those who were educated, was substantial and provided foundational teaching for Anabaptist congregations, but they did not provide authoritative answers to every doctrinal question or authoritative interpretations of every biblical text. Ordinary Anabaptists were more involved than their Reformed counterparts in interpreting Scripture. Though most relied on hearing and memorizing Scripture, they reflected on it and participated in the congregational process of discerning its meaning and application. This every-member approach had profound implications for Anabaptist hermeneutics.

Nevertheless, the frequency with which key texts and arguments appear in records of Anabaptists under interrogation indicates that their leaders provided tools for their brothers and sisters to explore Scripture. Often these comprised topical concordances – systematic collections of biblical quotations. More than biblical indexes, they provided hermeneutical assistance to help readers interpret an otherwise bewildering array of texts and guided congregations towards doctrines, practices, stories, and ethical stances regarded as having greatest significance for discipleship.

Anabaptism did not produce systematic theologians. Its focus was pragmatic rather than intellectual, concerned with obeying rather than analyzing and categorizing Scripture. Its confessions concentrated on ecclesiological and ethical rather than theological matters. Nor was there opportunity to produce many theological treatises. Most leading thinkers died young, before they had developed systematic presentations or had time and freedom to write at length. There is, therefore, no definitive Anabaptist statement on hermeneutics. But this does not mean a coherent hermeneutic cannot be discovered from their writings.

There are substantial discussions of hermeneutical issues, particularly in the writings of leaders who lived into the second generation. Menno Simons and Dirk Philips contributed thoughtful statements on methodology with copious applications. Pilgram Marpeck's *Testamentserleutterung* is an extensive treatment of the relationship between the Testaments, in which he explains his hermeneutical principles. There are, in various Anabaptist writings, sections on hermeneutical issues – the use of allegory, the Spirit's interpretative role, and the relationship between the Testaments. These sources must be augmented by considering how Anabaptist congregations functioned and how Scripture was used in practice.

Anabaptist hermeneutics developed in debate with opponents as well as through internal conversations. Anabaptist leaders were opposed not only by Reformers and Catholics, but also by other radical groups, such as Spiritualists. On some issues their stance differs depending on which opponents they were confronting. This must be recognized in attempting to discern hermeneutical norms.

Nevertheless, despite variations and difficulties in discovering an authoritative view, a coherent and distinctive Anabaptist hermeneutic emerges from their writings and practice. Contemporary opponents certainly assumed Anabaptist groups agreed on hermeneutical principles. And the fact that uneducated Anabaptists operated according to common principles of biblical interpretation indicates a shared outlook across the movement.

Six core convictions of Anabaptist hermeneutics

Six central Anabaptist hermeneutical principles can be identified, albeit expressed and nuanced in different ways across the movement.

1. Scripture is self-interpreting

A crucial component was the conviction that Scripture is self-interpreting. Statements from Anabaptist leaders demonstrate widespread confidence about the clarity of Scripture and its sufficiency without external additions. Repeatedly, Anabaptists on trial declared that their views were derived from no source other than Scripture, and that Scripture was sufficiently clear to justify these.

The Schleitheim Confession (1527) emphasized the importance to the Swiss Brethren of taking biblical teaching at face value. Balthasar Hubmaier, the leader with the most extensive theological training, strongly affirmed the right of private interpretation and insisted Scripture was straightforward enough to be understood and obeyed.

Marpeck advocated a similar approach in German congregations. Like Hubmaier, he resisted introducing complications rather than accepting biblical texts as they stood. This, he believed, produced theological wrangling, led to Scripture being downgraded, and confused ordinary Christians. Marpeck rejected the imposition of an interpretative grid on Scripture to force passages into consistency with preconceived theological positions. He defended private interpretation and insisted Scripture was sufficient without external additions. Among the Hutterites, Peter Riedeman expressed the same conviction.

Dutch Anabaptists shared this perspective, but only after recognizing the dangers of interpretative authority being concentrated in the hands of dominant leaders and of allowing unnecessarily complex and speculative systems to influence interpretation. Among apocalyptic Anabaptists, such as Melchior Hoffman, the conviction that all could interpret was accepted, but this did not mean all were equally skilled, or that all passages were susceptible to interpretation by every believer. Menno Simons, reacting against speculative systems, expressed his confidence in Scripture's clarity and simplicity.

Statements from Anabaptists on trial demonstrate that their leaders' attitudes had enfranchised the membership and produced tremendous faith and confidence, even in the face of clever questioning and severe pressure.

Multiple references in Anabaptist writings and testimonies to the clarity and sufficiency of Scripture indicate a significant hermeneutical claim. Anabaptists were concerned the Reformers were paying lip service to the plain sense of Scripture and the right of private interpretation, but hedging these about with many qualifications. Their repeated emphasis on Scripture being simple, clear, and plain urged a more radical approach. They challenged the Reformers' reliance on reason and increasing restriction of interpretation to pastors and scholars, bondage to doctrinal considerations and traditional interpretations, and use of external means to evade rather than explain Scripture. They disagreed about the inability of uneducated people to interpret Scripture and the value of scholarship, believing such training did more harm than good, obscuring rather than clarifying Scripture. They suspected predetermined doctrinal emphases were stifling biblical studies and precluding openness to fresh revelation. Anabaptists opposed the Reformers' tendency to regard Scripture as frequently ambiguous, regarding this as another device to evade its challenge. The Reformers agreed Scripture was clear on doctrinal issues but were not as decisive about ecclesiology or ethics; Anabaptists refused to separate these issues.

This stress on the clarity of Scripture has strengths and weaknesses. For example, Marpeck's resistance to imposing the interpretative grid of systematic theology on biblical texts is one this book passionately advocates. This stress on Scripture's clarity allows texts to speak for themselves. However, these very texts concerning, for example, the character of God, do turn out to be highly ambiguous as we shall see in Part 2. The Anabaptists' insistence on the lack of ambiguity was well-meaning, especially in their desire to put into practice the clear teachings of Jesus, but is ultimately flawed.

2. Christocentrism

Confidence that Scripture was clear and that all Christians could interpret it applied preeminently to passages containing the words and actions of Jesus. The belief that Jesus clarified what was previously obscure appears frequently in Anabaptist writings.

Among the Swiss this conviction appears repeatedly. Christocentrism, for Hans Pfistermeyer, meant that Jesus' words took precedence over all other words in Scripture, and that Christ was the interpreter of the Old Testament. It was by the words of Christ that Michael Sattler asked to be judged as to his faithfulness to the whole of Scripture. Similarly, Felix Mantz instinctively drew on the example and teaching of Jesus when arguing ethical or ecclesiological points.

Riedeman's writings demonstrate that Hutterites shared this christocentric approach. Comparing the Testaments, he concluded that what God really wants from his people could only be found by listening to Jesus, rather than hunting through Old Testament "shadows".

Among South German Anabaptists, Jesus' example and overall teaching thrust, rather than his explicit commands, was accorded primary significance. Hans Denck regarded Jesus' example as determinative, forbidding Christians treating Old Testament teachings and examples as normative.

It is arguable that a different approach was evident among apocalyptic Anabaptists such as Hoffman, Hans Hut, Bernhard Rothmann, and David Joris, who concentrated on prophetic and apocalyptic passages and interpreted Scripture in light of their interpretation of these. They adopted a dispensationalist approach, whereby different ethical requirements and spiritual responses were appropriate in different eras of history. Christocentrism was not absent, but it was harder to maintain as apocalyptic passages took center-stage.

In Münster, Christocentrism was abandoned and Old Testament practices became normative – with disastrous consequences for the Münsterites, whom the besieging armies massacred, and for the whole Anabaptist movement, regarded as equally dangerous.[3] This incident explains the determination of Menno and other

Dutch leaders to resist the still-popular apocalyptic approach and to be thoroughly christocentric. Menno, like Hubmaier, was confident that Jesus' words and example were clear and straightforward by comparison with other parts of Scripture. By the 1540s, as eschatological prophecies remained unfulfiled, apocalyptic interpretation waned and Christocentrism became normative.

Christocentrism meant that the Bible was not flat; some passages had greater authority for doctrine and practice than others. The New Testament took precedence over the Old, and Gospel accounts of Jesus' life and teachings were the pinnacle of God's revelation and primary in all questions of interpretation. Christocentrism meant that the whole Bible pointed to Jesus. The Old Testament prepared the way, pointing forward to him as the fulfilment of all God's promises. The New Testament pointed back to him as founder and head of the church, its source of life and power, and the example it followed.

For Marpeck, especially, Christocentrism was a deliberate policy to ensure Jesus was honored as the unique Son of God and authoritative interpreter. Anabaptists were deeply concerned to honor Christ, to give him first place in all aspects of life. They feared that the Reformers' emphasis on learning and reason enthroned Christ dogmatically, but dethroned him in relation to discipleship. For Marpeck, this had implications for biblical interpretation: Jesus was the preeminent revelation of God, who unlocked the secrets of Scripture.

Christocentrism, at its best, was not a literalistic and legalistic application of Jesus' teaching. Although some Anabaptists called Jesus the new lawgiver and treated his sayings as proof-texts, others regarded his example, lifestyle, spirit, relationships, and intention as crucial for interpreting the rest of Scripture. Christocentrism also meant that a living experience of Jesus was a prerequisite for hermeneutics. The historical Jesus was central to the text and the Christ of faith was central to the life-experience of interpreters. Anabaptists based their hermeneutics on a combination of the objective basis of Christ's human life and the subjective basis of their experience of him.

Reformed interpretations were *christological*: Jesus was the supreme revelation of God to humankind, and his death, resurrection, and ascension were God's central acts in history, through which salvation was available to believers. With this Anabaptists heartily agreed. However, the Reformers' emphasis was less on Jesus himself and more on his salvific acts and the doctrine of justification by faith. Their hermeneutics can be termed *soteriological*: their understanding of salvation provided the hermeneutical key to Scripture. Anabaptist hermeneutics were *christocentric*, focusing on Jesus himself rather than primarily on doctrines describing his redeeming work: Jesus was not only redeemer but also the example to imitate and the teacher to obey. Christocentrism was tied more firmly to the human Jesus and, consequently, their interpretations differed significantly.

Anabaptists were charged with literalism and legalism, naively trying to copy Jesus and turning him into a new lawgiver, rather than the unique Savior whose sacrifice freed them from bondage to law-keeping. Although some Anabaptists slipped into literalism and legalism in their determination to obey Jesus' teachings, their hermeneutic was often more sophisticated. Most refused to settle for the Reformers' generalities, but many heeded the spirit and intention of Jesus as well as his specific words and actions.

The Reformers suspected the emphasis on Jesus as example threatened the doctrine of grace alone and smacked of works-righteousness. Anabaptists argued repeatedly that they were not reverting to works-righteousness, and that the Reformers were unbalanced in teaching "faith alone". Anabaptists were accused of overemphasizing the human Jesus and underemphasizing the risen Lord. By emphasizing an aspect of Christology they felt was being neglected, Anabaptists have given an unwarranted impression that they were less committed to other aspects of Christology. They have also been criticized for selectivity, listening to sayings of Jesus that fit most naturally into their presuppositions and endorse their own convictions.

Christocentrism acted as a corrective to the Reformers' doctrinal approach. It was more radical in calling for a life of costly discipleship based on the example of Jesus, and less radical in mediating between the Reformers' emphasis on faith alone and traditional Catholic teaching. Constant reference to Jesus' words and actions challenged the Reformers, questioning the development of theology detached from the historical Jesus. And on ethical issues, the Anabaptist practice of starting with Jesus produced different conclusions from those reached by Reformers, who struggled to relate Jesus to their ethical convictions. In the next chapter I will focus specifically on an approach to reading the Bible, informed by the Anabaptists, which puts Jesus at the center of Biblical interpretation.

3. The two Testaments

In the sixteenth century, the relationship between the Testaments was much debated. Within Christendom many issues were decided by reference to the Old Testament, but those with new access to Scripture were questioning the legitimacy of this in light of New Testament principles.

Views about the relationship between the Testaments can be plotted between opposite poles of continuity and discontinuity. Anabaptists were generally located considerably closer to the discontinuity pole than Reformers. For Anabaptists, this under-girded many disagreements with Reformers, and they wrote extensively to explain and defend their practice.

Swiss Anabaptists assumed true interpretations could be found by carefully comparing the Testaments and treating the New Testament as primary, rather than imposing uniformity on Scripture, thereby leaving Old Testament practices unaffected. Participants in the Bern Debate (1538), though acknowledging the value of the Old Testament, curtailed its scope by granting it validity wherever Christ had not suspended it and wherever it agreed with the New Testament. Hubmaier expressed the same concern that using the Old Testament as if it were of equal authority should not compromise the New Testament.

Dutch Anabaptists were convinced the New Testament repre-sented a radical change from the Old Testament, so the Testaments could not be regarded as equivalent. Dirk Philips complained about his contemporaries' illegitimate use of the Old Testament. However strongly they emphasized discontinuity between the Testaments, most did not regard this as challenging Scripture's essential unity as the Word of God – but the primary focus was on discontinuity.

Marpeck was the most radical Anabaptist leader on this issue, convinced that the Old Testament functioned as the foundation of a house and the New Testament as the house itself; while the foundation was important, foundation and house must be distinguished. There were, however, important and influential exceptions to this approach. Hut, Hoffman, and others interested in eschatology used apocalyptic and prophetic passages regardless of which Testament these were in. The Münsterites treated the Old Testament as normative. Sabbatarian Anabaptists Oswald Glait and Andreas Fischer attempted to apply Old Testament laws in the contemporary context.

Anabaptists taught both continuity and discontinuity. They argued not for rejection of the Old Testament, or for divorce of the Testaments, but that the New Testament was radically new and could not be interpreted in unbroken continuity with the Old Testament. The New Testament did not revoke the Old Testament or make it worthless, but the Old Testament was subsumed in the New Testament and could not function in isolation from it.

Treating the Testaments thus had significant implications and led to major differences between Anabaptists and Reformers. Many ecclesiological and ethical practices, including persecution, were justified from Old Testament passages. Anabaptists believed this discounted the newness of the New Testament, subordinating it to the Old Testament. They argued with Reformers not about how to interpret Old Testament passages, but about whether this was the place to seek ethical and ecclesiological guidance.

Anabaptists have been criticized for their deprecation of the Old Testament, failure to appreciate the essential unity of Scripture, use of allegory to harmonize Old Testament texts with the New Testament, and inadequate recognition of the importance of the Old Testament as the necessary framework for reading the New Testament, a framework Jesus and the apostles used freely.

Neither Reformers nor Anabaptists succeeded in handling the Old Testament well. The Reformers' insistence on the unity of Scripture and on treating the Old Testament seriously was compromised by their tendency to justify practices from Old Testament texts in ways that marginalized Jesus. Anabaptists challenged this, but in the process some came close to jettisoning the Old Testament.

A major influence on the development of this Anabaptist perspective was their experience of being assaulted by Reformers with a battery of Old Testament texts to destroy their position on ethical and ecclesiological topics. Two responses were possible: to argue that the Old Testament was not authoritative, or to show how Reformers were misinterpreting it. Anabaptists, unable or unwilling to adopt the latter course, opted for the former. As a strategy to defend their convictions and provide a coherent approach to Scripture in the face of persistent challenges, this succeeded. But this position cannot be defended by those who recognize the significance of the Old Testament for Jesus himself. In this book I shall argue for an approach that respects the whole biblical witness but that still puts Jesus at the center of biblical interpretation.

4. Spirit and word

The relationship between Spirit and word was a major hermeneutical issue of the Reformation. Anabaptists were not alone in struggling to give sufficient room for the Spirit while safeguarding the normative authority of Scripture. They were charged with erring in both directions, accused of both literalism and spiritualism.

There were significant differences between Anabaptist groups and between first- and second-generation practices. Accusations of literalism generally focus on Swiss Brethren and Hutterites; accusations of spiritualism on South German Anabaptists and some followers of Hoffman. Spiritualism, more characteristic of the first generation, was gradually replaced by reliance on accepted interpretations.

Labeling Anabaptism as literalistic or spiritualistic fails to reflect its diversity. Some inclined towards literalism to be faithful to Christ's commands; others relied on the Spirit to communicate the essential truth of God's revelation. In certain groups these tendencies were held in tension or used without attempting harmonization, regarding reliance on the Spirit and adherence to the letter as complementary.

Anabaptists' emphasis on the Spirit in hermeneutics owed much to the influence of Andreas Karlstadt, Thomas Müntzer, and Caspar Schwenckfeld on different sections of the movement. Another factor was anticlericalism, evident in Anabaptism and the peasants' movement. Hermeneutical reliance on the Spirit enfranchised uneducated believers, challenging the clergy's interpretative monopoly. Anabaptists believed that relying on the Spirit would result in more faithful application of Scripture than relying on tradition, learning, or human reason.

Anabaptist writings contain numerous references to this feature of their hermeneutics. Reliance on the Spirit was expected to check naive and legalistic interpretations: believers, who, left to their own resources, would misinterpret or not comprehend Scripture, could rely on the Spirit for insight. Openness to the Spirit was preferred to reliance on education and scholarship: the Spirit was the true teacher and guide, on whom both educated and illiterate believers should depend. There was generally no opposition between reliance on the Spirit and common sense; approaches that polarized Spirit and reason were unwelcome. The Spirit's work included not only explanation of Scripture, but conviction and persuasion so that interpreters acted on it. And an important consequence of reliance on the Spirit was openness to correction and fresh revelation.

Safeguards were built into this principle and guidelines issued to protect the unwary from error. Marpeck warned interpreters not to force the Spirit or allow personal desires to masquerade as the Spirit's leading. Menno urged that reason be used to check against wild interpretations. Locating primary interpretative authority in the congregation was another safeguard; as it pondered Scripture, the congregation could anticipate the Spirit's direction in both individual contributions and emerging consensus.

Anabaptists shared in contemporary discussions about the relationship between word and Spirit, discussions given urgency by the recovery of the Bible, experience of spiritual phenomena, and challenges to traditional ecclesiastical authority. They offered alternatives to Reformers, who seemed to give inadequate room to the Spirit, and to Spiritualists, who seemed to give inadequate room to the word. Sometimes they erred in the direction of spiritualism or literalism; sometimes they were naive or overconfident. But many Anabaptists demonstrated a firm commitment to both word and Spirit, and challenged those tempted to denigrate either.

5. Congregational hermeneutics

What Anabaptists believed about ecclesiology, the Spirit, and the interpretative competence of all required a communal approach to biblical interpretation, and anticlerical and egalitarian impulses in the movement and its social context militated against tendencies to restrict the teaching office to recognized leaders.

Their congregational hermeneutics represented refusal to endorse the Spiritualists' autonomous individualism, rejection of the Catholics' drastic curtailing of private interpretation by the authority of ecclesiastical traditions, and qualification of the Reformers' application of *sola scriptura*, which disenfranchised most Christians and replaced priestly tyranny with tyranny of the preacher.

Some Reformers initially held similar views on the congregation's interpretative role and the limited rights of secular authorities. But as they abandoned this position, Anabaptists moved in the opposite direction, denying secular rulers jurisdiction over biblical interpretation. The concomitant divergence over ecclesiology ensured only Anabaptists would explore congregational hermeneutics, for a hermeneutic community must comprise committed believers, eager to obey Scripture and open to the Spirit. Anabaptists assumed such congregations existed. The Reformers, adopting a gradualist approach to reform and territorial rather than believers' churches, lacked congregations able to function as hermeneutic communities.

Sensitive congregational leadership was crucial for congregations operating as hermeneutical communities: their task was guiding rather than dominating, facilitators rather than sole participants. Their primary concern was to ensure Scripture was being read and, through the contributions of all members, understood and applied – very different from the role of Reformed pastors. Itinerant leaders, such as Grebel, Hut, and Denck, and theologically trained pastors, like Hubmaier, were respected teachers. Their contributions carried great weight and might discourage contributions from others who thought differently. However, the readiness of such leaders to submit to corporate discernment ensured this did not entirely undercut the congregational principle.

Menno agreed congregations needed teachers, but he did not expect them to dominate proceedings. Hubmaier wanted scholars to help with technical details, such as how to translate passages, and to explain how others had interpreted passages, but not to override other members of the congregation. In groups relating to Marpeck, leadership was regarded as a gift and allowed to operate freely, but leaders remained subject to the authority of the community. Congregational hermeneutics does not require that every contribution carry equal weight but that every contribution is weighed.

Another indication that some Anabaptist leaders encouraged dialogue and interaction is frequent encouragement that readers should search Scripture themselves to see if what leaders were teaching was correct. This openness to correction is especially evident in Marpeck's writings, but similar statements appear in Swiss and Austrian branches of the movement. Menno professed openness to correction and further revelation; he fell short of this ideal, but his writings indicate that openness to correction was influential in Dutch Anabaptism. Such statements are conspicuous by their absence in the writings of Reformers, who saw their task as providing authoritative interpretations.

A criticism of congregational hermeneutics is that it simply pools ignorance. However, Anabaptists, who were very biblically literate, believed interpretation involved listening to the Spirit and that Scripture was simple enough for all to understand, at least in part. Studying together enabled each to share insights the Spirit gave. Seeking consensus helped them discard unreliable interpretations and confirm those that were helpful. Furthermore, the Spirit's presence was promised in a special way in the congregation. Congregations were undoubtedly prone to domination by vocal characters and those with more experience or education. But its strength was its refusal to exclude its weakest members, since the Spirit was available to all. The ploughboy might sometimes understand Scripture better than the theologian.

A limitation on Anabaptist practice was the virtual exclusion of Christian wisdom from prior centuries. The focus was on present consensus and little attention was given to past consensus. Seeking freedom from binding traditions, and believing the church was fallen, Anabaptists drew sparingly on the wisdom of earlier Christians. This released them from dependence on past authorities to make fresh discoveries, but impoverished their interpretation and deprived them of scholarly and spiritual counsel.

There were weaknesses in this communal approach: Anabaptists had few precedents as they pioneered it, but those who persevered gradually refined it. And it had significant strengths, especially the conviction that every member of the congregation could contribute to the interpretative task, and their openness to correction. Their concern for truth, readiness to listen to anyone under the authority of Scripture, and willingness to consider fresh interpretations, rather than squeezing texts into conformity with set creeds, present a continuing challenge.

6. *Hermeneutics of obedience*

Anabaptists often complained that biblical interpretation was divorced from application: emphasis was placed on attaining a theoretical understanding of Scripture rather than putting this into practice. They were unimpressed by the quality of discipleship in state churches and by the Reformers' ethical teaching, and concluded these factors indicated deficiencies in the way Scripture was interpreted. Reformers argued that sound doctrine was the basis for Christian lifestyle: Anabaptists were unconvinced that their teaching resulted in true discipleship.

This concern led Anabaptists to emphasize the clarity of Scripture. They understood there were difficulties in interpreting Scripture, but highlighting interpretative problems was a disincentive to obeying Scripture. Uncertainties about the meaning of certain texts encouraged hesitation rather than bold and radical action. Emphasizing that much of Scripture was easy to understand and needed simply to be obeyed, not endlessly debated, removed excuses for compromise, delay, and inaction. Scripture, they insisted, was difficult to apply because of its costly challenge, but generally not difficult to understand. Anabaptists were frustrated by Reformers seeming to evade biblical challenges under cover of discussions about precise meaning of texts.

The decision to locate interpretative authority in congregations should be similarly understood. Academics were poorly placed to test the validity of their conclusions: although experts in linguistics, theology, and church history, their interpretative context was theoretical rather than practical. Congregations were better placed to test the adequacy of interpretations in their communal life, worship, and witness. The emphasis within communal hermeneutics was on application rather than interpretation.

Marpeck rejected any division between interpretation and application. Interpreters should not explain Scripture and abdicate responsibility for applying it. Not only was deference to secular authorities unbiblical and detrimental to reformation, it also drove an unacceptable wedge between interpretation and application.

This was why the Swiss Brethren deserted Zwingli. On the interpretation of Scripture, Zwingli and the Brethren essentially agreed, but they profoundly disagreed about its application. Zwingli left application to the Zurich Council, but the Brethren regarded this as compromise, undermining the hermeneutical process by stopping short of obedient action. Zwingli was concerned about implementing Scripture, but accepted a distinction between explaining its meaning and applying its implications. This the Brethren rejected: interpretation and application were aspects of a single process.

This contrast between the Reformers' theological approach and the more pragmatic Anabaptist approach reappears in the writings of Menno and Dirk Philips. Their interpretation was interrelated with their involvement in congregations. Tentative understandings of Scripture were tested and refined as they explored their practical implications in congregational settings; and the congregations' needs and concerns posed questions and perspectives with which to approach Scripture.

Anabaptists also regarded obedience as a crucial prerequisite of hermeneutics: ethical qualifications took precedence over intellectual abilities or official appointments. Living in obedience to Christ and submission to Scripture was more important than education, linguistics, or doctrinal correctness. Hut argued that discovering the truth was not achieved by studying in universities, but by following and obeying Christ. Menno argued that teachers should be judged by their obedience to Scripture: only those whose lives showed they were regenerate should be trusted as interpreters. Dirk Philips insisted on two qualifications: an experience of the Spirit and an upright life.

One aspect of this ethical qualification, which by definition excluded state church preachers, was that interpreters must be free from the influence of secular power and vested interests. Those wary of offending the authorities or disturbing the status quo were not free to interpret faithfully. Issues of finance and safeguarding a comfortable lifestyle were sometimes seen as determinative. These issues were raised throughout the Anabaptist movement.

This emphasis on obedience attempted to protect congregations from the falsehood that would creep in if ethical criteria were absent. Only those actively committed to discipleship could be trusted to interpret Scripture. They might be less equipped academically, but their ignorance was less perilous than the falsehood taught by scholars who were not truly following Christ.

Readiness to obey texts being studied was vital for effective interpretation. Without this one could expect no help from the Spirit and, consequently, no real understanding of Scripture. Contrary to accusations, Anabaptists did not suggest interpreters must be perfect before they could understand Scripture. They differentiated between occasional sins, which did not disqualify interpreters, and a sinful lifestyle, which did. Menno taught that blindness resulted from sinful living since interpreters wanted to justify their sinfulness, not to understand and obey God's will. Anabaptists regarded obedience to one's present understanding of Scripture, and openness to obey new understandings (appropriated by faith, eager desire, and diligent study) as hermeneutical prerequisites. They were confident such obedience would find a response from God, from whom true interpretation came.

Obedience played another crucial role in Anabaptist hermeneutics: interpretations were subject to ethical testing before being accepted. Menno and Dirk Philips placed great weight on the ethical consequences of interpretations and discounted any that led to unacceptable results. This principle was connected with Anabaptist Christocentrism: interpretations were judged by how they related to the life and teachings of Jesus. Conformity to Christ, rather than to abstract ethical norms, was the plumb line Anabaptists used to measure proffered interpretations.

Both Reformers and Anabaptists examined the ethical consequences of interpretations, but they disagreed about what norms to apply. For Reformers, social stability was crucial. For Anabaptists, obedience to Christ's specific teachings and imitation of his lifestyle outweighed this, as they committed themselves to establishing a new social order (in their churches, at least), rather than preserving the existing one. They can be criticized for failing to apply Scripture to social and political issues beyond their own communities, but freedom from concern about maintaining social and ecclesiastical givens enabled them to consider interpretations others excluded as dangerous and destabilizing.

Teaching that application was integral to interpretation; emphasizing ethical, rather than academic, qualifications for interpreting; and insisting Christians operate with an epistemology of obedience – these challenge traditional approaches to biblical interpretation and provide a historical basis for considering contemporary movements that emphasize reflection on action rather than the traditional movement from theory to practical application.

The continuing contribution of Anabaptist hermeneutics

These six principles were all operative within the Anabaptist movement in its early years, but the continuing hermeneutical tradition derived from this period has been selective. The congregational testing of hermeneutical principles led to some being abandoned or recast. The disappearance of apocalyptic and spiritualist groups resulted in their hermeneutical approaches being discredited and discarded; the balance between word and Spirit shifted towards the former. The charismatic phase developed into a settled tradition, in which widespread interpretative enfranchisement and experience of communal hermeneutics was largely replaced by the authority of leaders and accepted interpretations. But the legacy of the early years continues to inspire some interpreters today.

Anabaptist hermeneutics can be understood as comprising not six principles but six areas where competing tendencies were held in creative tension. Thus, the tension between adherence to the letter and reliance on the Spirit characterized the whole movement. Some groups emphasized one aspect more than the other but, throughout the movement, this tension was maintained in a way that differentiated Anabaptist hermeneutics from competing alternatives. Similarly, the tension between enfranchising all to interpret and relying on trusted teachers was resolved differently in various times and places. But agreement that enfranchisement was vital and attempts to explore its communal dimension differentiated Anabaptism from the Reformers' preacher/scholar domination and the Spiritualists' individualism.

For Anabaptist hermeneutics to be a useful contemporary resource, we must ask whether these principles can be combined into an integrated hermeneutical approach. Surveys of Anabaptist hermeneutics face two temptations, both of which result in artificiality. One temptation is to imagine that Anabaptists developed a fully integrated hermeneutic in which the six principles were carefully synthesized. The other is to imagine that Anabaptists operated with distinct and unconnected principles and to treat them in isolation.

Anabaptist hermeneutics was not a unified or fully integrated system. It developed in a piecemeal fashion under pressurized circumstances and among diverse groups. But common convictions produced an approach to biblical interpretation in which various principles acted as checks and balances. Not all were operative in every Anabaptist group nor was the balance between them uniform, nor was their integration often explicit. But from the movement as a whole emerges a paradigm offering a more sophisticated and nuanced framework than any sixteenth-century congregation would have recognized, but which is nevertheless true to the spirit and direction of Anabaptist hermeneutics.

The synthetic model that can be extracted from Anabaptist hermeneutical principles and practices is that of a Spirit-filled disciple, confidently interpreting Scripture within a community of such disciples, aware that Jesus Christ is the center from which the rest of Scripture must be interpreted.

This approach had weaknesses: marginalization of scholarship, depriving Anabaptist communities of helpful tools for interpreting Scripture; inadequate handling of the Old Testament and lack of interest in applying Scripture to society; and tendencies towards literalism and legalism that hindered a more sophisticated approach, not necessarily to be equated with dilution and evasion. However, even these inadequacies contain important warnings. The development of more sophisticated methodologies has demonstrated the relevance of Anabaptists' suspicions about dilution and evasion. The history of the interpretation of the Old Testament and its use to justify many practices that cannot be supported on New Testament grounds underscores their concern about its misuse. And a mutually helpful relationship between scholars and congregations has still not been satisfactorily established.

Anabaptism was one of several movements between the fourth and sixteenth centuries that rejected the Constantinian synthesis. Although detailed analysis of earlier radical movements is rarely possible because of the paucity of surviving records, there are indications they employed similar hermeneutical principles. Anabaptist hermeneutics represents the suppressed but persistent testimony of many other marginalized groups, a non-Constantinian hermeneutical tradition broader and longer than that embodied in sixteenth-century Anabaptism alone.

The primary contribution of Anabaptism to contemporary hermeneutics is as a conversation-partner, offering fresh historical perspectives on issues debated in the sixteenth century but unresolved centuries later, and surprisingly relevant insights on issues that have emerged in recent decades. And, because Anabaptist insights are appreciated across an unusually wide range of traditions, Anabaptist hermeneutics can be a catalyst for interaction between those who would not normally be conversation-partners, encouraging them to learn from each other. This book, for example, is profoundly indebted to this Anabaptist approach, and I shall advocate below that reading the Bible after Christendom requires an approach that is Jesus-centered, rooted in community reading, open to the Spirit and oriented to obedient response. These are all clear Anabaptist hermeneutical principles. However, I part company with my sixteenth-century conversation-partners on their refusal to accept ambiguity in the texts and their approach to the two Testaments.

Part 2

Reading the Bible

Jesus as the Center of Biblical Interpretation

Introduction

The previous chapter highlighted the Christocentrism of Anabaptist hermeneutics. It is, of course, commonplace to state that Christian biblical interpretation begins and ends with Jesus. However, there is no overall agreement as to what this actually means in practice. This was also true for the Anabaptists themselves. For some it meant mining the Old Testament for messianic proof texts. Others employed allegorical techniques to read Jesus back into Old Testament texts.[1] The predominant contemporary approach, however, is both to read the Old Testament in the "light of its climax in the death and resurrection of Jesus Christ" and to understand "the climax of the drama, God's revelation in Christ, in light of the long history of God's self-revelation to Israel."[2] This approach employs figural or typological readings of the Old Testament and sees Jesus as both recapitulating and fulfilling Israel's history.

While there are merits in all these approaches, I want to suggest alternative ways in which Jesus is central to biblical interpretation. First, Jesus[3] exemplifies what the Old Testament means by loving God "with all your heart, and with all your soul, and with all your might" (Deut. 6:5) and loving "your neighbour as yourself" (Lev. 19:18), which he states are at the heart of the Old Testament (Matt. 22:40). Second, Jesus expands on this by speaking of "justice and mercy and faith" as the "weightier matters of the law" (Matt. 23:23). So, any reading of Scripture which claims to be christocentric should enhance our love of God and neighbor and contribute to human flourishing in terms of justice, mercy, and faithfulness. This brings ethics and praxis to the forefront of biblical interpretation. Finally, reflection on the person of Jesus can provide us with particular lenses with which to read the Bible. It has been customary in systematic theology to speak of the offices of Christ: namely Christ as prophet, priest, and king.[4] Although these are thoroughly biblical images, it is arguable that Christ's role as priest and king has been too often viewed through the lens of Christendom. Christ's priestly role can too easily reinforce clerical readings that perpetuate the clergy-laity divide and Christ's kingly role can too easily reinforce images of power and authority that render the poor and marginalized mute. I shall, therefore, propose using images of Jesus as prophet, pastor, and poet as angles of vision with which to read the biblical texts. These images are not exhaustive but by using several in this way I hope to demonstrate that there is no monolithic way to interpret Scripture – our interpretations are inevitably plural and should be celebrated as such. Prophetic, pastoral, and poetic angles of vision correspond to specific biblical genres (prophecy, epistle, and Wisdom literature) but also provide perspectives with which to view the bible as a whole.

Jesus as prophet

Deuteronomy 18:15–19 speaks of a prophet like Moses being raised up and this text is specifically applied to Jesus in Acts 3:22–23. Matthew, as we shall see later, structures his gospel specifically so that Jesus should be seen as the New Moses. Furthermore, the Gospels regularly categorize Jesus as a prophet (Matt. 13:57; 21:11, 46; Mark 6:14–16; 8:28; 14:65; Luke 7:16, 39–50; 13:33; 24:19; John 4:19; 6:14; 7:40, 52; 9:17). As Tom Wright demonstrates, Jesus displays characteristics of a number of Old Testament prophets: Micaiah ben Imlach (1 Kgs. 22), Ezekiel, Jeremiah, Jonah, Amos and, above all, Elijah.[5] Jesus as prophet was mighty in word and deed, pronounced oracles of judgement and proclaimed the in-breaking of the kingdom of God.[6] His message involved an invitation to repent and believe; it was a welcome to sinners with its offer of forgiveness, a challenge to live subsequently as befits the people of God and a summons to take up the cross.[7] I will say more on all this later. Jesus' message of the kingdom of God inspired an alternative consciousness to that of the dominant culture as well as profoundly critiquing that culture. As a prophet, therefore, Jesus was engaged in prophetic consciousness raising, prophetic energizing and prophetic criticizing.[8]

Prophetic consciousness raising

First-century Judaism was by no means monolithic, as is now a commonplace in biblical scholarship. Judaism in Palestine responded in different ways to the reality of Roman occupation. As Josephus records, there were four main options: Sadducees, Pharisees, Essenes and "the Fourth Philosophy."[9] The priestly leadership in Judea was drawn predominantly from the aristocratic Sadducees, many of whom were notoriously pro-Roman. They had a vested interest in maintaining the status quo. The Pharisees were particularly interested in maintaining purity and this brought them into regular conflict with the Jesus movement as recorded in the Gospels. Their concern for purity led to mixed responses to Roman occupation. Some engaged in clear opposition to the Romans and undoubtedly were attracted to revolutionary movements while others broadly accommodated themselves to Roman rule focusing on purity within the community as the means of achieving liberation.

For both Sadducees and Pharisees, however, the temple in Jerusalem was highly significant. For them it was first and foremost the place where Yahweh chose to dwell. It was also the place where sacrifice was offered and consequently forgiveness of sins effected. Finally, it had enormous political significance; those running the temple enjoyed great prestige.[10] The Essenes, however, rejected the temple; they regarded the high-priestly dynasty as invalid and refused to take part in the cult. Instead they worshiped within their own communities, as exemplified at Qumran, and looked for the day when a new temple would be built. Lastly, Josephus states that the Fourth Philosophy was in all respects like the Pharisees except that it was resolutely opposed to Roman rule, claiming that only Yahweh was king. Although Josephus exaggerates the importance of this sect, undoubtedly its values fed into subsequent revolutionary movements culminating in the Jewish War in AD 66.

Into this mix Jesus proclaimed an alternative vision of the kingdom of God. Through word and deed, teaching and parable he was engaged in consciousness raising. His message of radical obedience to God echoed the claims of the Fourth Philosophy but Jesus clearly advocated nonviolence.[11] To embrace the kingdom meant learning to live free from the claims of the Domination System.[12] Jesus' healings and exorcisms released people from the crippling effects of disease and demonic oppression and restored them to full life in the community. His teaching and parables constructed an alternative world in which sins and debts were forgiven,[13] cares and anxieties were to be set aside,[14] sinners, tax collectors, and prostitutes were welcome,[15] women were accepted as equals,[16] the lust for wealth and power was challenged,[17] and community relations were built on mutual trust, forgiveness, and appropriate confrontation.[18] Furthermore, in offering forgiveness of sins, Jesus explicitly challenged the continuing validity of the temple.[19] In questioning the temple Jesus shared some of the concerns of the Essenes. So, Jesus shared the Pharisaic concern for purity but radically redefined what it meant to be pure; he shared the Essene critique of the temple but, unlike Qumran, did not call for communities to withdraw from society; and he shared the Fourth Philosophy's desire to be free from domination but opposed their violent ideology. His teaching on avoiding the temptation to wealth and power was an implicit critique of the Sadducees. In every way, therefore, Jesus was creating an imaginative alternative to the options confronting people living in first-century Palestine.

Prophetic energizing

As Brueggemann demonstrates, it is the role of the prophet first to articulate an alternative to the dominant "royal consciousness" and second to energize people to be able to engage this new vision.[20] He states that there are three moves involved in such prophetic energizing.[21] First, the prophet offers appropriate symbols to counteract feelings of hopelessness. Jesus' healings, exorcisms, and regular practice of table fellowship, thereby welcoming all who would join in, are powerful examples of such symbols. Second, the prophet brings to public expression hopes and yearnings that have been suppressed. Jesus' announcement of the coming kingdom of God serves this function. The Old Testament frequently speaks of God as king of both Israel and the whole earth.[22] It also speaks of a day when God shall become king.[23] In the midst of the stark reality of Roman occupation such texts must have been difficult to appropriate. Jesus' frequent talk of the kingdom of God would have powerfully rekindled the hope contained in these texts. Finally, the prophet must speak both metaphorically about hope and concretely about real newness. Jesus' use of parables and teaching about new life in the kingdom enable this.

Prophetic Criticizing

The final role of the prophet is to critique the existing order. Jesus' itinerant status challenges the prevailing convention concerning security, his trenchant critique of the Pharisees and scribes challenges the existing religious order and his words and actions concerning the temple strike at the heart of its legitimacy as a continuing symbol of the religious and political life of Israel.

Jesus, in particular, regularly warns Israel that if she continues on her current course judgement will be imminent. An example of this occurs in the Lukan version of the sign of Jonah saying (Luke 11:29–32). Matthew clearly equates the sign of Jonah with Jesus' death and resurrection (Matt. 12:39–40). But reference to three days and nights is absent from the account in Luke. Instead, for Luke, just as Jonah became the sign for Nineveh so Jesus *will be* the sign for the generation he addresses (Luke 11:30). Note the future tense. Just as Jonah preached that Nineveh would be overthrown within forty days so Jesus was in effect saying that in rejecting his offer of a new way of being Israel, Jerusalem would be overthrown within the lifetime of the generation hearing him. This, of course, happened in AD 70. This becomes more explicit in Luke 19:41–44. The irony is that the "city of peace" failed to recognize the "Prince of Peace" (Isa. 9:6; Luke 19:38) and embrace his message of peace (Luke 19:42) and so was destined for war within a generation.[24]

Jesus as pastor

The first reference to Jesus as shepherd is found in Mark 6:34. This occurs after Jesus had sent the Twelve out on a preaching and healing mission. As a result of their successful mission, the crowds sought them out to such an extent that Jesus suggested they should get away to an isolated place. However, the crowds discovered where they were and followed them. Mark, echoing Numbers 27:17, 1 Kings 22:17, Ezekiel 34 and Zechariah 10:2, describes the crowd as sheep without a shepherd. Jesus responds with compassion and begins to teach them. In other words, Jesus recognizes that the appropriate pastoral response for people lacking direction is to teach them. In Matthew 18:12–14 Jesus speaks of the person who has one hundred sheep and one goes away. The good shepherd will search for the one who went astray until he finds it and restores it to the fold. In John 10 Jesus specifically refers to himself as the good shepherd. According to this text, the shepherd is known by the sheep, protects the sheep from wolves and lays down his life for the sheep. Finally, in Matthew 26:31 Jesus, quoting Zechariah 13:7, predicts that his disciples will scatter when he is taken from them. Jesus' pastoral role, therefore, combines teaching, care, relationship, and protection.

Reading the Scriptures pastorally

The New Testament Letters themselves are the primary pastoral genre. Through them communities are encouraged, built up, admonished, and challenged. But the whole Bible can be read through a pastoral lens allowing texts to speak to us in this dimension. The key text here is 2 Timothy 3:14–17. This passage is often quoted in discussions on biblical inspiration and inerrancy but I want to focus on the practical dimension of this text. According to the writer the Scriptures are able to do six things. First, they are able to bring the reader to salvation "through faith in Christ". This is the author's version of the Lukan Jesus' claim that all the

Scriptures point to him. Second, they are profitable for teaching; this resonates with Jesus as shepherd teaching the crowds in Mark 6:34. Third, they are able to rebuke; and fourth, they provide correction. In this way they can provide material to guard against false teaching (a prime concern of the Pastoral Epistles). Fifth, they provide training in righteousness. This could be construed as making upright and virtuous but such concepts cannot be divorced from the clear biblical use of righteousness as that which makes for right relationships and, therefore, its clear link to issues of justice. In this way there is also here a resonance with Jesus speaking of justice, mercy, and faith as "the weightier matters of the law" (Matt. 23:23). Sixth, they are able to equip readers "for every good work". Reading the Bible, according to this definition, equips us for praxis. Once again ethics comes into focus.

A clear example of this in practice comes from 1 Corinthians 10:1–22. Paul draws on the exodus narrative to remind the Corinthians that the wilderness account provides clear instruction for them. In particular, despite their "baptism" and spiritual sustenance many of them perished due to a combination of idolatry, sexual immorality, and lack of trust. In the same way, the Corinthians should not presume that their baptism (1:13–16) or their spiritual gifts (1:7) guarantee their standing before God (10:12). In particular, Paul refers back to this narrative to warn his readers against idolatry (10:14).

Paul's use of the exodus narrative in this way is highly instructive and provides a paradigm for reading the Bible through a pastoral lens. Other retellings of aspects of the Old Testament narrative can be found, for example, in Acts 2:14–36, 7:2–53 and Hebrews 11. The narratives concerning biblical characters and significant events can be powerful sources for building up the Christian community. They provide warnings as to how not to behave, examples of obedient response to emulate, puzzling encounters with God to challenge our preconceived notions of how God should behave, and so on. As we shall see, even difficult texts, such as the "texts of terror", can provide material for instruction that equips us for the task of proclaiming the gospel of the kingdom of God.[25] Outrage is sometimes the most appropriate response to a biblical text and this outrage can be the most effective route to spiritual insight and growth.

The paradigmatic Old Testament text for reading through a pastoral lens is, of course, Psalm 23. Here Yahweh is described as the shepherd who provides for all needs. The language is richly evocative and speaks of rest, well-being, and restoration as prerequisites for engaging in social justice ("paths of righteousness") which can prove dangerous and make enemies (23:4–5). But Yahweh's presence and provision are found in the midst of conflict – for social justice is engaged in "for his name's sake." As a result the psalmist experiences Yahweh's *shalom*. Here in a nutshell, in this most pastoral of psalms, we find the biblical exhortation: love God and do social justice.

In Mark 6:34 Jesus is described as having compassion for the crowd because "they were like sheep without a shepherd". This is a prelude to a feeding miracle which is so significant that it is told no less than six times in the Gospels. The feeding of the five thousand is the only miracle in Jesus' ministry that is recounted in all four Gospels (Matt. 14:13–21; Mark 6:32–44; Luke 9:10–17; John 6:1–15) and the feeding of the four thousand occurs in Matthew 15:32–39 and Mark 8:1–10. In John 6 the feeding miracle precedes Jesus' discourse on the bread from heaven, which has clear eucharistic references (there is no account of the Last Supper in John). The first feeding miracle, which takes place in the wilderness, clearly echoes both Yahweh's provision for Israel in the wilderness in Exodus and 2 Kings 4:42–44. The latter occurs in the context of famine in the land (2 Kgs. 4:38). The combination of the feeding miracle and the phrase "sheep without a shepherd" (echoing Ezek. 34:2–6) suggests "a criticism of the political economy of Palestine and the ruling class who profits from it".[26] Furthermore, the miraculous provision of food for the hungry masses also suggests a profound anti-imperial emphasis. Rome famously had the bread dole to feed its hungry citizens from the bread baskets of the empire. Jesus' role in feeding the masses out of compassion is implicitly contrasted with Rome's ability to do the same by means of military conquest (as Rome itself could not provide the grain to meet the needs of its population). The account in John is more explicit – as a result of the feeding miracle the crowd want to make Jesus king (John 6:15). The crowd perceive the provision of food as an imperial claim. Jesus specifically repudiates this. Finally, the combination of themes from

Psalm 23 (the "green grass" of Mark 6:39 echoes Ps. 23:2) and the Eucharist suggest the imagery of a table prepared in the midst of occupied territory (Ps. 23:5). Eucharistic feasting is to be a profound means of economic sharing which subverts the economy of empire.[27] This gospel rendering of Psalm 23 highlights that pastoral care helps to shape a community that is profoundly engaged with the world. One cannot read the Scriptures pastorally without also reading them politically!

Jesus as poet

> After the seas are all cross'd (as they seem already cross'd),
> After the great captains and engineers have accomplish'd their
>   work,
> After the noble inventors, after the scientists, the chemist, the
>   geologist, ethnologist,
> Finally shall come the poet worthy that name,
> The true son of God shall come singing his songs.[28]

According to the Gospels, Jesus' parables were enigmatic and not easily understood (Mark 4:11–13); indeed, Mark claims that parables were Jesus' characteristic form of speech (Mark 4:33–34). The poet, like the prophet, surprises us by using word imagery to unmask systemic injustice, evoke visions of an alternative world, and inspire action. "[T]he power of poetry [is] shattering, evocative speech that breaks fixed conclusions and presses us always toward new, dangerous, imaginative possibilities."[29]

Jesus was a peasant artisan in a predominantly agrarian, peasant society. His parables were generally drawn from this world and consistently deal with political and economic issues highly relevant to peasant society.[30] As Josephus records, social bandits (*lēstai*) were generally considered as heroes by peasant villagers.[31] The crowd cried out for the release of Barabbas, a *lēstēs*, instead of Jesus at the crucifixion (John 18:40) and Jesus was crucified with two *lēstai* (Mark 15:27). Jesus draws specifically on the example of such social bandits in the parable of the good Samaritan (Luke 10:30–35). It would appear that Jesus was attracted to the goals of social banditry in terms of social and economic justice but refused to endorse their violent methods. The parables of Jesus have a long history within Christendom of being read for the single moral point they are meant to be making. However, those reading from the margins have regularly produced readings of the parables sensitive to their political and socioeconomic setting.[32]

I have already drawn attention, in Chapter 3, to the parable of the ten minas in Luke 19:11–27. In this section I will highlight a couple of other parables which have lost their cutting edge over centuries of interpretation in Christendom.

The parable of the mustard seed (Mark 4:30–32)

Mark effectively only has four story parables: three seed parables in chapter 4 and the parable of the wicked tenants in 12:1–12. The inclusion of the parable of the mustard seed, as the last of the seed parables, is therefore significant for Mark. Most commentators note the proverbial nature of the smallness of the mustard seed in Jesus' time and see the point of comparison as being the largeness of the mature plant compared to the smallness of the seed. They also note reference to the birds nesting in its shade as echoing Ezekiel 17:22–24; 31:3–9 and Daniel 4:10–12. Thus the point of the parable is that the kingdom of God, which begins in such an insignificant way with the ministry of Jesus, will grow spectacularly and provide protection for many.[33] This interpretation fits well with Christendom as the triumph of Christianity.

However, if the point of the parable were to emphasize simply the growth of the kingdom into something significant then it would have made more sense to use the example of a tree, like the cedar, precisely as in the Ezekiel passages. But Jesus specifically draws on the mustard seed. The fully grown mustard bush cannot compare with the cedar if this were the point Jesus was trying to make. Rather, as Pliny notes in the first century AD, in his *Natural History* 19.170–71, the mustard plant, although beneficial, quickly gets out of hand and tends to take root where it is not wanted. Furthermore, as Jesus had already stated in the parable of the sower, the fact that it attracts birds is problematic for areas under cultivation (Mark 4:4). So, Jesus is much more likely to be emphasizing the problem the kingdom of God poses to the establishment. It tends to flourish precisely where it is not wanted and attracts undesirables (as far as those in control are concerned).

The point, in other words, is not just that the mustard plant starts as a proverbially small seed and grows into a shrub of three or four feet, or even higher, it is that it tends to take over where it is not wanted, that it tends to get out of control, and that it tends to attract birds within cultivated areas where they are not particularly desired. And that, said Jesus, was what the Kingdom was like: not like the mighty cedar of Lebanon and not quite like a common weed, like a pungent shrub with dangerous takeover properties. Something you would want in only small and carefully controlled doses – if you could control it.[34]

The parable of the dishonest manager (Luke 16:1–9)

This has proved to be one of the most puzzling of the parables in that Jesus appears to approve in some way the dishonest behavior exhibited in the story. Particularly problematic is the master's commendation of his manager's actions which apparently had lost him money. Every detail of this parable is significant and highlights the harsh realities of economic life in first-century Palestine.

First, this parable follows on immediately from the parable of the prodigal son and shows some affinity with it through the concept of "squandering" (same verb in Greek) property (15:13; 16:1). This is important because the hearers of the parables in Luke 15 included tax collectors, sinners, and Pharisees (15:1–2). The Pharisees are still listening at 16:14 so, by implication, the tax collectors and sinners, as well as the disciples (16:1), are also listening to this parable (and the subsequent one concerning the rich man and Lazarus). Jesus is particularly associated in the Synoptic Gospels with tax collectors and sinners. In Luke they appear, either in combination or separately, in 3:12; 5:27, 29, 30, 32; 6:32–34; 7:29, 34, 37, 39; 15:1–2; 18:10, 11,13; 19:2, 7.

Tax collectors should more appropriately be translated as toll collectors. In first-century Palestine direct taxes were collected by tax collectors known as *dēmosiōnes* (a word never used in the

New Testament), who were directly employed by the Roman authorities. The collection of other taxes was auctioned off to the highest bidder who became the chief toll collector, or *architelōnes* (Luke 19:2). The *architelōnes* would have a number of agents, *telōnai*, and these are the "tax collectors" of the Gospels. They acted as tax farmers in the indirect taxation system. The *architelōnes* had to pay over the amount bid in advance to the authorities and then was expected to collect this by assessing and collecting tolls. This naturally led to abuse as unscrupulous collectors sought to maximize their own profits in the process (Luke 19:8).[35]

The sinners were those who, by virtue of not being included among the righteous, were of low socio-religious status and were "counted among the excluded, even damned".[36] On the other hand, it is possible that the term functioned in a quasi-technical way to refer to those in a state of irretrievable indebtedness.[37] Either way, the sinners would certainly be numbered among the "poor" to whom Jesus was bringing good news (Luke 4:18).

Second, the parable occurs in a decidedly Jewish context. For the terms used to describe the debts in verses 6–7 are Jewish rather than Roman measures (*bath* as a liquid measure and *cor* as a dry measure). This is significant when considering the percentage of debt written off in these verses as we shall see.

Third, the rich man (*plousios*) is both very rich and is no hero. The amount of debt owed in verses 6–7 is vast and indicates a landowner with considerable estates. In the context of Jesus' day these rich landowners ruthlessly exploited their tenant farmers. The rich, therefore, are regularly condemned in Luke. This is already hinted at in the Magnificat (1:53) and made specific in 6:24–25. The rich landowner of Luke 12:16–21 is condemned for accumulating wealth and not distributing it and it is virtually impossible for the rich to enter the kingdom of God (18:18–25). To be commended by such a person (16:8) demonstrates just how entrenched in the economic system of exploitation the manager is.

Fourth, the main character in the parable, the dishonest manager, would have been a retainer in the household of the rich landlord. He would not have been a slave as he is dismissed from his post. However, as a retainer, he was in a precarious position.

He occupied a privileged place but enjoyed none of the security of a slave whose status as property of the master at least ensured ongoing accommodation. If the retainer should be dismissed he would no longer have a roof over his head and, deprived of his livelihood, he would become one of the expendables in society. To engage in digging (16:3) was the hardest kind of labor for the uneducated workman in the context of the day.

> With nothing left to offer but his animal energy, the former steward will have little chance of competing for jobs with peasants who have worked all their lives or with the excess of village artisans who have fallen into the class of expendables. Having been accustomed to regular meals, he will adapt poorly to irregular meals interspersed with long periods of hunger. As he loses what little strength he has, he will become a beggar until, like Lazarus and thousands of others, he dies from the complications of malnutrition and disease. His dismissal from the stewardship is a death sentence.[38]

The position that this retainer currently occupies, and which he dreads losing, is that of estate manager. As such he would have been given wide powers by his master to enter into binding contracts on the master's behalf. Under the laws of the day he could not be prosecuted for wrongdoing but could be shamed or dismissed. However, as estate manager, he would have been fully complicit in the exploitative economic activities of his rich master. The rich landowner would be concerned to receive maximum profit from his estate manager and would require proper accounting. However, it was common practice (and expected) that the manager would make his cut, outside of the books, before properly accounting to his master. This is significant and cannot mean that the reduction in debt was just the manager foregoing his cut, as many commentators state. For the original debt is clearly accounted for in the books.

Fifth, the debtors, due to the vast amount owed, would not be peasant tenants of the rich landlord. Instead they are to be seen as merchants in their own right and, as such, equally part of the economic system condemned in Luke. These merchants would have secured distribution rights to the landowner's crops. The

fact that the debts are stated in terms of goods rather than monetary amounts means that they have contracted to dispose of those
measures of goods.

Sixth, the different percentages of debts written off is significant. In the case of olive oil it represent 50 percent of the full
amount; for wheat it represents 20 percent. It was common in
those days to state the total amount of the debt incurred as a single figure that included principal plus interest. This amounted to
charging interest (forbidden under Torah – the Jewish context is
important) but hiding the fact by simply stating a single (inflated
by the hidden interest) figure. These hidden interest rates varied
depending on the degree of risk attached to the goods. Olive oil,
as more susceptible to adulteration, is of higher risk than wheat;
hence the greater interest rate. So what the estate manager is
doing here is writing off the (unlawful) hidden interest charged
on the transaction.

Seventh, the estate manager summons the debtors privately,
one by one, and insists that they renegotiate the contracts quickly
(16:5–6). At this stage the debtors do not know that he has been
dismissed and so they assume he has full authority to conduct
these reductions in debt. In this way each of the debtors becomes
indebted to the manager and, in the context of the day, would now
be under an obligation to repay the favor. In this way the manager has secured for himself the means to avoid inevitable desti-
tution following dismissal.

Eighth, the deliberate reduction of the debts by the amount of
hidden interest sends a clear message to the rich master.

> By this move, the steward reminds the master just who has been
> taking chances to accumulate his wealth, including the question-
> able practice of charging de facto interest in spite of the prohibi-
> tions of the Torah and oral torah. To preserve his social status, the
> master needs a steward who is willing to engage in these kinds of
> practices. This the steward has done. Whatever faults he may have
> do not include indolence in looking after the master's concerns. By
> his actions, therefore, the steward reminds the master of his value.
>
> Finally, the steward displays his resourcefulness to the master.
> The debtors think that they have received a generous dividend
> from their master/patron, and in their joy, they overlook the

obligation they have taken upon themselves. When the patron gives, he also indebts. By signing their revised [contracts] with the reduced amounts, the debtors have also signed a new contract with a different kind of hidden interest, and they will pay for their good fortune. Clients always do. The steward has not cheated the master; he has placed new cards in the master's hand. Seeing the steward's strategy and tactics, the master commends him for his shrewdness. The master has taken a short-term loss and has been reminded of the value of the steward, but he will realize long-term gains.

Little wonder that the master "commended the steward of unrighteousness for operating shrewdly" (author's translation). The praise is in keeping with the master and forms a fitting conclusion to the parable. The steward belongs to the system of injustice (*adikia*) and has never left it; he has no intention of giving up and dropping out just because another anonymous enemy has launched a campaign to remove him. The master, who belongs to the same system of exploitation, recognizes a gifted steward when he sees one.[39]

Using the example of how reducing debt "works" in a fundamentally unjust economic system, Jesus urges similar "shrewdness" in the use of money from his followers (16:8b–9). Specifically, this means practicing Jubilee as proclaimed in the programmatic announcement of Luke 4:18–19.[40] Debts are to be forgiven and possessions are to be given to the poor and in this way his followers inherit the kingdom (Luke 12:33–34; 14:33; 18:28–30; 19:8–9). However, there may also be a further point here. Given that the toll collectors form part of Jesus' audience, and given that Jesus is noted as keeping company with toll collectors, it may well be that Jesus himself actually commends the actions of the dishonest manager. Commentators have noted the ambiguity of "the master" (*ho kyrios*) in 16:8a as this could either refer to the master of the parable or to Jesus. This ambiguity may be deliberate. If Jesus is commending the actions of the manager in the parable in the hearing of the toll collectors then implicitly he could be encouraging the toll collectors to reduce the taxes they are collecting. This would be part of a strategy of tax resistance that is well documented among the peasant classes.[41] It is, of course, only in Luke that the specific charge of tax resistance is raised against Jesus (23:2).[42] Jesus the tax-resister would not be championed by Christendom. But in the contemporary environment, where in particular our taxes support the military machine, it should give us pause for thought.

Lament

Jesus the poet is not afraid to use lament as an appropriate response as can be seen particularly in his lament over Jerusalem (Matt. 23:37–39). The lament form, with its outrage against injustice and longing for God's deliverance, is a regular feature of the Old Testament, as we shall see. As texts of lament are read today it is appropriate to take them up as protests to God against the apparent senselessness of the violence and injustice we see all around us.

Summary

If we use the prophetic lens with which to read the Bible we will allow biblical texts to enable us to imagine an alternative reality to the dominant culture – a reality in which God is powerfully at work, yet predominantly in hidden ways. We will also allow the biblical texts to energize us, bringing us hope of a future in which righteousness and justice are manifestly exercised, and we will allow the biblical texts both to challenge us and to provide resources with which to confront the contemporary world we inhabit. Reading the Bible through a pastoral lens will enable us to be comforted, rebuked, and equipped for the task. Finally, reading through a poetic lens will enable false certainties to be challenged and open us up to fresh possibilities.

Furthermore, as stated above, these particular lenses coincide with specific genres: prophecy, Epistle, Wisdom literature, and lament, so that reading the Bible christocentrically involves being sensitive to issues of genre. In the next few chapters I will seek to summarize the whole Bible paying particular attention to genre.

6

Reading the Whole Bible

Introduction

In Chapter 1, I argued that Christendom relied on the Old Testament for its approach to ethics. However, in Chapter 5 I suggested that any *Christian* interpretation of the Bible must be christocentric in its approach. This does not mean that the Old Testament is now ignored and this chapter will seek to suggest ways in which the whole Bible can be read christocentrically.[1] Usually the attempt to place Jesus at the center of biblical interpretation results in some variation of a promise-fulfilment schema, with the Old Testament seen as promise pointing to fulfilment in Jesus and the New Testament seen as involving the tension between what Jesus has already accomplished in his life, death and resurrection and what remains to be accomplished at his Parousia – the tension between the "now" and the "not yet." The order of the Protestant canon suggests such an interpretation with the prophets prophesying a future that is fulfilled in the Gospels, continued in Acts, worked out in the Epistles and culminating in Revelation. This schema has often been articulated as encompassing creation, fall, redemption, and consummation.

Tom Wright, in adapting the above schema, provides a helpful analogy as to how contemporary Christians can engage with the Bible.[2] He suggests the example of a Shakespearean play whose fifth act has been lost. However, there is such a wealth of plot, characterization, and so on within the first four acts that it is deemed appropriate that the play should be performed. Nevertheless, it is decided not to write a script for the fifth act, but to allow the actors to so immerse themselves in the first four acts that they are able to work out a fifth act for themselves. Each performance of the play thereby involves improvisation based on the authority of the first four acts and would necessarily consist of both innovation and consistency. Each performance could then be judged on the basis of its degree of faithfulness to the known script. Wright suggests that the Bible functions as the first four acts (and the first scene of the fifth act); in addition he notes that the Bible gives some indication as to how the play should end (Rom. 8; 1 Cor. 15; Rev. 21 – 22). The first four acts correspond to:

(1)   Creation;
(2)   Fall;
(3)   The story of Israel; and
(4)   Jesus.

The New Testament corresponds to Act 5, Scene 1.[3] In performing the rest of Act 5, "[t]he church would then live under the 'authority' of the extant story, being required to offer something between an improvisation and an actual performance of the final act."

This model rules out any notion of the Bible as a rule book or repository of timeless truths but sees it instead as providing an authoritative foundational script for an unfinished drama that requires sensitive performance in the present to move the drama towards its ultimate conclusion. However, continuing with the analogy, the church finds itself in the present having enacted numerous scenes over the past two millennia without reaching the conclusion of the drama hinted at in the New Testament. This period has been dominated in the West by Christendom and the question naturally arises as to what it means to provide a faithful performance of Scripture today and to what extent such a performance should depend on church tradition (previous scenes of the fifth act)?

Wright himself provides an interesting example from the Old Testament – that of the prophet Micaiah, son of Imlah, in 1 Kings 22. He notes that, in fact, the false prophets had everything going for them – they quote Scripture (Deut. 33:17 in 1 Kgs. 22:11); they had the tradition of Yahweh as the God of battles on their side; and they had reason on their side – the combined forces of Israel and Judah should prove more than a match for their northern enemies. Yet this passage subverts the usual appeal to Scripture, tradition, and/or reason – the three generally accepted criteria for acceptable theological interpretation of Scripture. Instead it is Micaiah's *experience* of standing in the council of Yahweh that counts (1 Kgs. 22:19–23).

It would appear then that faithful performance of this fifth act requires careful attention to the script but not in such a way that repeats it verbatim but rather works imaginatively with it, sensitive to the leading of the Spirit. The biblical text, therefore, acts as a means of funding the prophetic imagination of the church.

Both Jesus and Paul provide us with examples of this process within Act 4, and in Act 5, Scene 1. Jesus pays attention to the script he inherits: "Do not think that I have come to abolish the law or the prophets; I have come not to abolish but to fulfil" (Matt. 5:17); but that fulfilment involves both genuine innovation: "You have heard that it was said . . . but I say" and a substantial critique of the tradition (e.g. Mark 2:23–28; Matt. 23). Paul likewise insists that we cannot slavishly follow Scripture without reference to the life-giving Spirit (2 Cor. 3:6). Furthermore, just as Jesus felt free to disregard both Scripture and tradition, so Paul is able to disregard a specific command of Jesus (1 Cor. 9:14–15; cf. Matt 10:10; Luke 10:7). What was appropriate for wandering disciples in Palestine has to be recontextualized in the very different circumstances of urban life in the wider Greco-Roman world.

The nature of the script

The above model still begs the question as to what is the underlying nature of the script the church actually inherits? What is the overall plot that informs faithful performance today? Wright's view of the five acts follows the prevailing Protestant understanding since the Reformation, which is that the Bible provides us with a compelling story of the plight of humanity: humankind through sin is estranged from God and is incapable by its own efforts to be reconciled to God. The Old Testament graphically portrays how Israel, despite the provision of the Law and the Prophets, fails to meet God's standards. However, God comes to humanity's rescue in providing his own son as an atoning sacrifice, thereby effecting reconciliation. All that is required from humanity is faith in Christ and his atoning work. The biblical script is thus construed as a narrative concerning creation, subsequent fall and redemption.

> Human beings (generically speaking), originally created good, are now fallen, sinful, and rebellious against God at the core and incapable of redeeming themselves by their own effort or "works." Instead, God alone can redeem human beings from their sinful state, and he does so by atoning for their sins through the substitutionary and salvifically efficacious sacrifice of Jesus Christ. Rather than relying on the merits of our own (outward) effort or works to save us – which is always the greatest human temptation and source of pride before God – we must cast ourselves on the undeserved mercy of God shown in Jesus Christ, through whom we are saved strictly out of God's own gracious goodwill and through his work. Human beings must therefore have faith *in* Jesus Christ and his atoning sacrifice in order to be rescued from bondage to sin and saved from the wrath of God. Faith itself, in many tellings of this story, is not something that human beings can muster or do or achieve, but is that purely passive (inner) *receiving* of God's grace made possible by the Holy Spirit working in the human heart. Thus the very core of the gospel which Paul preached is thought to be this: the individual sinner is caught in an inescapable plight and thus in desperate need of salvation, of being made right – justified – before God. This "righteousness" is found in one's faith in Jesus Christ alone, rather than through one's own striving; through faith, Christ's righteousness is "imputed" to the sinner, who is thus enabled to stand before God without guilt or shame.[4]

This understanding of justification by faith in Christ is seen as central to Paul's theology and has recently been affirmed by Roman Catholics as well as Protestants.[5]

However, this story of creation-fall-redemption, which pervades Christian thinking, is problematic in a number of ways. First, astonishing as it may seem, Genesis 3 is not a central passage in Jewish reflection on their Scriptures and is generally not interpreted as a mythic account of humanity's fall. Apart from Ezekiel 28 there are no clear subsequent references to it in the Old

Testament. Paul's interpretation of this text in Romans 5:12–21 has, of course, been decisive for subsequent Christian identification of this passage as a narrative of the fall. However, as Brueggemann states, Paul draws judgements that are not based on the text as such but depend on later theological developments and furthermore he cites Genesis 3 in a specific context; it is not a passage that features prominently elsewhere in Paul's thinking. Indeed, Brueggemann emphatically states:

> Frequently, this text is treated as though it were an explanation of how evil came into the world. But the Old Testament is never interested in such an abstract issue. In fact, the narrative gives no explanation for evil. There is no hint that the serpent is the embodiment of principle of evil. The Old Testament characteristically is more existential. It is not concerned with origins but with faithful responses and effective coping. The Bible offers no theoretical statement about the origin of evil. And, indeed, where the question of theodicy surfaces, it is handled pastorally and not speculatively (cf., for example, Habakkuk).[6]

Second, this understanding of the overall biblical narrative bypasses the crucial Gospel narratives in which Jesus freely offers forgiveness and welcomes the outcasts of society. The Jesus of the Gospels apparently expects humanity to be capable of loving God and neighbor (Luke 10:25–28) and of practicing justice, mercy, and faithfulness (Matt. 23:23). The understanding of the atonement as dealing with humanity's estrangement from God does not do justice to the notion of Jesus as "God with us" in the incarnation. Third, recent Pauline scholarship has questioned both the centrality of the notion of justification by faith for Paul's theology and the prevailing understanding of justification.[7]

On the other hand, Catholic theology standing in the tradition of Thomas Aquinas has tended to emphasize creation ordinances and natural law built upon Genesis 1 and 2. The problem here is that, once again, these two chapters do not figure prominently in the rest of the Old Testament.

So, in summary, Wright's model is a useful one in that it rightly draws attention to the notion of the church performing the text in the present. However, the content of the previous acts is misconstrued. In particular, Acts 1 and 2 do not bear the weight that Wright or Catholic tradition assigns them in the biblical narrative and Act 3, the story of Israel, is depicted by Wright as one of failure resulting in Israel's continuing experience of exile as God's punishment. What Wright's linear model fails to see is that the story of Jesus, according to the New Testament, means that the preceding acts have to be fundamentally reconfigured and reread in the light of the Christ event. Furthermore, the grand schema of creation-fall-redemption-consummation ignores the complexity of the biblical material in which a multiplicity of voices offer competing perspectives on the God of Israel.[8]

Post-Christendom Bible reading

Reading the Bible after Christendom requires a sensitivity to both aspects of the composite term "post-Christendom". The term requires engagement with Christendom and its received tradition of over two thousand years of interpretation of the Bible. It would be naive, arrogant, and impossible to ignore this long history of interpretation. Nevertheless, this tradition should be approached with a hermeneutic of suspicion, recognizing all the effects of Christendom outlined in Chapter 1. Furthermore, in recognition of our postmodern context, any such reading should maintain suspicion of any *controlling* metanarrative which seeks to ignore or minimalize difference. It is proposed, therefore, that any post-Christendom reading of the Bible should critically engage with the received tradition. As such the traditional notion of an overarching story should be taken seriously as should the overall canonical shape of the Bible, which moves from creation to new creation.[9] On the other hand, we also need to pay equal attention to the specificities of particular biblical texts and to recognize that narrative is not the only biblical genre. In paying attention to what Brueggemann calls "little stories" over against "the great story" we will become sensitized to the Bible's ambiguity and complexity and learn to appreciate dissenting voices within the text.[10] Once again Brueggemann puts this well:

In the Bible, the little pieces that constitute the text do more or less flow toward a central narrative, but not easily, obviously, or uniformly. To make the little pieces fit requires our most heavy-handed, systematic propensity . . . I am proposing that as we attend to the minor, unincorporated dramas of the Bible, we give folk freedom and permit to attend to the minor, unincorporated dramas of our own life, which are not to be run over roughshod, either by imperial orthodoxy, by imperious ego-structure, or by rationalistic criticism.[11]

By paying detailed attention to particular texts we avoid the temptation to move too quickly to some systematic synthesis of the data. In particular, this applies to the Bible's central character – God. We are used to naming the attributes of God according to the discipline of systematic theology and so envisage God as omnipotent, omniscient, and unchanging. However, close attention to specific texts shows, for example, a God who is revealed in the powerlessness of the cross (what Paul in 1 Cor. 1:25 dares to call "God's weakness"),[12] a God who does not know that the Israelites would engage in child sacrifice (Jer. 32:35) and a God who changes his mind (Jonah 3:10). Furthermore, this God at times (even if only "for a moment") abandons his people (Isa. 54:7) and is at times violent (Josh. 8:1–2, 24–27). Brueggemann insists that "the canonical text is indeed the full telling of the tale of YHWH, a tale that has odd and unpleasant dimensions to it".[13]

Brueggemann suggests that to deal with these "dark" texts concerning God's absence and even violence we need to see God as a character in the text. As such "it is clear that YHWH 'moves on' as a character in the text, as any character surely will move on in the drama. Thus these texts are in YHWH's *past*, but they are assuredly *in* YHWH's past."[14]

This means that a "truer" picture of YHWH cast in canonical or theological form has moved beyond these texts, but has not superseded these texts, as no human person understood in depth ever supersedes or scuttles or outgrows such ancient and powerful memories. There linger in the character of YHWH ancient memories (texts) that belong to the "density" of YHWH and that form a crucial residue of YHWH's character. YHWH may not be in a "truer" "canonical" understanding, a God who abandons [or is violent]. But that past marking of YHWH is still potentially available in the current life of YHWH (for the text lingers), and must in any case be taken as a crucial part of the career of YHWH. YHWH cannot simply will away that past, nor can the interpreters of YHWH.[15]

Brueggemann also employs the metaphor of drama and script with the biblical text as the "fixed and settled" script which can be rendered in a variety of ways by contemporary actors. However, he refuses to prescribe specific acts to the script in the way that Wright does.[16] In what follows I hope to do justice to both "the great story" and the "little stories".

7

Reading the Pentateuch

The first five books of the Bible are significant for both Jews and Christians. They contain the opening narratives concerning creation, the stories of Abraham, Isaac, Jacob, Joseph, and Moses, the Decalogue (the Ten Commandments), and the promises of Deuteronomy. However, Christians have also had an ambiguous attitude to these books. The sacrificial demands, the dietary requirements and the purity regulations all reflect an alien and problematic environment.

Genesis 1 – 11

The opening chapters of Genesis serve as a fitting introduction to the whole Bible. The majestic opening chapter declares God as the Creator who creates by means of his word. It is widely recognized that the final form of the first creation account in Genesis 1:1 – 2:4a comes out of Israel's experience of exile in Babylon. As such it parallels, but deliberately counters, Babylonian creation myths. The primary text, the *Enuma Elish*, portrays creation as an act of violence, so that violence is structured into creation. The gods are intrinsically violent; the cosmos is formed from the murder and dismembering of the goddess Tiamat and humans are formed from the blood of an assassinated god to serve as slaves to the gods. So, according to the prevailing creation account of the day, killing is in the very blood of humans. In stark contrast, the Genesis creation account poetically portrays the creation of the cosmos by the speech of God and the text subsequently denounces violence in the strongest terms (Gen. 4:10–11).[1]

The opening chapters of Genesis, then, are not meant to be read as a scientific account of the origins of the cosmos but rather as a theologically rich statement concerning the nature of God and the intrinsic goodness of creation. In the context of the predominant Babylonian "myth of redemptive violence" (Wink's apt phrase) this is a profound subversion of the dominant reality. So, the very opening chapter of our Bibles invites us to imagine a world vastly different from that proclaimed by the dominant culture: a world alive with the creative speech of God, in which violence has no place and in which humanity is called to play its part in the unfolding of God's creative purposes (Gen. 1:26–28).

Nevertheless, we all realize that the pristine world of Genesis 1 – 2 is not the world we currently inhabit. This problem is actually embedded in the creation account itself. In Genesis 1:2 the earth is described as a "formless void". Gordon Wenham renders the Hebrew *tohu wabohu* as "total chaos".[2] God shapes this chaos into structured order by his creative word. Nevertheless, the threat of the return to chaos remains throughout the biblical narrative.[3] As Brueggemann states, "[f]or much of the Bible, the energy of chaos (antiform) continues to operate destructively against the will of the Creator, and sometimes breaks out destructively beyond the bounds set by the decree of the Creator."[4] Genesis 3 – 4 provides a profound narrative concerning the issue of evil. Sin and violence are not structured into creation, and thus inevitable, but confront humanity from without. Here, in rudimentary form, what Paul would much later refer to as "principalities and powers" are introduced. Most significant is Genesis 4:7 where, even after the events of Genesis 3, sin is regarded as an external power which seeks to grip humanity but can be overcome. These opening chapters of Genesis indeed form a powerful introduction to the whole Bible. Creation, decreation, and recreation are all played out in these chapters.[5] In powerful, mythic form the whole drama of God's good creation, humanity's propensity to spoil that creation and God's gracious provision is laid out. There is a tension here between two perspectives – "whatever God creates man tends to spoil by sin" and "however drastic man's sin God always starts afresh."[6] This tension reoccurs throughout the biblical narrative.

Genealogies

Genesis itself is divided into sections beginning with the initial creation account in Genesis 1:1 – 2:3 and then following sections are introduced by the Hebrew phrase "these are the generations of" (Gen. 2:4; 5:1; 6:9; 10:1; 11:10, 27; 25:12, 19; 36:1, 9; 37:2).[7] Four of these sections contain actual genealogies and, of course, genealogies occur throughout the Bible (including elsewhere in Genesis). Genealogies are usually glossed over by readers,[8] but they do serve significant functions. They operate to convey a sense of tradition and/or historical connectedness; often they are used to provide a sense of cultural and social location and/or to give a reason for the emergence of various cultural factors.[9] For example, the genealogy in Genesis 4 juxtaposes violence, technological advances in society (the building of the first city), agriculture (herding), music (lyre and pipe), metal work, and confessional religion. In this way the chapter brilliantly maps out central issues that have occupied humanity ever since – how those who seek to follow Yahweh deal with violence, science, and technology.[10]

The God of Abraham, Isaac, and Jacob

The rest of Genesis narrates the stories of Abraham, Isaac, Jacob and Esau, and Joseph, and their encounters with Yahweh. After the wide sweep of Genesis 1 – 11 the pace slows down and the narrative focus is on one family as the text portrays the origins of the nation of Israel. Genesis 12:1–3 is programmatic, both for the rest of Genesis and for the whole of the Pentateuch. It introduces the motif of journey and contains a fourfold promise to Abram: land, descendants, a special relationship with Yahweh, and blessing for the whole world. The intention of God, according to this programmatic text and echoed just before the giving of the Decalogue at Sinai in Exodus 19:5–6, is that the nation of Israel in the land is specially chosen by him in order to model to the rest of the world what it means to follow Yahweh and thereby to bring blessing to all. So the particularity of Israel is necessary for subsequent universality. Foretastes of this universality are found in the historical writings in the Old

Testament (Rahab and Ruth) but the promise is most pronounced in the Prophets.

Genesis 12 – 50 consists of three major narratives: Abraham (11:27 – 25:11), Jacob and Esau (25:19 – 35:29) and Joseph and his brothers (37:2 – 50:26) interspersed by two genealogies (Ishmael [25:12–18] and Esau [36:1 – 37:1]). As Wenham points out, all three narratives have a similar shape: each of the main characters has a divine revelation, they each leave home, and each narrative ends with a burial at the ancestral grave of Machpelah.[11] These and other parallels suggest that the stories are not meant to be read in isolation but shed mutual light on each other. The carefully crafted final redaction of these stories highlights the struggle involved in realizing the fourfold promise of Genesis 12:1–3.

The Joseph cycle is particularly interesting for a post-Christendom reading. Although Yahweh is with him (Gen. 39:2) through the twists and turns of his career, he ends up in a position of royal power in a foreign land, second only to Pharaoh in power and authority. He is given the chariot of second-in-command and the people are ordered to bow to him (Gen. 41:43). He is also given an Egyptian name and an Egyptian wife. The careful reader will be aware of the problematic nature of this rise to power. In the light of Genesis 24:1–9; 26:34–35 and 27:46 – 28:9, the taking of a foreign wife is disapproved of in the narrative. Abram is renamed as Abraham and Jacob as Israel by Yahweh but Joseph is renamed by Pharaoh. Chariots were the Egyptian technology of war and were the means by which Pharaoh pursued the fleeing Israelites in Exodus 14:5–9; they are specifically mentioned again in Exodus 14:26, 28. Chariots are clearly the symbol of Egyptian military power. Finally, royal power is particularly problematic; although at one moment it can be the means of Israel's salvation at another it is bent on Israel's destruction. Brueggemann (commenting that, although the Genesis story focuses on Abraham, Isaac, Jacob, and Joseph, the latter is dropped from the subsequent mantra "the God of Abraham, Isaac, and Jacob"), suggests that it is precisely because Joseph's counsel to Pharaoh results in an Egyptian monopoly of food that becomes an economic tool and political weapon in Pharaoh's hands that Joseph's name is dropped.[12]

Joseph senses no moral dilemma in his imperial work. The narrative signals nothing. But Israel's long and wise memory knows, and so drops him from the theological mantra. This Joseph, willed by God's providence and rooted in Israel's oldest, deepest promises has, in these chapters, sold out. He has distanced himself from old covenantal dreams, trading them for the deep nightmare of the empire, sinking deeply into its fear of scarcity . . . I think he is, in the end, dropped from Israel's theological summary because Israel was unclear about his God. Israel might confess "the God of Joseph" who then turned out to be the Egyptian author of slavery. Joseph had to be dropped because he understood so little and valued so thinly the God of the promise that he served greedy interests that victimized his own people.[13]

Exodus

The Exodus story of liberation from Egypt is referred to on numerous occasions in the rest of the Old Testament and is also paradigmatic for contemporary liberation theology. The dramatic reversal of fortunes in chapters 12 – 14 is echoed in Hannah's prayer in 1 Samuel 2:1–10 and, of course, in the Magnificat (Luke 1:46–55). However, apart from the dramatic narrative concerning release from Egypt, the book also contains the giving of the law at Sinai (19 – 24) and detailed instructions for the construction of the tabernacle (25 – 40).

The Decalogue

The Ten Commandments form the heart of the law. The text begins (in both Hebrew and English) with "I am the LORD your God" and ends with "your neighbour" (Exod. 20:2–17). Thus Jesus' statement that the two greatest commandments are to love God and to love neighbor (Matt. 22:34–40) reflects the structure of the Decalogue, which expands on what it means to love both God and neighbor. The first two commandments go together: exclusive allegiance to the one God and the prohibition of idolatry. The former becomes the basis of Israel's daily confession in the *shema* (Deut. 6:4) and the theme of idolatry is regularly taken up in the Prophets. In our contemporary world these two commandments remain fundamental when it is obvious that the ancient gods are alive and well and demand our allegiance. For example, Mars (the god of war), Mammon (the god of economics), and *Technē* (the goddess of science and technology) form an unholy trinity in contemporary society where so much is dictated by the military-industrial complex. These gods are aided and abetted in our culture by Venus (the goddess of love), Hebe (the goddess of youth), and Dionysus (the god of revelry/hedonism).[14] The third commandment is still regularly invoked by conservative forces concerned about blasphemy. However, this debate is often trivialized. It is all too easy to invoke the name of God to give apparent legitimacy to a particular point of view. This commandment should give pause for thought to all who want to claim that they are speaking in the name of God. The Sabbath command that follows is unique to Israel. In the ancient Near East units of time were universally based on solar and lunar cycles. Through this command rest is structured into the rhythm of creaturely life on a weekly basis.

> The order of Creation is translated into a social pattern and woven into the fabric of society. By proscribing work and creativity on that day, and by enjoining the inviolability of nature one day a week, the Torah delimits human autonomy and restores nature to its original state of pristine freedom. Human liberty is immeasurably enhanced, human equality is strengthened, and the cause of social justice is promoted by legislating the inalienable right of every human being, irrespective of social class, and of draft animals as well, to twenty-four hours of complete rest every seven days. Exodus 23:12 emphasizes the social function of the Sabbath – "in order that your ox and your ass may rest, and that your bondman and the stranger may be refreshed."[15]

The rest of the commandments address familial and societal relations. However, a striking characteristic of the Decalogue is that "you" and "your" throughout is singular. Each individual is addressed by these words and called to respond.

The tabernacle

A considerable proportion (nearly one-third) of Exodus is taken up with regulations concerning the construction of the tabernacle. Detailed descriptions occur twice and sandwiched between them is the episode concerning the golden calf in chapters 32 – 33. In the context of detailed instructions concerning worship the issue of idolatry – whom shall we worship? – once again is central. The movement of the book of Exodus is thus from slavery in Egypt to worship in the wilderness. It is a movement from the enforced building of Pharaoh's demands to the glad and obedient construction of a worship sanctuary for Yahweh.[16] Creation themes abound in this section of Exodus – a place of order and beauty is constructed "in the midst of the chaos of the wilderness."[17] Tabernacle imagery is used of Jesus in John 1:14; it is a focus of sustained reflection in Hebrews and imagery from the construction of the tabernacle is further explored in Revelation.

Leviticus

With its focus on ritual, priestly duties and sacrifice, Leviticus is often neglected. However, anthropologists in particular have found a rich amount of material in the book as they point out that ritual is a key to understanding the central values of society. Mary Douglas, for example, has demonstrated that purity systems reflect the cohesiveness of the social order.[18] At the heart of the book is the "Holiness Code" of chapters 17 – 26 following immediately from regulations for the Day of Atonement in chapter 16. The New Testament commentary on Leviticus 16 is found in Hebrews 6 – 9 where Jesus' death is portrayed as the sacrifice to end the entire sacrificial system. The language of sacrifice is thereby transformed in the New Testament; no longer is the requirement for the sacrifice of produce and animals but rather sacrificial language is used of the believer's ongoing relationship with God (Rom. 12:1–2; Heb. 13:15–16; 1 Pet. 2:5).

The detailed regulations in Leviticus are, of course, no longer to be followed slavishly. Instead, the clear concern for holiness and purity should cause modern believers to reflect on what it means to live as a "holy priesthood" in contemporary society. Furthermore, the very specificity of these laws can stimulate our thinking. For example, the law of gleaning in Leviticus 19:9–10 was an appropriate means of providing for the poor in an agrarian society.[19] This should stimulate us to think about appropriate ways of providing for the poor and marginalized in our society. Another key text in Leviticus concerns the Year of Jubilee (25) and I will deal with this text in Chapter 14.

Numbers

Numbers is similar to Exodus in combining narrative and legal material. In Exodus the crucial problem facing the Israelites is idolatry; in Numbers it is unbelief. After setting off from Sinai bound for the promised land in 10:33 there are complaints about their misfortunes (11:1), about the lack of meat (11:4–6) and about Moses' leadership (12:1). This culminates in the report of the spies concerning the land (13:25–33) and the resulting unbelief leads to forty years of wandering in the wilderness until the entire generation (excluding the two faithful spies, Joshua and Caleb) die out (14:30–35). The narrative pauses for three chapters (22 – 24) to recount the story of Balak, the king of Moab, and Balaam the seer in which four oracles of Balaam are recounted. Balak hires Balaam to curse Israel but he can only pronounce blessing. Despite Israel's disobedience (graphically highlighted in the very next chapter [25]), God intends her well-being. The book ends with Israel at the edge of the promised land in Transjordan.

In Numbers 6:24–26 we have the extraordinarily crafted Priestly Benediction consisting of fifteen words in Hebrew over three lines (3–5–7) with increasing consonants in each line (15–20–25), with the name of God, Yahweh, occurring as the second word in each line and with *shalom* as the last word.

Deuteronomy

The last book of the Pentateuch also forms a bridge into the narrative running from Joshua to 2 Kings. This narrative (excluding

Ruth, which appears among the Writings in the Hebrew Bible) is shaped by the concerns of the book of Deuteronomy as Martin Noth recognized in 1943.[20] In Deuteronomy Moses recapitulates all that has gone before from Mount Sinai onwards. As Israel stands on the verge of the promised land they are reminded of their history with Yahweh in the wilderness and urged to embrace covenantal obedience. The consequences of disobedience, and especially idolatry, are spelled out in terms of loss of the land (e.g. Deut. 4:25–31; 28:63–68; 30:1–5). This is, of course, the perspective of exile and Deuteronomy in its final form dates from this period. However, the book has a long and complex literary history with some materials clearly dating to before the fall of the northern kingdom in 722 BC (chapters 27 – 28 concern a covenant ceremony based on Mounts Ebal and Gerizim at Shechem in the northern kingdom). The scholarly consensus is that the material was decisively shaped during the reign of Josiah and the "discovery" of the book of the law in 622 BC (2 Kgs. 22:8–13).

The book consists of three speeches by Moses (1:6 – 4:40; 5:1 – 28:68; 29:2 – 30:20) and a concluding section made up of the appointment of Joshua as Moses' successor, Moses' song, his final blessing on Israel, and an account of his death (31 – 34). The first speech recapitulates the wilderness wanderings and warns against idolatry. The third speech looks to the future in the promised land and offers Israel a clear choice between obedience and life in the land and disobedience, death and exile. Between these two speeches concerning life in the wilderness and life in the land is sandwiched the long, central speech of Moses. Here the Decalogue is revisited (5:1–21) and the *shema* is pronounced (6:4–5). Here too is the legal corpus of Deuteronomy, which is concerned primarily with ethical reflection rather than the predominantly cultic material of Leviticus. In this section, for example, there is provision for the regular cancellation of debts (15:1–18), concern for the potentially marginalized (orphans, widows, and resident aliens [24:17–22]) and regulations for governance in the land whereby an excessive concentration of power (especially in the hands of the monarch) is prohibited (16:18 – 18:22).

Deuteronomy is one of the most quoted books in the New Testament. Jesus answers each of the temptations by quoting words from Deuteronomy. He quotes the *shema* as the greatest commandment. In particular, Jesus is presented as the prophet like Moses of Deuteronomy 18:15–19 in Acts 3:22–26.

8

Reading the "Historical" Narratives (Joshua – Esther)

These narratives consist of the "Deuteronomistic History" (Joshua – 2 Kings, excluding Ruth), a revisionist, post-exilic retelling of this history (1 and 2 Chronicles), the rebuilding of Jerusalem and the temple following the exile (Ezra and Nehemiah) and two tales of extraordinary women (Ruth and Esther) – the first set in the period of the judges before the monarchy and the second set in the Persian Empire. Together they span the period from occupation of the land to the exile and return from exile.

The Deuteronomistic History

As mentioned above, Martin Noth formulated the hypothesis that the books Joshua to 2 Kings (excluding Ruth) have been decisively shaped by the concerns of Deuteronomy. His thesis has been substantially refined and subjected to critique but nevertheless the description of the overall narrative remains. The "Deuteronomists" are profoundly interested in obedience to Yahweh and are thus generally antagonistic towards the monarchy, as the request for a monarch "like other nations" is viewed as a rejection of Yahweh's rule over Israel. In this connection 1 Samuel 8 is pivotal. The monarchy will give rise to a standing army, heavy taxation, and forced labor. The constant refrain in the ensuing summaries of the kings concerns their evil ways (1 Kgs. 15:3, 26, 34; 16:13, 18, 25, 30; 22:52; 2 Kgs. 3:2; 8:18, 27; 10:31; 13:2,

11; 14:24; 15:9, 18, 24, 28; 16:2; 17:2; 21:2, 20; 23:32, 37; 24:9, 19). A number of kings of the southern kingdom, Judah, are said to have done "what was right in the sight of the Lord" but they were unable to remove the "high places". Only in the reign of Hezekiah were these alternative places of worship to the temple at last removed (2 Kgs. 18:4). Consequently, Hezekiah, and later Josiah, are presented as heroes in the same mould as David.

Joshua 23, 1 Samuel 12, 1 Kings 8, and 2 Kings 17 serve as "narrative signposts, reviewing previous events and pointing forward to future developments".[1] The longest portion of this narrative takes up the story of David. In contrast to Saul, the first king, whose physical height marks him out as a potential ruler (1 Sam. 9:2; 16:7), David is presented as an unlikely candidate (out tending the sheep) but one whose heart is in the right place. David thus is portrayed as the shepherd-king and this portrayal is significant for subsequent reflection on the nature of Yahweh's rule. Another key text is 2 Samuel 7 in which David is promised that his throne will be established forever. This promise is cited as the prime reason that Judah is allowed to continue despite the reigns of kings considered evil by the Deuteronomists (1 Kgs. 15:3–5; 2 Kgs. 8:18–19). However, the subsequent reign of Manasseh is portrayed as so evil that judgement on Judah is inevitable (2 Kgs. 24:3–4). The failure of the promise to David becomes a matter for subsequent messianic speculation.

Clear Deuteronomistic concerns emerge in the summary of 2 Kings 17 where Israel's captivity is blamed on her idolatry, and the syncretism which accompanies the Assyrian resettlement of Samaria is contrasted with the Decalogue's prohibition of idolatry. Furthermore, Joshua and Josiah form bookends for the narrative. Obedience to Torah by not turning to the right or to the left is exhorted four times in Deuteronomy (5:32; 17:11, 20 [concerning the king]; 28:14); it reoccurs in Joshua's farewell address (Josh. 23:6) and does not appear again in the narrative until Josiah fulfils it (2 Kgs. 22:2).[2]

The Deuteronomists' ambiguity over the monarchy is also expressed through prophetic critique. The true prophets in the narrative appear outside royal control and address kings concerning idolatry and social justice. This is true of Elijah, Elisha, and Micaiah (1 Kgs. 22:5–28). The overall message of the Deuteronomistic History is thus that if rulers rule wisely according to Torah then the people live in *shalom* but the norm actually is that rulers rule in ways predicted in 1 Samuel 8 thereby incurring the judgement of Yahweh. Whenever rulers depart from the norms of social justice, prophetic denunciation occurs and this is true even of David (2 Sam. 12:1–15).

Joshua

Joshua is particularly problematic for any post-Christendom reading of the Bible. Within Christendom the narrative of the conquest of Canaan has been used to justify, for example, the conquest of North American Indians and the forcible occupation of their land, and the European occupation of Southern Africa and the eventual emergence of apartheid. The narrative not only condones genocide (Josh. 6:21; 8:22–27; 10:20, 28–39; 11:8–14) but asserts that Yahweh commanded it (Josh. 8:1–2; 10:40; 11:6, 12–15, 19–20). Various interpretational moves have been made to deal with this problem and the main lines of interpretation are as follows:

- The conquest narrative is straightforward history. Although difficult for modern sensibilities, ancient warfare was particularly bloody and brutal. This has been the mainstream approach in Christendom and poses no problems for those who view war as justified in particular circumstances, especially in combating evil. The evil of the Canaanites was, therefore, sufficient grounds for conquest.
- The archaeological evidence suggests such a conquest is problematic. There is no evidence of destruction at Jericho or Ai, for example. An increasing number of scholars are persuaded that ancient Israel emerged *within* Canaan, rather than conquering from without. Consequently, the conquest account has little or no historical basis. The text is late and reflects either the political realities of the reign of Josiah following the collapse of Assyrian power or the post-exilic dream of re-entering the land. In either case Israel possessing a large, conquering army was simply not a military possibility. The texts are, therefore,

ideological and reflect the desire for separation, purity, and holiness. This is particularly the case with the notorious **ḥĕrĕm** or sentence of total destruction on the population. Canaanites are viewed as idolaters and thus a potential source of pollution. The injunctions to annihilate them reflect later Israelite concern to be totally separate and are, therefore, a literary device with little or no historical foundation.

• In generic terms Joshua reads like an ancient Near-Eastern conquest narrative as found in Egyptian, Hittite, and Neo-Assyrian texts. Such texts typically include references to divine aid and power, use exaggerated language, and contain descriptions of fear inspired in the enemy.[3] In particular, the language of **ḥĕrĕm** is hyperbole typical of such accounts. So, although the texts may have some historical basis, the reportage follows the literary conventions of the day.

• The notion that only Yahweh is a warrior and that victories are achieved by miraculous intervention rather than military might. This is the thesis of Millard Lind who, although recognising that battles were actually fought by Israel, suggests that the exodus narrative is the paradigmatic text for all subsequent battle narratives. In other words, Yahweh is the warrior who alone decisively wins the battle. Any human activity is merely mopping up. This is particularly true, Lind argues, of the conquest narrative which begins with the crossing of the Jordan in terms reminiscent of Exodus.[4]

The ideological and literary interpretations above have great merit but we still have to deal with the actual presentation of Yahweh in the text and recognize that this presentation has informed the violent action of Christians throughout Christendom.[5] We must, therefore, take seriously the violence of God articulated in this and similar biblical texts but recognize that this is not the last word in Yahweh's textual history. If Jesus is the supreme revelation of God, as suggested by Hebrews 1:1–3, then the nonviolence of Jesus must be the ultimate arbiter in the complex and ambiguous biblical characterization of Yahweh. Thus ultimately we can affirm a nonviolent, *shalom*-inspiring God but, in doing so, we have to recognize that this God has a violent (textual) past.[6]

However, even in Joshua this violence is somewhat attenuated. First, there is the clear ambiguity in the narrative. The first twelve chapters speak of the conquest of the whole land but the second half (and Judges 1) indicate that the land was not wholly conquered. Even in the first half the outsiders Rahab and her family and the Gibeonites are preserved, the former becoming fully part of Israel but the latter remaining as resident aliens. Although ambiguous the narrative thus leaves open the possibility that other cities might have been spared had they, like the Gibeonites, thrown themselves on the Israelites' mercy.[7] Second, there is not a strict binary opposition between Israelite/Canaanite or insiders/outsiders. Rahab becomes an insider and Achan an outsider with the two accounts juxtaposed in Joshua 6:22 – 7:26. Third, Joshua's vision of the "commander of the army of the Lord" (Josh. 5:13–15), placed just before the Jericho incident, should be a commissioning vision but Joshua is left acknowledging he is on holy ground and without a specific commission at this point. Instead he has a revelation that this mysterious figure is the Lord's commander in all that follows. This reinforces the notion that the land is a divine gift and not actually won through military conquest, despite the rhetoric of the text (Josh. 1:1–9).[8]

Brueggemann notes the observations of two scholars concerning the account of land distribution in the second half of Joshua. Blenkinsopp suggests that the comment in Joshua 19:51 "they *finished* dividing the land" echoes the language of both Genesis 2:1 ("Thus the heavens and the earth were *finished*, and all their multitude") and Exodus 39:32 ("In this way all the work of the tabernacle of the tent of meeting was *finished*"). So creation, tabernacle, and land are the three key elements of order for Israel. Von Rad focuses on the formula of Joshua 21:43–45 which he sees as a fitting conclusion to the Hexateuch (Genesis – Joshua). The initial promise of land to Abraham is finally fulfilled.[9]

"Texts of terror"

This is the title of a book by Phyllis Trible in which she examines the biblical accounts of four female victims: Hagar, Tamar, the unnamed woman of Judges 19, and the daughter of Jephthah. Three of these accounts are found in the Deuteronomistic History.

For reasons of space I will focus on the last two which are found in Judges.[10]

Judges 19

This horrendous story, whose consequences are played out in the remaining chapters of Judges, concerns an unnamed concubine of a Levite from the hill country of Ephraim. At no point in the entire narrative does she speak. The story is told from a male perspective throughout. The Levite and the woman's father eat and drink together (19:4–8); the Levite and his male attendant converse (19:10–15), as do the Levite and an old man residing in Gibeah (19:16–21); the old man and the men of Gibeah converse (19:22–24); and, finally, the Levite addresses his concubine for the first time in 19:28 but she is silent – no conversation takes place. The incident with the men of Gibeah echoes the Sodom narrative of Genesis 19:1–11 but whereas at Sodom there is deliverance and Lot's daughters escape gang rape, no such deliverance occurs for the concubine who is gang-raped, tortured all night and left for dead at daybreak (19:25).

The woman is the subject of verbs only twice in the narrative. In 19:2 she leaves the Levite and returns to her father in Bethlehem. In 19:26, having now been abandoned to her fate by the Levite, she falls down at the door at daybreak – she may be subject of the verbs again but here she certainly has no power to act. Finally, as if her rape and torture were not enough, she is dismembered by the Levite (and the Hebrew text leaves open the possibility that she is still alive at this point)[11] and her dismembered body is sent to all the tribes of Israel. The narrator frames the entire story and its aftermath with "there was no king in Israel" (19:1; 21:25) and adds in 21:25 (RSV) "every man did what was right in his own eyes."[12] This addition plays on the words of the old man to the men of Gibeah in 19:25, which literally in the Hebrew reads: "Do to them the good in your own eyes." There is heavy irony from the Deuteronomist narrator here: the absence of kings leads to anarchy and violence but we know from the rest of the Deuteronomistic History that the rise of the monarchy is no antidote to the evil perpetrated by Israel.

Trible concludes her analysis of this text with the following words:

What can we, the heirs of Israel say in the presence of such unrelenting and unredeemed terror? First of all, we can recognize the contemporaneity of the story. Misogyny belongs to every age, including our own. Violence and vengeance are not just characteristics of a distant, pre-Christian past; they infect the community of the elect to this day. Woman as object is still captured, betrayed, raped, tortured, murdered, dismembered, and scattered. To take to heart this ancient story, then, is to confess its present reality. The story is alive, and all is not well. Beyond confession we must take counsel to say, "Never again." Yet this counsel is itself ineffectual unless we direct our hearts to that most uncompromising of all biblical commands, speaking the word not to others but to ourselves: Repent. Repent.[13]

Furthermore, as Trible notes, in the canonical ordering this text does not have the last say about women in the narrative. In the Hebrew Bible it is immediately followed by the story of Hannah who does speak and act in her own right. In the Christian Old Testament it is immediately followed by the story of Naomi and Ruth and the women of Bethlehem – a contrasting tale of female hospitality which also occurs "[i]n the days when the Judges ruled" (Ruth 1:1).

Jephthah's daughter (Judges 11:29–40)

The story of Jephthah's vow to offer up to Yahweh as a burnt offering whatever came out of his house to meet him after victory over the Ammonites (11:31) is so tragic that attempts have been made to tone down the sacrifice. Some commentators suggest that rather than being sacrificed, the daughter remains unmarried and a virgin throughout her life in fulfilment of the vow.[14] However, this is unconvincing in the light of the parallels with Abraham and Isaac (especially 11:34 when compared to Gen. 22:12). Jephthah makes his vow to Yahweh and we are told that it was indeed Yahweh who gave the Ammonites into his hand (11:32), a detail that is repeated both by his daughter (11:36) and after her sacrifice in 12:3. Clearly the narrator wants to highlight Yahweh's role in the victory. However, the battle against the Ammonites is reported in just two verses – the narrative slows down immediately after this to focus on the daughter. As was customary after victory in battle, the daughter fulfils the role of jubilant women coming out to greet the victors (Exod. 15:20–21; 1 Sam. 18:6–7). Although Jephthah's original vow is ambiguous (it could be possible, given the construction of houses of the day, that an animal would be the first to meet him), this possibility should have presented itself to him. Jephthah is, of course, devastated but cannot retract his vow apparently – a view which his daughter accepts.

The tragedy of this story concerns not only the vow in the first place (something which Anabaptists from the sixteenth century onwards would never have entertained given the words of Jesus in Matt. 5:33–37), but also the lack of intervention by Yahweh. Yahweh specifically intervenes at the crucial point in the Isaac narrative (Gen. 22:10–14). Similarly, when Jonathan is in danger of being put to death for innocently violating a rash vow made by his father, Saul, the people save his life (1 Sam. 14:24–45). This lack of intervention is the occasion for female lament, initially for two months with the daughter herself and subsequently annually in solidarity with her. Lament with and for the daughter of Jephthah is also protest against a God who fails to intervene. This protest, as we shall see, is taken up in the Wisdom literature, particularly Job and the Psalms. It is outrageous, therefore, that Hebrews can simply name Jephthah as one of the heroes of faith without further comment (Heb. 11:32–34).

1 Chronicles – Nehemiah

These books both recapitulate what has gone before from Adam to the exile and take the story further to the return from exile and the rebuilding of the temple (Ezra) and Jerusalem (Nehemiah). Chronicles is particularly significant because it specifically mentions Kings as a source and so we have a clear example of Scripture using Scripture. The extended account of David in 1 Chronicles 11 – 29 offers an alternative to that in the books of Samuel. In particular, David makes extensive preparations for the temple and its cultic practice.

The book of 2 Chronicles begins with a focus on Solomon and the building of the temple and contains no negative verdict on his reign. The rest of the book focuses on the Davidic dynasty in Judah with little attention given to the northern kingdom. Famously, Manasseh, the archetypal evil king in 2 Kings, repents in 2 Chronicles and subsequently removes foreign gods. Finally, the book closes with mention of Cyrus, the Persian king and the possibility of return to the land. These verses, of course, form the end of the Hebrew Bible as Chronicles is the last book in the Hebrew canon. Thus the Hebrew Bible ends with both the recognition of the reality of empire – Persia – and the anticipation of temple and land.

The end of Chronicles is also the beginning of Ezra-Nehemiah, although current scholarship rejects any formal link between the two. Ezra-Nehemiah, with its focus on the rebuilding of the temple and Jerusalem, is primarily concerned with Torah observance and purity. The dangers of assimilation have been fully experienced in exile and now returnees are concerned to define themselves over and against others. This is taken to extremes with the breakup of mixed marriages for the sake of community purity in both Ezra and Nehemiah. This, as Brueggemann states, "may be understood as a necessary undertaking if the communal identity is to survive at all".[15] On the other hand, this demonization of the "Other", which has also been a real characteristic of Christendom, is to be firmly rejected in the light of Jesus' exhortation to embrace the "Other" and also in the light of biblical concern for the resident alien.

Esther

Esther is set in the midst of the Persian Empire and concerns a perceived threat to Jewish identity in Diaspora. It negotiates the difficult terrain between assimilation and distinctiveness through sectarian withdrawal.[16] Furthermore, it does this without any reference to God. In particular, the threat of Jewish extermination is met with "fasting, weeping and lamenting" but no specific cry to God. Instead Esther, with her access to royal power, is able to provide deliverance through her own cunning and by "a huge act of subversive, dissenting imagination".[17] Brueggemann states that although "[t]he book of Esther is intractably and wondrously Jewish":

Christians in the West, in a now increasingly deprivileged situation, may be instructed by the book of Esther. The book of Esther invites readers – contemporary as ancient, Christian as Jewish – away from the certitudes of modernity that have long been an instrument of Christendom. It instructs too the fragile strategies of drama and narrative by which to maintain a distinct identity. The point at which characteristic Judaism (short of the state of Israel) and contemporary Christianity (now deabsolutized) may read together concerns narrative strategies and playful features that generate particular identity out beyond the leveling, generic humanity of military consumerism. The cases of Judaism and Christianity are not at all symmetrical, of course, but there is now enough of a crisis in Western Christianity to ask about the practice of subversion in the interest of communal survival.[18]

9

Reading Wisdom Literature
(Job – Song of Solomon)

Biblical Wisdom literature explores in various ways the richness, complexities, and perplexities of human experience in a world created by God. These five books offer rich reflection on this experience and are engaged in an inner-canonical dialogue as we shall see.

Job

Job in its final form is a carefully constructed work of great artistry exploring the huge mismatch between lived reality and orthodox theological wisdom. The book consists of a short prologue and epilogue in narrative form with an extended dialogue forming the bulk of the work. The prologue sets the scene and raises the question as to whether Job, who is described as "blameless and upright", only fears God because of his status and wealth. The reader is informed, through this prologue, that Job's loss of all his wealth, his ten children, and ultimately his health is entirely due to a heavenly wager! Job and his counselors are, of course, unaware of this. It should give us pause for thought that Yahweh, according to this text, can behave so capriciously and with apparent disregard for human and animal life. God is not referred to again as Yahweh after the prologue until he speaks in chapter 38. The bulk of the work explores traditional concepts of God and how conventional wisdom asserts that God rewards the faithful and punishes the wicked. Job does not dispute this conventional wisdom but insists throughout on his innocence. However, it is Yahweh himself who has allowed these calamities and so it is with Yahweh alone (and not conventional wisdom) that Job has ultimately to contend.

The extended dialogue consists of three cycles of speeches in chapters 3 – 27. Each cycle is structured: Job to Eliphaz to Job to Bildad to Job to Zophar. In the final cycle Bildad says very little (25:1–6) and Zophar does not speak. They literally run out of words! In chapter 28 there is an interlude meditating "on the reality that human wisdom – that is, the wisdom of both Job and his friends – cannot penetrate the mystery of creation that only God knows."[1] The placement of this meditation at this point in the book serves to highlight that "God's intentionality is beyond human explanation or challenge."[2] Nevertheless, Job continues to protest his innocence in the strongest possible terms in chapters 29 – 31. In particular, he accuses God of violence, cruelty, and persecution in 30:18–21. Finally, he demands an answer from "the Almighty" (31:35) and, with this demand, his protest ends (31:40).

However, an answer has to wait for six more chapters. Elihu now appears, has four speeches in 32 – 37, and then disappears. Elihu is the voice of youth who has waited until the conventional wisdom of his three elders has been exhausted before speaking. Nevertheless, Elihu persists with conventional wisdom and what he declares about God belies what we know about him from the prologue. He asserts that God is not capricious but Job has insisted that he is (23:13–14) and, from the prologue, it would appear that Job, not Elihu, speaks truthfully.[3]

At last, Yahweh speaks in two speeches in 38 – 41. However, Yahweh does not address Job's complaint. As Brueggemann notes, there is a massive "disconnect" between the speeches of Yahweh and the discourse to date.[4] He twice asks Job to respond (38:2–3; 40:1–2) and Job does respond twice (40:3–5; 42:1–6). In his first response Job acknowledges he has nothing to say when confronted by a God of such awesome power. However, his final response is much more enigmatic. Traditional interpretation has rendered this as Job at the end repenting when confronted by the truth of Yahweh. But is this really what is going on here? First, Job reaffirms the caprice of Yahweh (42:1–2), then, in verses 3a and 4, he quotes what Yahweh has previously said back to him (38:2–3; 40:7). Job acknowledges that his discourse hitherto has been beyond him (42:3bc) but now this is no longer the case because finally "verse 5 brings to a positive conclusion the question which Job has posed in great anguish throughout the dialogues: Will the silent God *speak*, that Job may *hear*? and will the absent God *appear*, that Job may *see*?"[5] The end result is that Job both repudiates and abandons dust and ashes. In other words, Job, having now both heard and seen Yahweh, no longer needs to engage in groaning and lamentation. He has uttered his complaint against Yahweh *and won*![6] This is indicated by Yahweh's own words in 42:7–8 – only Job has spoken truthfully of Yahweh throughout.

> What is primary is whether or not God succeeds in forcing Job's attention away from God and back upon Job himself. If God can force Job somehow to stop blaming God and start blaming himself, God wins. If God cannot do that, God loses. In contemporary political language, the question is whether God can make his opponent the issue. Despite spectacular effort, God, in my judgment, fails in his attempt to do this, and Job becomes as a result the turning point in the life of God, reading that life as a movement from self-ignorance to self-knowledge.
>
> If God defeats Job, in short, Job ceases to be a serious event in the life of God, and God can forget about his garrulous upstart. But if Job defeats God, God can never forget Job, and neither can we.[7]

Resolution of the narrative occurs in the prologue of 42:10–17 where Job's fortunes are restored. Nevertheless, Job's past history is not obliterated in this resolution. It is acknowledged, in line with Job's protest, that Yahweh had brought evil upon him (42:11). Furthermore, although Job has a further seven sons and three daughters they can never replace those lost to him so that his final state "is marked by durable loss."[8] Remarkably, however, in this state of restoration Job's three daughters are named, whereas the sons are not and they share an inheritance with their brothers. It is as though, at the conclusion of Job, not only conventional wisdom concerning the way God rewards the righteous and punishes the wicked is overturned but patriarchal assumptions themselves are profoundly questioned.

Psalms

Psalms functions in many ways as Israel's "hymnal." In its final form it consists of five books: 1 – 41; 42 – 72; 73 – 89; 90 – 106; 107 – 150. Each book culminates with a doxology (41:13; 72:18–20; 89:52; 106:48; 150). In fact the last six psalms form a collection of doxologies. The final shaping of the Psalter into five books forms a liturgical counterpart to Torah and clearly Psalm 1 is designed to introduce the collection and place it firmly within the framework of Torah. The longest psalm (119) is a carefully constructed acrostic poem focusing on Torah. Scholarly research has identified several types of psalm of which the most significant are hymns of praise, individual and corporate lament, the royal psalms, and individual and corporate thanksgiving. Brueggemann usefully divides the psalms, based on their underlying genre, into psalms of orientation, disorientation, and reorientation respectively.[9] The psalms of disorientation (lament psalms) continue in the line of Job's protest and their form is typically as follows (using Psalm 13 as an example):

Plea

Address to God (v. 1)
Complaint (v. 2)
Petition (v. 3a)
Motivations for God to act (vv. 3b–4)
Imprecation (none in Psalm 13; cf. Ps. 35:4–6, 8)

Praise

Assurance of being heard (v. 5)
Payment of vows (none in Psalm 13; cf. Ps. 22:25)
Doxology and praise (v. 6)

The move from plea to praise is striking and is characteristic of these psalms. Some decisive action takes place "off psalm" to make this move possible and the psalmist experiences deliverance, or assurance of deliverance, as a result. However, three psalms stand out: Psalm 88 is the darkest psalm in the Psalter – its last word in Hebrew is "darkness". There is no response from God and consequently there is no move from plea to praise. Psalm 109 is the most vindictive psalm with a sustained attack on the Psalmist's opponents and thus has an imprecation section out of all proportion. Psalm 137 finishes infamously with the longing that Babylonian infants should be dashed against a rock.

These psalms, in particular, are "limit" psalms. They speak to the most extreme situations that humanity experiences. Psalm 88 resonates with Job in that the Psalmist continues to address their plight to Yahweh even though he does not answer and seemingly will never answer as the Psalmist remains in darkness.

Christians are familiar with the use of psalms of orientation and reorientation in worship. These psalms speak of the order of creation or of the hope of transformation in new creation. But, in my experience, Christians find it difficult to integrate the psalms of disorientation into liturgical life. Yet, if our worship is to reflect with integrity the realities of lived experience, then all parts of the Psalter should inform our personal and corporate spirituality.

Proverbs

If Job represents a sustained protest against conventional wisdom then Proverbs provides a fount of such wisdom! In Proverbs the right way to live is wisdom/righteousness whereas the wrong way to live is folly/wickedness. Here the wise definitely do prosper and the foolish are punished. Proverbs thus promotes conventional wisdom in the whole of life. Such wisdom is, however, not just to be found in Israel. The book in its final form consists of six broad collections:

- Proverbs of Solomon (1:1 – 22:16);
- Sayings of the wise (22:17 – 24:34);
- More proverbs of Solomon transcribed by officials of King Hezekiah (25 – 29);

- Sayings of Agur (30);
- Maternal instructions to King Lemuel (31:1–9);
- In praise of a capable wife (31:10–31).

Eleven of the sayings of the wise derive from the *Instruction of Amenemope*, which originated in Egypt. Agur and Lemuel are non-Israelites. The example of Proverbs thus serves to highlight that wisdom is not only to be found in Israel – it is a universal phenomenon and Israel can thus learn from, and incorporate in its sacred Scriptures, received wisdom from other cultures.

Ecclesiastes

Ecclesiastes (Qoheleth) offers another way of wisdom in the world. This is the sustained voice of cynical wisdom. It lacks much of what is central elsewhere in the Hebrew Scriptures. For example, there is no mention of God's saving acts, especially the exodus; God is never referred to as "Yahweh"; and life is seen as ultimately meaningless for "there is nothing new under the sun" (1:9).

> The voice of Qoheleth, however, is not one of passionate protest against the futility of life; there is here none of the rage of the psalms of lament. Rather, his attitude is one of jaded resignation. "Utterly absurd!" runs his refrain. "Everything is absurd. Everything is wearisome." These are the words of someone who has heard it all and has no appetite for more . . . Not that Qoheleth is an atheist. He believes that life is to be received as a gift from God – but we cannot hope to make sense of it. The wise may make claims to knowledge but they do not impress him (8:16f.). Ecclesiastes provides a haven for those who continue to believe in God but are disillusioned or cynical or have lost interest. And Ecclesiastes' advice? Eat, drink and enjoy your toil! We may not be able to understand life, but we can relish it as our portion from God. Qoheleth does not claim that his advice makes any ultimate sense, for any such suggestion would, of course, be vanity. Nevertheless, this does provide a way of being in the midst of an incomprehensible world.

Yet he does not allow this revelling in life to lead to hedonism. We are invited to fear God and keep his commandments (12:13). Life is still to be lived and savoured in the context of obedience to the Torah – even if this seems to make no sense. This is deeply important. Ecclesiastes may be a voice from the margins but the function of the epilogue is to remove any doubt about its canonical context. 12:9–12 identifies it as wisdom literature and 12:13f. places it in relationship to the Torah. In the wisdom of God, this voice of resigned negativity finds its place in Israel's and then the Church's scriptures. It is neither the only voice, of course, nor the most prominent; nevertheless, it is one that we must listen to carefully.[10]

Song of Solomon

The move to allegorize this highly erotic, evocative, and sometimes explicit poetry is deeply embedded in both Jewish and Christian tradition. However, it must first and foremost be taken at face value as part of the Wisdom tradition celebrating erotic love as an integral part of human experience. Those Christian interpreters who rightly focus on the book's eroticism want to "rescue" the book by declaring that it describes the love between a husband and wife but there is no mention of the couple being married! On the contrary, there are clear hints of disapproval of the relationship (5:7; 8:1–2). As Brueggemann rightly states: "it is clear that this is human love expressed erotically and without restraint. It is love of an innocent kind unrestrained by morality or even a suggestion of matrimonial context."[11] The poetry consists of "a set of episodes hovering between reality and dream, centered on the relationship between lovers, but exploring a number of other themes."[12]

The book divides into two halves (1:1 – 5:1; 5:2 – 8:14) with clear links as 3:1–5 is paralleled in 5:2–9 and 2:6–7 in 8:3–4, for example. Other themes explored include that of nature and culture (2:2–5 // 7:1–9; 4:1–8 // 3:6–11); country and city (2:8–15 // 5:2–9); and the garden as sanctuary (4:12 – 5:1; 6:2–3, 11–12). The book celebrates erotic love in an ecologically sound environment! As such there are clear echoes of the garden of Eden.

Although the book should rightly be read as a celebration of human sexuality, the move to allegorize should not be dismissed as those from theological traditions open to a mystical dimension have insisted. The mystical literature on spirituality draws heavily on this text. Brueggemann, once again, summarizes this well:

> The articulation of such romantic passion means that we are invited in these poems to move even beyond the *ethical* perspective of the prophets to the *erotic* hunger of the Song as a disclosure of God. That is, if this text is theological disclosure, then it must be taken without weakening the force of the passion or diminishing the delight that God takes in God's beloved, either by moralism or by institutional constraints. What is given us here is a God who is a true lover, one who loves with unrestrained delight and unqualified lust that constitute the fullness of self-giving.[13]

10

Reading the Prophets
(Isaiah – Malachi)

There is a widespread misconception that the biblical Prophets primarily foretell the future. Writings on biblical prophecy have been popular particularly in more fundamentalist Christian circles where the Prophets have been mined both for supposedly messianic prophecies and for predicting the contemporary world scene. The following report, from a Christian magazine in February 1989, neatly encapsulates this approach to biblical prophecy.

> The radio broadcast last June began with a bold claim: "1988 is the rapture of the church . . . 5.7 billion people will either die or be raptured within the next seven years."
>
> The claim was made by Edgar C. Whisenant, a former electrical engineer retired from NASA, who had spent over 14 years *studying 886 biblical prophecies*. He had arrived finally at the dates September 11–13, 1988, as the period during which the church would be supernaturally taken out of the world . . . Not surprisingly for an engineer, Whisenant made his claims on the basis of calculation rather than special revelation. The predictions were printed in a booklet entitled *88 Reasons Why the Rapture Will Be in 1988* and sent out in a massive mailing intended to reach every church and Christian broadcast ministry in [the USA].
>
> Apparently, thousands found Whisenant's calculations intriguing or even convincing. In the months leading up to the appointed dates, the book sold hundreds of thousands of copies, sometimes several thousand in a single bookstore. Meanwhile,

radio and TV stations featuring Whisenant in interviews were swamped with anxious callers.

Closer to mid-September, stories began to circulate in the secular news media about the "hysteria" of some who were so fully convinced Whisenant was correct that they had sold all their possessions. Others reportedly ran up immense credit-card charges because they believed they would never have to pay them.

Needless to say, September 1988 came and went, but the church remains on planet earth. Whisenant is in fact only the most recent in a long line of end-time calculators who missed the mark. His predecessors over the last two thousand years confidently predicted the end of the age again and again: in the years 200, 380, 1000, 1260, 1533 and 1844, to name only a few.[1]

Rather than a vehicle for predicting what is happening in the world today, biblical prophecy should be seen primarily as a revelation of Yahweh, summed up in Amos 4:12, "prepare to meet your God, O Israel!" The prophets spoke in a specific, historical context and predictive elements in their prophecies generally concern the immediate future which is, of course, now past for us. Furthermore, generally predictive prophecy is not like history written in advance of events. There is a lack of detail and chronology is not important.

> The modern mind is interested in chronology, in sequence, in time. The prophetic mind usually was not concerned with such questions but took its stand in the present and viewed the future as a great canvas of God's redemptive work in terms of height and breadth but lacking the clear dimension of depth. The prophets usually saw in the background the final eschatological visitation of God; but since they primarily concerned themselves with God's will for his people in the present, they viewed the immediate future in terms of the ultimate future without strict chronological differentiation and thus proclaimed the ultimate will of God for his people here and now.[2]

Genuinely predictive prophecy is cast in a form which is historically and culturally conditioned. For example, Isaiah's vision of transportation in the new Jerusalem involves camels and ships of

Tarshish (Isa. 60) and Ezekiel's vision of transformed, eschatological worship involves the temple and animal sacrifice (Ezek. 40 – 48).

The Prophets are passionately concerned about Torah obedience. They cannot be understood canonically apart from the foundational text of Torah (Prov. 29:18). The prophets call for covenantal faithfulness (e.g. Mal. 2:10–16), they demand social justice (e.g. Amos 5:21–24), and denounce idolatry (e.g. Isa. 44:9–20). Finally, they look forward to the renewal of creation (e.g. Isa. 116–9; 65:17–25).

In contrast to the stories of prophets such as Elijah and Elisha in the Deuteronomistic History, the prophetic books generally say very little about the lives of the prophets. They are more interested in what the prophets had to say. In reading the Prophets, therefore, the primary unit of investigation is the prophetic oracle. Often this is introduced with a messenger formula: "Thus says the Lord," and contains an announcement of Yahweh's action together with the reason for this action. Prophetic utterances take a number of forms of which the most important are:

- The *covenant lawsuit*, which typically contains a summons to court to hear Yahweh's charge. Evidence is presented and a verdict is proclaimed. For example, in Isaiah 13, the court is convened (vv. 13–14a), the charge is read out (vv. 14b–15), evidence is presented (v. 16) and the sentence is announced (vv. 17–26).
- The *woe* (e.g. Hab. 2:6–8), which consists of an announcement of distress, the reason for the distress and a prediction of disaster.
- The *salvation oracle* (e.g. Amos 9:11–15), which refers to the future, mentions radical change, and promises blessing.[3]

In the Hebrew Bible the Latter Prophets consist of Isaiah, Jeremiah, Ezekiel, and the Book of the Twelve so there are four books corresponding to the four books of the Former Prophets: Joshua, Judges, Samuel, and Kings. In the Christian Old Testament the Prophets consist of Isaiah, Jeremiah, Lamentations (considered as an appendix of Jeremiah), Ezekiel, Daniel, and the Twelve Minor Prophets.

Isaiah

Isaiah in its final form has gone through a long traditioning process. Scholarship divides the book into chapters 1 – 39; 40 – 55; and 56 – 66. First Isaiah probably has some historical roots with an eighth-century BC prophet of that name (Isa. 1:1) but the chapters contain material that cannot easily be dated to the eighth century. This is true of chapters 13 – 23 (oracles against the nations) where Babylon (which would not be in focus in the eighth century) is prophesied against in chapters 13 – 14. It is also true of the "Little Apocalypse" of chapters 24 – 27, and the judgement on the nations and the promise of restoration of Jerusalem in chapters 34 – 35. Second Isaiah reflects the demise of Babylon and the rise of the Persians under the leadership of Cyrus (45). Third Isaiah is primarily concerned with internal community life.[4]

The concern for social justice pervades the whole book. Israel is indicted in the famous "Song of the Vineyard" (5:1–7) for injustice. The Servant of Second Isaiah is introduced in the first Servant Song (42:1–9) as one who will "bring forth justice to the nations" and who will not rest "until he has established justice in the earth." Third Isaiah begins with the exhortation to "[m]aintain justice and do what is right" (56:1). Chapter 9 looks forward to the fulfilment of the Davidic promise of 2 Samuel 7 and the establishment of a rule of justice and righteousness. Chapter 11 likewise anticipates a coming king who will practice righteousness and equity. It is no wonder that the early church saw fit to apply these texts to Jesus. Furthermore, texts such as 2:1–4; 25:6–10; 35; 44:1–8; 60 – 62 and 65:17–25 speak of the restoration of Jerusalem with a focus on Mount Zion. God's rule in Jerusalem goes out to the nations, bringing *shalom* in all its dimensions and resulting in blessing and fruitfulness for the whole earth. Such texts inform the New Testament's understanding of "a new heaven and a new earth" (e.g. 2 Pet. 3:11-13; Rev. 21 – 22).

Jeremiah

Jeremiah too is complex and multilayered and focuses on the crisis of exile in 587 BC. The book certainly reflects the prophetic utterances of the prophet Jeremiah in Jerusalem at the end of the seventh century BC. Jeremiah is influenced by the Deuteronomists – his call in 1:7–9 echoes the call of the Mosaic prophet in Deuteronomy 18:18. Furthermore, his links with Anathoth (1:1) reflect 1 Kings 2:26–27 and the banishment of the priest Abiathar (who had been loyal to David throughout his life) by Solomon. This places Jeremiah as an outsider to the royal court in Jerusalem. This is most clearly seen in chapter 36 where the scroll of Jeremiah is a threat to the king, who burns it.

The book itself intersperses prose narrative and prophetic oracles throughout. Decisive moments occur in chapters 45 and 51:59–64. Both these passages refer to a scroll and to scribes (Baruch and Seraiah). Furthermore, in the Greek tradition of the book of Jeremiah, the oracles against the nations of chapters 46 – 51 are placed immediately after 25:14. As chapter 52 forms an appendix, the main work ends either at the end of chapter 51 in the Hebrew tradition or at the end of chapter 45 in the Greek tradition.

It is worth noting that in scenarios wherein Jeremiah 45 or Jeremiah 51:64 ends the book of Jeremiah, both versions bespeak a scribal future; in one case represented by Baruch, in the other by Seraiah and his scroll. Either way, the completed book of Jeremiah recognizes and anticipates that the restored Judaism will take on a wholly new form, a form brought to fruition by the scribe, Ezra.[5]

Jeremiah proclaims both judgement on Jerusalem and the hope of future restoration. Judgement is due to the lack of social justice (e.g. 5:1, 26–29) and idolatry (e.g. 7:16–20). The "temple sermon" (7:1 – 8:3) contains a profound plea for repentance cast in Deuteronomistic language (7:5–7). This provocative sermon in the temple precincts is repeated in 26:1–6 and Jeremiah is arrested and sentenced to death by the religious leaders. He is rescued from death by an appeal to earlier prophetic tradition (including the citation of Mic. 3:12) and by the protection of an insider in the royal court (Jer. 26:24).

The book is particularly memorable for the prayers of Jeremiah, which are in the tradition of the lament psalms (11:18 – 12:6; 15:10–21; 17:14–18; 18:18–23; 20:7–18). These "laments" of Jeremiah are the prime reason that the book of Lamentations is traditionally thought to be associated with Jeremiah and why it immediately follows Jeremiah in the Old Testament canon.

Lamentations

This book is a sustained example of Hebrew poetry concerned with the destruction of Jerusalem in 587 BC. It graphically portrays the immense grief outpoured when theological certainties are dashed. It consists of five chapters which all have 22 verses (corresponding to the number of letters in the Hebrew alphabet), apart from the middle chapter, which has 66 verses. The first four chapters are structured as acrostic poems with each verse beginning with a fresh letter from the Hebrew alphabet (in the third chapter each letter begins three successive verses) but the final chapter deliberately breaks this pattern. The book as a whole functions as a psalm of lament. The move from devastation to hope, characteristic of the lament psalms, occurs in 3:21–24 and comes from remembering the steadfast love of Yahweh. Nevertheless, although these particular verses are cherished by Christians, the book does not end with these words of hope. Grief persists and the book ends enigmatically in 5:22. It ends with uncertainty as to whether Yahweh has indeed utterly rejected Israel.

> The text expresses the community's doubt about God's care and about God's character. It utters the unthinkable – that God has utterly and permanently rejected them, cast them off in unrelenting anger. The verse is fearsome, a nightmare of abandonment, like a child's terror that the only ones who can protect her and give her a home have rejected her forever. Such is the ending of this book, and I think it is wonderful.[6]

Ezekiel

Ezekiel, as a prophet in exile, is crucial reading in a post-Christendom context. He is described as a priest and receives his first vision in exile in Babylon in 593 BC. This places him with the exiles of the first deportation of 598 BC (2 Kgs. 24:10–17; Jer. 24:1–10). At this point Jerusalem and the temple are still standing but Judah is now a vassal state of Babylon. Hope for those remaining in the land still persists but it is fast fading. Indeed, seven years later, in 586 BC, word reaches Ezekiel that the city has fallen (33:21). So Ezekiel prophesies for those in exile, as does Jeremiah in Jeremiah 29, where the latter exhorts the exilic community to settle down and seek the welfare of Babylon, promising return after seventy years (Jer. 29:4–14). It is of interest that sixteenth-century Anabaptist writers quote Ezekiel extensively. These writers found the notion of exile appropriate to their circumstances as they sought a third way between the Protestant and Catholic Christendoms confronting them. Furthermore, the theme of exile has proved fruitful for the contemporary context in which the church finds itself increasingly marginalized and immersed in an alien culture in the West.[8]

A key to the book is found in Ezekiel 33:32 where Ezekiel is described as a musician. Although this text is an indictment on those who come to hear him, it nevertheless gives us insight into the structure of the book. For Ezekiel is modeled on the ancient "Song of the Sea" found in Exodus 15:1–18. The latter has a three-fold structure: the victory of Yahweh over the enemy (Exod. 15:1–12); Yahweh leading the people to the mountain (15:13–17a); and the establishment of the sanctuary from which Yahweh reigns forever (15:17b–18). Similarly, Ezekiel has three predominant themes: the victory of Yahweh over all enemies, including apostate Israel (1 – 34:10); the return to the land and final defeat of imperialism (34:11–39); and the vision of an eternal sanctuary (40 – 48).[9]

The profoundly disturbing experience of exile necessitated extreme measures to get the message across. Ezekiel is well known for his bizarre street theatre and pantomime (4:1 – 5:4; 12:1–7, 17 – 20; 21:18–27; 24:15–18; 37:15–23). He also uses extreme language to indict the apostasy of Israel in chapters 16, 20, and 23. The portrayal of Yahweh as a jealous lover and Israel as a faithless harlot, with language bordering on the pornographic, has rightly attracted devastating critique from feminist scholars. Nevertheless, without excusing the patriarchal framework in which the message is cast, the anguish and anger of

Yahweh over the breakdown of this covenantal relationship makes for powerful and disturbing reading.

The book ends with a vision of a restored temple, a new redistribution of the land, and a description of a new capital city. Significantly, Ezekiel does not name this "Jerusalem". For him, Jerusalem was a rebellious city and, apart from one reference to appointed festivals at Jerusalem (36:38), it is never mentioned again after its fall in 33:21. The redistribution of the land is re-envisioned as an equal distribution between the tribes, with allotments provided for resident aliens. The center of the land, 25,000 cubits square, is set apart for the sanctuary, the priests, and the city. Significantly, the area proscribed for the city is described as "ordinary", or "secular", as opposed to the "holy" portion allotted to the sanctuary and the priests. This is very different from other biblical notions of the "holy city" (e.g. Ps. 87:1–3; Isa. 52:1; Dan. 9:24; Zech. 8:3). In Ezekiel's vision, temple and city occupy different spaces. Yet, astonishingly, the city is finally named in the very last verse as "Yahweh is There". This clear separation of the city from sacred space delegitimizes all economic and political claims to speak for Yahweh. On the other hand, the very naming of the city demonstrates Yahweh's claim over the whole of life. In our post-Christendom context this speaks to issues concerning the clear separation of church and state but does not suggest thereby that the claims of God over the whole of life are abrogated.[10]

Daniel

Daniel speaks powerfully to the relationship between the believing community and the wider empire. In its final form it clearly dates to the crisis in Palestine in 167–164 BC when Antiochus IV (Epiphanes) of Syria ruled and tried to eradicate Judaism through a process of radical Hellenization. Daniel knows of the abolition of regular sacrifice in the temple and the erection of a pagan altar, which took place in 167, but not of the circumstances of the death of Antiochus in 164. This makes the dating of the visions in Daniel to between 167 and 164 one of the most precise in the entire Bible.

The book itself is complex in form. It divides naturally into two halves with chapters 1 – 6 consisting of narrative and concerning Daniel in Babylon, and chapters 7 – 12 consisting of apocalyptic visions. However, Daniel is written in both Hebrew and Aramaic and the language division does not follow the genre division. Daniel 2:4b–7 is written in Aramaic with the rest in Hebrew. Furthermore, the Aramaic section has a clear chiastic structure – a literary device in which the order of the first half of a section is inverted in the second half:

A vision of four empires (2)
   A trial of faithfulness and a marvelous deliverance (3)
      An omen interpreted and a king challenged and chastised (4)
      An omen interpreted and a king challenged and deposed (5)
   A trial of faithfulness and a marvelous deliverance (6)
A vision of four empires (7)

The book displays a clearly ambiguous relationship to empire. In the first half Daniel and his three friends rise to prominence in the court of the Babylonian king, Nebuchadnezzar. However, the question of idolatry is raised in chapters 3 and 6. Idolatry, as we have seen, regularly came under the condemnation of both the Deuteronomists and the Prophets. Daniel and his friends, however, refuse to bow down to royal power and suffer the consequences. In both cases they are miraculously rescued from death. The first half suggests that the believing community can prosper in an alien environment; however, this prosperity must not compromise unswerving loyalty to Yahweh and when empire demands worship, as it inevitably does, this must be resisted at all costs. In the second half, empire is clearly evil and opposed to the purposes of God. This has been already hinted at in chapter 4 when Nebuchadnezzar is reduced to beastly status. In chapter 7 empire is unambiguously described in beastly terms and there is a clear contrast between the "beasts" of empire and the Human One of 7:13.

The apocalyptic language of chapters 7 – 12 is unusual in the Old Testament and is found elsewhere primarily in Isaiah 24 – 27 and Zechariah 9 – 14. The genre of apocalypse became popular in the period 200 BC – AD 150. It arose out of times of crisis and alienation and is a particularly apt form for bringing, as a revelation from God, comfort and exhortation to beleaguered believers. "[An apocalypse is] intended to interpret present, earthly circumstances in light of the supernatural world and of the future, and to influence both the understanding and the behavior of the audience by means of divine authority."[11]

The use of apocalyptic language in the second half, and particularly the introduction of heavenly beings such as the princes of Persia and Greece (10:13, 20), sets up a deliberate contrast with the first half. By projecting earthly realities onto a cosmic screen a much more complex notion of empire emerges than is found in the first half. For nations are not simply instruments of the divine will, they can oppose the will of God and delay, although not ultimately thwart, his purposes. Such a view of empire opens the way for fresh contemplation of Israel's continuing exile. Now her misfortune can be seen not simply as divine punishment for sin (as in the Deuteronomistic History and the Prophets), but rather as the result of being caught up in a heavenly conflict involving the angels of the nations. As Wink notes, Daniel introduces a third element besides God and Israel into the prayer equation: the Powers. The angels of the nations have a will of their own and are capable of resisting the will of God. In the New Testament this concept is taken up in the Pauline language of "principalities and powers".[12]

The Minor Prophets

The Book of the Twelve in Hebrew takes up one scroll and consists of the prophetic books from Hosea to Malachi. Historical-critical scholarship, as elsewhere in biblical studies, has dominated the discussion, seeking to situate each individual book in its historical context. The consensus of such scholarship is that nine of the books fall into three groups of three. Hosea, Amos, and Micah are situated in the eighth century BC; Nahum, Habbakuk, and Zephaniah in the seventh century; and Haggai, Zechariah and Malachi from the Persian period. Of the remaining three books, Jonah constitutes a narrative tale of great artistry, problematizing Israelite nationalism and parodying the traditional role of the prophet. Obadiah, the shortest book, is probably to be situated in the fifth century. In genre it is an oracle against the nations, specifically Edom. Obadiah 1:6 is paralleled in Jeremiah 49:9–10, 14–16. Finally, Joel is impossible to date, although it is usually dated late. It is most well known due to being quoted by Peter in Acts 2 on the day of Pentecost.

Each of these books (apart from Jonah), in its own way, looks forward to an eschatological future of great blessing (e.g. Hos. 2:14–23; Joel 3:17–18; Amos 9:11–15; Obad. 17-21; Mic. 4:1–4; Nah. 1:15; Hab. 2:14; Zeph. 3:14–20; Hag. 2:19–23; Zech. 14:8–9; Mal. 4:2).

The overall shape of the Book of the Twelve suggests, as throughout the Old Testament, that the judgement of Yahweh takes place through historical processes but that this judgement is never the last word as there is always, however muted, the hope of future blessing. This emphasis on future hope is precisely why, in the Christian Old Testament, Malachi appears as the last book. First, 4:4 looks back and reemphasizes Moses and the importance of Torah. Second, 4:5–6 focuses on Elijah and the prophetic tradition. Thus the Law and the Prophets are brought together in this summarizing statement. Third, the book ends on a note of hope for the future. Thus Torah obedience and prophetic hope are the last words in the Christian Old Testament and form a fitting introduction to the New Testament and particularly the Synoptic Gospels in which Jesus is presented as both teacher and prophet. Furthermore, the transfiguration narrative (Matt. 17:1–13; Mark 9:2–8; Luke 9:28–36) specifically draws on this juxtaposition of Moses and Elijah.[13]

Summary of the Old Testament

I have spent a long time on the Old Testament, mindful of the fact that traditions which emphasize the centrality of Jesus for biblical interpretation have generally found it difficult to do justice to it. Of course, in the space of these chapters I have only scratched the surface of the rich, complex, multifaceted material within the Old Testament. Reading from a post-Christendom perspective has, hopefully, allowed elements of the text to emerge which are often hidden in Christian readings previously aligned to patriarchy and the maintenance of political power. In particular, these readings have revealed a God more complex than the omnipotent, omniscient, unchanging, impassible, benevolent, patriarchal god of Christendom. The Old Testament reveals God as one with a dark side and a violent past, as well as a God of compassion, love, and passionate concern for social justice. Of course, a hermeneutic committed to a Jesus-centered interpretation of the Bible will eventually see this picture of God resolved into a God of immense love who has recovered from his abusive past and is thus ultimately revealed to us in Jesus. This reading, which claims to take these Old Testament texts seriously, argues for a God who really does change and learns from his textual past.

11

Reading the Gospels and Acts

I am treating these five books together, conscious that John is very different from the three Synoptic Gospels, and that Acts is not a gospel but rather the second volume of Luke-Acts. But, unlike the rest of the New Testament, they are all narrative in genre. It is impossible to overemphasize the Gospels for Christians. For in them we encounter the Jesus whom we, as Christians, claim to follow. Each gospel offers a different portrait of Jesus and, by allowing the four witnesses to stand side-by-side, each is given its own distinctive place with no attempt made to harmonize them or elevate one gospel over the others within the New Testament canon. Burridge has demonstrated, to the satisfaction of most scholars, that all four Gospels should be regarded as Greco-Roman biographies in genre. Some doubt remains about Luke, because of its relationship to Acts, but even Acts can be regarded as a collection of biographies of Stephen, Peter, and Paul (or even God).[1]

Ancient biographies cannot be compared to either modern biographies or modern historical accounts. For example, words were often put into the subject's mouth in order to convey some aspect about the person or situation that the author wanted to get across.[2] On the other hand, neither were ancient biographies fictional accounts such as ancient novels or romances. This poses limits on the extent to which imaginative material can be included. "This indicates the room for maneuver the evangelists have in creating their pictures of Jesus: we should not expect modern criteria of history, but nor the creativity of legend or novel."[3] The significance of the Gospels as ancient biography, as Burridge points out, is that they are really about the person of Jesus of Nazareth, rather than, say, early Christian experience.[4] Paul could write about early Christian experience, but he does not write a biography. "That Paul says little about the person of Jesus in his epistles does not necessarily mean that he was not interested in his earthly ministry; it might be that he is writing epistles and not [biography]."[5]

Chapter 5 dealt specifically with the central significance of Jesus for biblical interpretation. In this chapter I will simply summarize the main features of each of the gospels.[6]

Matthew

Matthew opens with *biblos geneseōs* – a phrase which occurs twice in the LXX (Septuagint) of Genesis (2:4; 5:1). Canonically, therefore, it is fitting that the New Testament begins by echoing the first book of the Old Testament. Jesus is immediately introduced as "the Messiah, the son of David, the son of Abraham". These titles reflect Matthean emphases. He is concerned to demonstrate Jesus as the messianic fulfilment of the Hebrew Scriptures. The phrase "son of David" appears only on the lips of Bartimaeus in Mark (Mark 10:47–48) but in Matthew it occurs again at 9:27; 12:23; 15:22; 20:30–31 and 21:9, 15. Furthermore, in Hebrew as in Greek, letters are used to represent numbers and the Hebrew letters for David add up to fourteen. Consequently, Matthew constructs his genealogy of Jesus to give three sets of fourteen generations with David forming the culmination of the first set and thus standing at the head of the second set. Finally, "son of Abraham" looks back to the Abrahamic promise (Gen. 12:3; 18:18; 22:18; 26:4) and anticipates Matthew 28:19.

Matthew's structure

Matthew has grouped all Jesus' teaching into five blocks (5:1 – 7:28; 10:1 – 11:1; 13:1–53; 18:1 – 19:1; 23:1 – 26:1), here is the new Moses with the new Torah.

- Prologue (1:1 – 4:16)
- Introduction to public ministry (4:17–25) "From that time Jesus began to proclaim"

- Discourse 1: The Sermon on the Mount (5:1 – 7:29) "Now when Jesus had finished saying these things"
- A series of miracles and summary statement (8:1 – 9:38)
- Discourse 2: Mission (10:1 – 11:1) "Now when Jesus had finished instructing his twelve disciples"
- Varying responses to Jesus' ministry (11:2 – 12:50)
- Discourse 3: Parables (13:1–53) "When Jesus had finished these parables"
- Varying responses to Jesus' ministry (13:54 – 16:20)
- Beginning of more private ministry with disciples (16:21 – 17:27) "From that time on Jesus began to show his disciples"
- Discourse 4: Community instructions (18:1–35) "When Jesus had finished saying these things"
- On the way to Jerusalem (19:1 – 20:34)
- Controversies and questions in Jerusalem (21:1 – 22:46)
- Discourse 5: Woes and eschatology (23:1 – 25:46) "When Jesus had finished saying *all* these things"
- The death and resurrection of Jesus (26:1 – 28:20)

From the above analysis it is easy to see the narrative markers that Matthew places in his gospel. After the fifth discourse he indicates that the teaching sections have come to an end by adding "all" to his usual narrative marker (26:1) thus indicating the transition to his Passion Narrative.

Matthew also has a series of "bookends" at the beginning and end of his gospel. First, there is the emphasis on "God with us" (1:23; 28:20). Second, mountains appear frequently in Matthew: as a setting for Jesus' temptation (4:8–10); where the first discourse takes place (5 – 7); where Jesus goes alone to pray (14:23); where Jesus heals many and feeds four thousand plus (15:29–38); where Jesus is transfigured (17:1–8); the Mount of Olives (21:1; 24:3; 26:30); and finally the mountain in Galilee (28:16). The first and last form narrative bookends. At the mountain of temptation Jesus is promised all the kingdoms of the world if he worships Satan but he refuses; at the mountain in Galilee the disciples worship Jesus spontaneously (28:17) and are commissioned to demonstrate the kingdom of God throughout the world by making disciples. The final bookend concerns

Gentiles who call Jesus "King of the Jews". Magi from the East do so in 2:1–2 and the Roman governor from the West does so in 27:11, 37.

Matthew's plot

As with any coherent narrative, Matthew has a clear plot. Jesus summons Israel to fulfil her destiny and embrace his message of "the kingdom of heaven" (10:5–7). But the Jewish leaders become increasingly resistant to his teaching, culminating in the woes pronounced against them in chapter 23 and their conspiracy to have Jesus arrested and killed (26:3–4). On the other hand, throughout Jesus' ministry his disciples (unlike Mark) grow increasingly in understanding and faith. As a result of Jesus' rejection by the Jewish leaders, Gentiles will be invited to embrace his message and the disciples will be the instrument of proclamation (21:42–46; 28:19–20).

Some Matthean themes

- Gentiles as co-heirs of the Abrahamic promise
  - The genealogy emphasizes Jesus' Jewishness but also includes four women, apart from Mary, and these are Gentiles:
    - Tamar, a Canaanite
    - Rahab, from Jericho
    - Ruth, a Moabite
    - The wife of Uriah, a Hittite
  - Gentiles worship Jesus (2:1–12)
  - Gentile faith (8:5–13; 27:54)
  - Galilee of the Gentiles (4:15; 28:16–20)
- Jesus as a New Moses
  - Child saved from evil king intent on slaughtering infants (2:16–18; cf. Exod. 1:15 – 2:10)
  - Flight from king and growing up in another land (2:13–15; cf. Exod. 2:15–22)
  - Return after death of the king (2:19–20; cf. Exod. 2:23)
  - Sermon delivered from a mountain (cf. Moses and Sinai)
  - Five discourses

- Jesus as the fulfilment of Torah (5:17–18)
- Jesus as the fulfilment of Scripture
  - "This was to fulfil what had been spoken through the prophet"
    - Birth (1:22–23)
    - Flight to Egypt (2:15)
    - Massacre of infants (2:17–18)
    - Nazareth (2:23)
    - Living in Galilee (4:14–16)
    - Healing and ministry (8:17; 12:17–21)
    - Parables (13:35)
    - Entry into Jerusalem (21:4–5)
    - Judas' blood money (27:9–10)
  - Other fulfilment passages (2:5–6; 13:14–15; 26:54, 56)
  - Around sixty references or quotations from Old Testament (approximately three times more than Mark)
- Righteousness
  - Never in Mark, once in Luke, but seven times in Matthew (3:15; 5:6, 10, 20; 6:1, 33; 21:32). Five of these occur in the Sermon on the Mount
  - Related adjective "righteous" or "just" occurs seventeen times (twice in Mark; eleven times in Luke)
  - Beatitudes highlight Matthew's concern for ethical conduct
- Jesus' identity
  - Opponents and questioners call him "teacher" (8:19; 9:11; 12:38; 17:24; 19:16; 22:16, 24, 36)
  - Judas calls him "Rabbi" (26:25, 49; cf. 23:7–8)
  - Disciples and those asking for help call him "Lord" (8:2, 6, 8, 21, 25; 9:28; 14:28, 30; 15:22, 25, 27; 16:22; 17:4, 15; 18:21; 20:30, 31, 33; 26:22)
- Kingdom of heaven
  - Kingdom occurs fifty times
  - Parables of the kingdom in Matthew 13 form the central section of the gospel
- Church
  - Three times, not in any other gospel (16:18; 18:17)
  - In Matthew there is a clear expectation of a continuing community

Death and resurrection in Matthew

Jesus' cry of abandonment (27:46) is answered (unlike in Mark) by apocalyptic events. First, the splitting of rocks by an earthquake echoes Judges 5:4; 2 Samuel 22:8; 1 Kings 19:11; Psalm 68:8 and Psalm 77:15–20). Second, the dead rising from tombs echoes Ezekiel 37:12–13. Similarly, an earthquake accompanies the resurrection (28:1). The risen Jesus meets both the women (28:9) and the disciples (28:16–17). The disciples are commissioned by the risen Jesus who promises to be with his disciples always.

Mark

The scholarly consensus is that Mark was the first of the Gospels to be written and that Matthew and Luke both used Mark as a source. Scholars differ as to whether they used Mark independently (the majority) or whether Luke also used Matthew. There are a number of passages which occur in both Matthew and Luke, but not Mark, and so the question arises as to the source of these passages. Either Matthew and Luke had access to another source (referred to as Q) or Matthew used Mark and his own sources (M) and Luke used Mark, Matthew, and his own sources (L). For technical reasons, beyond the scope of this book, it is not thought likely that Matthew used Luke.[7]

Mark's structure

Mark is carefully constructed so that Peter's confession of Jesus as the Messiah occurs at the mid-point of the gospel:

- Prologue (1:1–15)
- Galilee and beyond (1:16 – 8:26)
- Peter's confession at Caesarea Philippi (8:27–30)
- On the way to Jerusalem (8:31 – 10:52)
- Jerusalem (11:1 – 16:8)

Mark's pace

Mark's narrative is a masterpiece in the use of pace. In the first half of Mark the pace is unrelenting. Mark achieves this in two ways. First, by the use of *euthus* (immediately) which occurs forty-one times in Mark (eleven in chapter 1; twenty in chapters 2 – 8; ten in chapters 9 – 16) and only ten times in the rest of the New Testament. Second, by the use of the "historic present" – using the present tense to narrate events in past time (e.g. 1:12). Mark does this 151 times. In 8:27 – 10:52 the pace slows down as Jesus' identity and destiny become clearer on the way to Jerusalem.

Finally, in the last six chapters the pace really slows to focus on the Passion Narrative and there are precise time indicators covering one week in Jerusalem:

- Sunday (11:1-11)
- Monday (11:12–19)
- Tuesday (11:20 – 13:37)
- Wednesday (14:1–11)
- Thursday (14:12–72)
- Friday (15:1–47)
  - Morning (15:1)
  - 9:00 a.m. (15:25)
  - 12:00 noon (15:33)
  - 3:00 p.m. (15:34)
  - Evening (15:42)
- Saturday (not narrated)
- Sunday (16:1–8)

Mark's narrative framework

Like Matthew, Mark too has narrative bookends. In 1:10–11 the heavens are "torn apart" (Matthew and Luke have "opened") followed by a voice from heaven declaring Jesus to be God's Son. In 15:38–39 the curtain of the temple is "torn apart" (same Greek word) followed by the centurion declaring that Jesus is God's Son.

Although Mark opens with a declaration of Jesus as Messiah (Christ), this identity of Jesus remains a secret throughout the first half of the gospel. Jesus commands silence concerning his messianic status of: the demons (1:24–25, 34; 3:11–12); those healed (1:43-45; 5:43; 7:36); and the disciples (8:29–30; 9:7–9). Mark highlights the misunderstanding of the disciples in ways not emphasized by the other evangelists (e.g. 4:13; 8:17–18). Finally, the Markan Jesus makes it clear that the mystery of the kingdom of God is given to insiders only (4:10–12).

Markan themes are introduced in chapter 1 and developed as the story unfolds:

- Jesus as Messiah (8:29; 12:35; 14:61; 15:32)
- Jesus as Son of God (3:11; 5:7; 9:7; 14:61; 15:39)
- Conflict with Satan and demons (3:22–30; 5:1–20)
- Jesus as preacher, teacher and healer
- Discipleship
- The messianic secret

Mark's literary features

Besides the use of pace, Mark employs two other key literary devices. First, there is the Markan "sandwich" in which one story provides the "filling" between two pieces of "bread":

- 3:20–35 (family – Jesus empowered by Satan – family)
- 5:21–43 (Jairus' daughter – woman with hemorrhage – Jairus' daughter)
- 6:6–30 (mission of Twelve – death of John the Baptist – report of the Twelve)
- 11:12–25 (fig tree – cleansing of temple – fig tree)
- 14:1–11 (plot against Jesus – anointing of Jesus at Bethany – plot against Jesus
- 14:54–72 (Peter in courtyard – Jesus before the Jewish Council – Peter in courtyard)

Second, Mark uses groups of three increasing in intensity:

- Three boat scenes (4:35–41; 6:45-52; 8:14–21)
- Three passion predictions (8:31; 9:31; 10:32–34)
- Three commands to "keep alert/awake" (13:33, 35, 37)

- The disciples sleep three times in Gethsemane (14:37, 40, 41)
- Peter denies Jesus three times (14:66–72)
- Pilate asks the crowd three questions (15:9, 12, 14)
- Three time references at three-hourly intervals when Jesus is crucified (15:25, 33, 34)

Jesus as teacher and healer

Although Mark presents Jesus as a teacher (1:14, 21–22, 39; 4:1–2; 6:6, 34), there is very little actual teaching compared with Matthew and Luke. There are four main parables (4:3–20; 4:26–29; 4:30–32; 12:1–12) and an eschatological discourse (13:1–37). Mark has seventeen miracles including exorcisms, healings, and nature miracles.

Conflict

The theme of conflict runs throughout Mark's Gospel. There is conflict with Jesus' own family (3:21, 31–35) and in his home town (6:1–6). As the story unfolds there is increasing conflict with the authorities (2:6–8, 16, 24; 3:1–6; 7:1–15; 8:11–15; 10:1–12; 11:18, 27–33; 12:12–40; 14:1–2). Ultimately, the primary conflict is seen to be with Satan (1:13; 3:23–27).

Discipleship

Jesus' disciples are called (1:16–20; 2:13–14), chosen (3:13–19), and sent out (6:7–13). However, they fail to understand (4:13; 6:52; 7:18; 8:17–18, 32–33); fail to exorcise a demon (9:18, 28); Judas betrays Jesus (14:10–11); Peter denies Jesus (14:66–72); and the disciples desert Jesus and flee (14:50). Mark makes it clear that Jesus is hard to understand and tough to follow!

There are two pivotal texts, which occur either side of Peter's confession of Jesus as the Messiah. In 8:22–26 there is no immediate healing. This is most unusual given the prevalence of the word "immediately" up to this point. Furthermore, the blind man only sees partially at first (just like the disciples). He requires a second touch before he can see clearly. Then, in 10:46–52, Jesus is addressed in messianic terms and does not demand silence (instead the crowd does). This is in complete contrast to the emphasis on the messianic secret in the first half of Mark. Bartimaeus "immediately" regains his sight and follows Jesus "on the way". This ends the middle section; now Jesus' identity is no longer secret, the blind see immediately and follow Jesus on the way.

For Mark, discipleship is conceived as a journey "on the way". John the Baptist prepares the way (1:2–3); the crowd is fed lest people faint on the way (8:3); the disciples are questioned about Jesus' identity on the way (8:27); they dispute about greatness on the way (9:33); and, ultimately, the way leads to Jerusalem and the cross (10:32–34). Discipleship is "following Jesus" on the way (1:16–20; 2:13–14) and, for Mark, this entails suffering (8:34–38; 10:28–31; 13:9–13).

The cross

In Mark the death of Jesus ends in unrelieved darkness with the unanswered cry of dereliction (15:33–34). Jesus' baptism is recapitulated with the reappearance of "torn apart" (as mentioned above) but this time there is no affirming voice from heaven.

The Markan ending

Mark 16:8 is the best attested ending in the manuscripts. Here there is a final Markan irony. The women are told to tell (16:7) and fail to do so (16:8), whereas in 1:44–45 the healed leper is told not to tell and does! There is an empty tomb but no resurrection account. Instead the resurrection is referred to earlier in the narrative (8:31; 9:9, 31; 10:34; 14:28). So Mark ends with the ambiguity of following Jesus – terror, amazement, and fear.

Luke

The overarching theme of the Gospel of Luke is "salvation in Jesus Christ". The full breadth of what this salvation means is seen in the gospel's many socio-political themes with its emphasis on the poor and the outcast, and its themes of prayer, joy, the Holy Spirit, and freedom for women.

The scene is set in the Nazareth proclamation (4:18–19) quoting from Isaiah 61:1–2; 58:6, proclaiming the "acceptable year of the Lord" (i.e. Jubilee – Leviticus 25). Jesus says this anticipated time has now come and is present in his proclamation and acts, which he demonstrates to John's disciples in 7:21–22.

Luke as narrative

Luke is seeking to write an "orderly account" (1:1, 3). The Greek is *diēgēsis*, which suggests a long narrative composed of a number of events. Luke's "order" means narrative order rather than chronological order. The gospel is part of a wider work: Luke-Acts. Many of the themes in Luke continue in Acts and incidents in Luke anticipate aspects of the story in Acts. As stated above, for Luke, God's purpose is to bring salvation to all people. This is anticipated by God's messengers in Luke 1 – 2, made possible through the ministry of John the Baptist and Jesus, and realized in the mission of the early church in Acts.

Luke's structure

- Preface (1:1–4)
- Infancy narrative (1:5 – 2:52)
- John the Baptist and Jesus (3:1 – 4:44)
- Galilee (5:1 – 9:50)
- The journey to Jerusalem (9:51 – 19:44)
- Jesus in the temple (19:45 – 21:38)
- Death and resurrection (22:1 – 24:53)

The preface (1:1–4)

These verses form one sentence in Greek and consist of arguably the best stylized Greek in the whole of the New Testament. Its reference to *diēgēsis* suggests that the work will consist of a reasonably long narrative composed of a number of events and arranged using major developments and patterns. Luke aims to write the well-ordered, polished product of the ancient biographer. Furthermore, Luke's narrative should be seen as proclamation designed to persuade. For he uses the related verb *diēgeomai* (to give a detailed account of) in the context of proclamation in Luke 8:39; 9:10; and Acts 9:27; 12:17. The emphasis throughout the preface is on the reliability and trustworthiness of the account. Finally, Luke declares that his theological intention is that the reader should "know the truth." This stands emphatically as the last word of this long sentence in Greek.

Infancy narratives

The stories of John and Jesus are presented in parallel in Luke's infancy narratives. Luke uses repetition, an increasing disclosure of God's purposes, and the alternation of joy and pathos as narrative techniques. These infancy stories are patterned on Old Testament birth annunciations (e.g. Ishmael, Isaac, and Samson). This literary type consists of the appearance of an angel; the fear and/or prostration of the one receiving the vision; a divine message; some sort of objection from the visionary; and the giving of a sign to reassure the visionary.

Luke begins in the temple and ends (unlike Matthew and Mark, which both have the disciples in Galilee) with the disciples praising God regularly in the temple. This forms Luke's narrative bookends. Acts too begins in the temple (2:46) but ends in a house (28:23), anticipating the move of the early church from its roots in Jerusalem to the wider environment of the Greco-Roman city.

In addition, as well as the annunciation stories, there are a number of other intertextual allusions in the infancy narratives. For example, 1:25 echoes Genesis 30:23; 1:42 echoes Judges 5:24; 2:25 reflects Isaiah 40:1; 49:13; and 2:38 echoes Isaiah 52:9.

John the Baptist (3:1–20)

John is presented as a prophet (cf. Jeremiah, Hosea, Joel, Jonah, Micah, Zephaniah, Haggai, Zechariah). The references to the desert, Jordan, and the crowds reflect the story of Joshua about to enter the promised land. However, they also suggest to the discerning reader the political dangers involved in John's actions. For Josephus tells of the consequences that befell other "prophets" who attracted crowds in the wilderness:

There was also another body of wicked men gotten together, not so impure in their actions, but more wicked in their intentions, who laid waste the happy state of the city no less than did these murderers. These were such men as deceived and deluded the people under pretense of divine inspiration, but were for procuring innovations and changes of the government, and these prevailed with the multitude to act like madmen, and went before them into the wilderness, as pretending that God would there show them the signals of liberty; but Felix thought this procedure was to be the beginning of a revolt; so he sent some horsemen and footmen, both armed, who destroyed a great number of them.

But there was an Egyptian false prophet that did the Jews more mischief than the former; for he was a cheat, and pretended to be a prophet also, and got together thirty thousand men that were deluded by him; these he led round about from the wilderness to the mount which was called the Mount of Olives, and was ready to break into Jerusalem by force from that place; and if he could but once conquer the Roman garrison and the people, he intended to domineer over them by the assistance of those guards of his that were to break into the city with him, but Felix prevented his attempt, and met him with his Roman soldiers, while all the people assisted him in his attack upon them, insomuch that, when it came to a battle, the Egyptian ran away, with a few others, while the greatest part of those that were with him were either destroyed or taken alive; but the rest of the multitude were dispersed every one to their own homes and there concealed themselves.[8]

Luke 3:5–6 does not appear in Matthew or Mark. The filling of valleys and lowering of mountains echoes 1:52–53 and the salvation of all people, as we have already seen, is a major Lukan theme.

Lukan introductions to mission

Luke introduces the mission of his main characters in a similar way. First, he places a sermon at the beginning of their ministry: John (3:7–9); Jesus (4:16–27); Peter (Acts 2:14–36); and Paul (Acts 13:16–41). Second, he introduces scriptural quotation as the key to their mission: John (Isa. 40:3–5 in Luke 3:4–6); Jesus (Isa. 61:1–2 in Luke 4:18–19); Peter (Joel 2:28–32 in Acts 2:17–21); and Paul (Isa. 49:6 in Acts 13:47).

Baptism of Jesus (3:21–22)

The affirmation of Jesus as God's beloved Son is the culmination of development in the narrative concerning Jesus' early years from 2:40 to Jesus in the temple at the age of twelve (2:52) and finally to his baptism. The descent of the Spirit initiates a series of events (4:1, 14, 18). This is paralleled in Acts, where the descent of the Spirit at Pentecost results in mission. Jesus at prayer during his baptism (3:21) is only mentioned by Luke. For Luke, prayer is the setting for divine revelation: Zechariah (1:9–11); Anna (2:37–38); Cornelius (Acts 10:2–6); Peter (Acts 10:9–16); Paul (Acts 9:11–12; 22:17–21); and the prophets and teachers at Antioch (Acts 13:2).

Temptation of Jesus (4:1–13)

The temptation is seen as an initiative of the Spirit and echoes Israel's testing in the wilderness (Deut. 8:2–3; 6:14–16). There is a narrative link between the descent of the Spirit and Jesus' realization of the reason for his anointing in 4:18–19. The temptations concern what does it mean to be the "Son of God"? Jesus demonstrates solidarity with the starving in their reliance on God (cf. 1:53) and he refuses to grasp for power and glory (cf. 1:52 but note 1:32–33 and Ps. 2:7–8). Finally, Jesus faces the question of glory or suffering in Jerusalem (cf. 22:39–53; 23:35–37). These temptations anticipate the divine-diabolic contest throughout Luke-Acts.

Nazareth manifesto (4:16–30)

This is a programmatic statement for Luke, emphasizing the role of the Spirit, the good news for the poor, the notion of eschatological reversal which figures strongly in the Magnificat, and the introduction of Jubilee themes from Leviticus 25: the concept of a fallow year; remission of debts; liberation of slaves; and the redistribution of capital wealth. This liberating good news is too radical for many and inevitably results in division and opposition.

Lukan themes

These have already been outlined above but Luke particularly emphasizes:

- The gospel as good news for the marginalized
  - Poor (4:18; 6:20–21; 14:12–14; 16:19–31; 19:1–10)
  - Sinners (5:29–32; 15:1–2; 19:7)
  - Women (Elizabeth, Mary, Anna, women disciples in 8:2–3, Mary and Martha in 10:38–42, etc.)
  - Non-Jews (2:32; 4:24–27; 10:29–37; 17:11–19; 24:47)
- Prayer (3:21; 5:16; 6:12; 9:18, 29; 11:1–3; 22:31–32, 41–42)
- The Holy Spirit (1:15, 35, 41, 67, 80; 2:25–27; 3:16, 22; 4:1, 14, 18; 10:21; 11:13; 12:10, 12; 24:49)
- Joy and praise (1:14, 44, 47, 58, 64, 68; 2:10, 13–14, 20, 28, 38; 5:25–26; 7:16; 13:13; 15:6, 9, 23–24; 18:43)
- Salvation (1:47, 69, 71, 77; 2:11, 30; 3:6; 6:9; 7:50; 8:12, 36, 48, 50; 9:24; 13:23; 17:19; 18:26, 42; 19:9–10; 23:35, 39)
- The divine plan (1:70; 4:21; 7:30; 10:22; 22:22, 37; 24:44)

Discipleship

Discipleship for Luke, like Mark, involves a journey on the way. "The Way" is actually Luke's description of the early Christian community in Acts (9:2; 19:9, 23; 22:4; 24:14, 22). John the Baptist "prepares the way" and disciples are "on the way" to Jerusalem, and later to Emmaus (10:38; 13:22; 14:25; 17:11; 18:31; 19:11; 24:32).

Luke 12 is a key chapter in which there is a clear interplay between the crowd and the disciples (12:1, 13, 22, 41, 54). The crowd stands for outsiders and the disciples for insiders. The Pharisees and the crowd are described as hypocrites (12:1, 56). The question is whether the disciples will end up like the crowd or whether the crowd will become disciples. The context concerns persecution and possessions: the fear of death and worry about subsistence are key issues. To the crowd Jesus says "guard against greed" (12:13–21), but to the disciples he says, "do not be anxious" (12:22–34). For Luke, discipleship is tantamount to giving up possessions (12:32–34; 14:33; 16:13; 18:18–30; 19:8–9). Luke sums this up in 14:25–33. Discipleship means abandoning security and identity, carrying the cross (living a life so radically opposed to the "domination system"[9] that disciples are considered a threat by the ruling powers and will consequently inevitably be persecuted), counting the cost, and giving up all possessions.

Death and resurrection

In Luke one of the bandits crucified with Jesus responds (23:39–43). Unlike Matthew and Mark, Jesus' final cry is one of commitment (23:46). Following this cry a centurion proclaims Jesus' innocence (23:47) and the crowds respond (23:48). Unlike the crowds, who return home, the women continue to watch with others from a distance (23:49). The women see two men in dazzling clothes and tell the disciples (24:1–11) who, apart from Peter, do not believe them (24:11–12). Luke alone tells the story of two disciples who encounter the risen Jesus "on the way" to Emmaus (24:13–35). Jesus is made known to them as they break bread together – an incident with clear eucharistic overtones. Finally, Jesus appears to the disciples (24:36–49) and ascends into heaven (24:50–51). The disciples now worship Jesus and carry that worship back to the temple (24:52–53).

John

Andrew Lincoln has persuasively demonstrated that John should be viewed from the perspective of the cosmic lawsuit motif found particularly in the Prophets.[10] He uses this motif to shape his gospel, as ancient biography, in a significantly different way from the Synoptics. Unlike the Synoptics, John has no trial of Jesus before the Jewish Sanhedrin. "Instead, throughout his public ministry, Jesus can be viewed as on trial before Israel and its leaders."[11]

John's structure

- Prologue (1:1–18)
- Jesus' public ministry (1:19 – 12:50)
  - Seven signs
  - Seven discourses

- Summary (12:44–50)
- Jesus' departure from the world (13:1 – 20:31)
  - Interpreted for the disciples (13:1 – 17:26)
  - Passion and resurrection (18:1 – 20:31)
- Epilogue (21:1–25)

Jesus' public ministry

- First sign (2:1–11)
- First discourse (3:1–21)
- Second discourse (4:1–42)
- Second sign (4:46–54)
- Third sign (5:1–18)
- Third discourse (5:19–47)
- Fourth sign (6:1–15)
- Fifth sign (6:16–21)
- Fourth discourse (6:22–71)
- Fifth discourse (7:1–39)
- Sixth discourse (8:12–59)
- Sixth sign (9:1–41)
- Seventh discourse (10:1–42)
- Seventh sign (11:1–53)

John as lawsuit

- Prologue
  - Interrupted by references to John the Baptist in 1:6–8, 15. In these verses John's role is as a witness
- Public ministry
  - 1:19–28 John's testimony about himself
  - 1:29–34 John's testimony about Jesus
  - 5:19–47 The trial motif is explicit in the controversy with Jews (22, 24, 27, 30–39, 45)
  - 8:12–59 The trial motif is explicit (13–18, 26, 50)
  - 12:44–50 Jesus as judge concludes this section
  - John 13 – 17
  - The Holy Spirit as Paraclete or advocate (14:16, 26; 15:26-27; 16:7–11)
- John 18 – 20

- Dominated by the trial of Jesus
- Epilogue
  - Testimony of the beloved disciple (21:24)

Testimony thus forms clear narrative bookends in John, encouraging us to view the whole gospel from the perspective of a trial. The prologue provides the cosmic backdrop. The lawsuit is between Jesus and Israel (1:11) but also between God and the world (1:1, 10) with the notion of truth at stake (1:9, 14).

Trial

As stated above, John has no trial of Jesus before the Sanhedrin. Instead, Jesus is on trial before Israel's leaders throughout his public ministry. In this trial seven witnesses are called:

- John the Baptist (1:6–8, 15)
- Jesus himself (8:14, 17–18)
- Jesus' works (5:36; 10:25)
- God (5:32, 37; 8:18)
- The Scriptures (5:39)
- The Samaritan woman (4:39)
- The crowd who witness the raising of Lazarus (12:17)

Charges and plot

Jesus is charged with: deceiving the people (7:45–52); violating the Sabbath (5:16; 7:23; 9:16); blasphemy (5:17–18; 8:58–59; 10:30–39); and being an enemy of the Jewish nation (11:46–53). John's plot concerns Jesus being commissioned to witness to the truth about God (18:37). The plot is complicated by the world not receiving his testimony (1:10–11). Instead, there is a counterplot against Jesus taking the form of a counter-trial – the Jewish trial of his public ministry and the Roman trial leading to Jesus' crucifixion. Resolution of the plot occurs by the counter-trials achieving the purpose of the overall lawsuit. The world's verdict on Jesus results in his crucifixion which, ironically, allows him to complete his commission – "it is finished" (19:30). Jesus' death thus becomes "the paradigm for faithful witness in the hostile world".[12]

Key stages in the trial

- The testimony of John the Baptist (1:6–8, 15, 19–34; 3:25–30)
- The testimony from above (3:11–21, 31–36)
- Jesus as the just judge and the testimonies to Jesus (5:19–47)
- The truth of Jesus' own testimony and judgement (8:12–59)
- The interrogation of the man born blind (9:1–41)
- Jesus and the judgement of the world (12:37–50)
- The preparation of the disciples for testifying and the role of the Paraclete (14:16–17, 26; 15:26 – 16:15)
- The trial before Pilate (18:28 – 19:16a)
- Resurrection as vindication (20:1–29)

Truth at stake

Truth is the final judgement in the lawsuit ("What is truth?" 18:38). As such truth is contested and depends on witnesses to that truth. The truth which is at stake involves: Jesus as Messiah and Son of God (20:31):

- Christological; God as the one who is known in the crucified Jesus (19:30)
- Theological; the divine verdict of life through the death of Jesus (3:16; 6:47–51)
- Soteriological; and
- The relationship of love (3:16; 14:21, 23; 17:23, 26) – relational.

Acts

We have already noted above some features of Luke's Gospel that carry forward into Acts. In particular, Luke's understanding of the divine plan as being fulfilled (Luke 1:1) continues in Acts with the mission of the church.

> The plot of Luke is simply put: conceived, empowered, and guided by the Holy Spirit, Jesus both embodies the Way and makes provision for others to follow in it, thereby fulfilling the divine plan. Here the focus is on Jesus but against the background of the divine plan.

The plot of Acts is equally straightforward: between the ascension and parousia, empowered by the Holy Spirit, the Messianists bear an unstoppable, universal witness to Jesus by word and deed, thereby fulfilling the divine plan. Here the focus is on the church but against the background of the divine plan.[13]

In genre Acts is a form of ancient biography known as the succession narrative. If Luke functions as a biography of Jesus, then Acts functions as a biography of Jesus' successors, particularly Stephen, Peter and Paul.[14] A key text is Luke 22:28–30 where Jesus speaks of bequeathing to his disciples a kingdom just as a kingdom had been bequeathed to him. This sets up the notion of succession. Talbert notes that the elements of this text are fulfilled in Acts where the apostles act as appointed representatives making key decisions for the early church in ways similar to the ancient judges in Israel.[15]

Acts 1:8 is a key verse for understanding how the work unfolds. The mission of the church, empowered by the Holy Spirit, begins in Jerusalem (1:12 – 8:1), spreads out into Judea and Samaria (8:2 – 11:18) and then to the ends of the known world, culminating in Rome (11:19 – 28:31).

In common with ancient biographies, Acts contains a number of speeches made by the key characters. Particularly significant are Peter's speeches in 2:14–36; 3:11–26; 10:34–43; and 11:4–17; Stephen's speech in 7:2–53; and Paul's speeches in 13:16–41; 17:22–31; 20:17–35; 22:1–21; 24:10–21; and 26:1–23. Two of Peter's speeches and four of Paul's speeches end with reference to the resurrection of Jesus and in one other of Peter's speeches the resurrection is central. In two out of the four Pauline speeches, mention of the resurrection is problematic – for the intellectual Athenians (17:32) and the Roman governor, Festus (26:24).

The mission strategy of the early church, according to Acts, is instructive. To the Jews, Peter, Stephen, and Paul all connect the story of Jesus to the wider biblical narrative. To the Gentile, Cornelius, Peter begins with the story of Jesus and emphasizes that his message concerned peace (10:36). This echoes the angelic chorus of the Lukan birth narrative (Luke 2:13–14). This peace is thus not restricted to Israel but is intended for the whole world, for Jesus is "Lord of all" (Acts 10:36). To the Athenians, Paul begins with their own religious proclivity, appeals to God's creation of all humanity as his offspring and suggests that the Athenian altar to "an unknown God" reflects the desire that God has put in all humanity to search for him. In Ephesus, a center for magical practices in the ancient world, Paul combines two years of daily teaching with "extraordinary miracles" (Acts 19:9–11). I have much more to say about mission in Chapter 14 but at this stage it is important to note that Acts, which is all about the mission of the early church, demonstrates the process of contextualization from the outset as the message is creatively adapted for each new context.

12

Reading the Letters and Revelation

The Pauline Corpus (Romans – Philemon)

The scholarly consensus is that, of the thirteen letters in the Pauline corpus in the New Testament, only seven are genuinely from Paul (Romans, 1 and 2 Corinthians, Galatians, Philippians, 1 Thessalonians, and Philemon). Along with a minority of scholars I also regard Colossians and 2 Thessalonians as genuine but consider Ephesians and the Pastoral Epistles (1 and 2 Timothy and Titus) to be pseudepigraphical. Nevertheless, all thirteen letters claim to be by Paul and certainly all of them, in my opinion, represent Paul's thought, either because they were written by him or they are attempts to update (i.e. recontextualize) Paul for a subsequent generation. I believe this is true even of the Pastoral Epistles, which many Pauline scholars see as representing a fading, or even betrayal, of the Pauline vision.[1]

Paul's letters, like letters generally, address situations in his absence. They are written to specific communities (with the possible exception of Ephesians which may have been a circular letter), addressing specific issues. Consequently, there is a certain contingency to each of the letters reflecting the particular situations addressed. This is as true of Romans as of all the other letters. On the other hand, Paul's letters are clearly an application of his coherent gospel to the specific situation so we can discern a coherent center to Paul's thought amidst the specificities of the individual letters.[2] The letters follow the conventional form of ancient Greco-Roman letters.

Letter form

The form of the Greek letter remained relatively unchanged from the third century BC to the third century AD. The following elements are usually present:

Salutation

"From A to B (many) greetings [(*polla*) *chairein*]." The salutation often included additional greetings and/or a wish for good health.

Thanksgiving

On occasions the writer gives thanks (*eucharistō*) to the gods and this is followed by reasons for the thanksgiving. This is usually because the gods have saved the sender or the recipient from some catastrophe.

Body

Introduced with characteristic formulae such as:

- "When I found someone . . ."
- "I want you to know . . ."
- "When I arrived . . ."

The body of the letter is usually split into two parts: the first part giving information about the sender and the second asking about the recipient.

Conclusion

- Greetings
- Wishes for the good health of the recipient
- Farewell
- Date

The form of Paul's letters

Salutation

Paul elaborates on the standard "A to B (*polla*) *chairein*." He includes some self-description here and often mentions co-workers. Most significantly he changes *chairein* to *charis* (grace) and adds *eirēnē* (peace) from the standard greeting in Jewish letters: *shalom*. This is true of every letter in the Pauline corpus (1 and 2 Timothy add "mercy"); it is also true of 1 and 2 Peter and 2 John (the latter also has "mercy" added). Hebrews reads much more like an essay in letter form (it has no salutation), as does 1 John (no salutation or closing greetings). James has the standard Greek salutation (*chairein*) and Jude has "mercy, peace and love".

Thanksgiving

Paul begins this section either with some form of *eucharistō* (give thanks) or with *eulogētos* (worthy of praise, 2 Cor. 1:3).

Body

Formal opening
- I urge/appeal (1 Cor. 1:10; Phlm. 8–9)
- I want you to know/do not want you to be unaware/you yourselves know (Rom. 1:13; 2 Cor. 1:10; Phil. 1:12; 1 Thess. 2:1)
- I am amazed (Gal. 1:6)

Main body
This section usually includes Paul's intention or desire to visit.

Conclusion

- Peace wish
- Greetings
- Holy kiss
- Benediction

Not all of Paul's letters contain all of the above elements but the above framework is comprehensive enough to cover all of the Pauline corpus.

Thanksgiving section

This section of the letters of Paul has received the most attention, in terms of form, in New Testament scholarship.[3] Schubert's analysis highlighted the following features:

- Immediately follows and, therefore, serves to close the letter opening;
- Signals the basic intent of the letter; and
- May serve to highlight the major topics to be considered in the body of the letter.

The body of the letter

The main body in Paul's letters opens with either a request or a disclosure formula and usually concludes with an announcement of Paul's travel plans (e.g. 1 Cor. 16:5–12; 2 Cor. 12:14 – 13:10). The body often contains a section of *paraenesis* (ethical instruction) and this can take the following forms:

- A string of moral maxims (e.g. Rom. 12:9–13)
- Virtue/vice lists (e.g. Gal. 5:19–23)
- Prolonged exhortation on a particular topic (e.g. 1 Thess. 4:13–18)

Types of letter

As well as the *form* of the letter, ancient handbooks classified letters by *content*. The epistolary handbook of Pseudo-Demetrius (probably first century BC in its present form) lists twenty-one types and Pseudo-Libanius (fourth century AD) lists forty-one. The key classifications, as far as New Testament letters are concerned, are:[4]

- *Friendly letter* These letters express the desire to be present with the recipient and the letter becomes a form of friendly conversation.

- *Family letter* This is a sub-type of the friendly letter reserved for letters between members of the same household. As Paul regularly uses the language of fictive kinship ("brothers" or parent/child) his letters can be construed as an adaptation of the family letter.
- *Letter of praise* Paul regularly uses the language of praise in his letters, usually in the thanksgiving section. 1 Corinthians 13 follows the form of a letter of praise.
- *Letter of blame*
  - Admonition – this occurs regularly in Paul and members of the community are encouraged to engage in mutual admonition (e.g. Col. 3:16; 1 Thess. 5:12–14).
  - Rebuke – this is harsher than admonition and is only found in Galatians, which is the only one of Paul's letters not to have a thanksgiving section.
  - Reproach – this is the harshest form of the letter of blame and is not found in the New Testament. Indeed, Paul and his followers specifically distinguish their approach from that of reproach (1 Thess. 2:6–7; 2 Tim. 2:23–26).
- *Paraenetic letter* These letters consist of moral exhortation in which the writer typically encourages patterns of behavior which conform to certain well-known characteristics and urges the avoidance of negative characteristics. Paul's letters are full of such *paraenesis*.
- *Letter of advice* This is very similar to the previous type but has a much more specific focus on a particular course of action that is either to be pursued or avoided. For example, 2 Corinthians 9 falls into this category.
- *Protreptic letter* These letters are more wide-ranging than paraenetic letters. Whereas the latter focus on specific exhortation, protreptic letters urge the recipient to take up a whole way of life. Romans is widely regarded as such a protreptic letter.
- *Letter of consolation* These letters were written to provide consolation at a time of crisis. In Paul the most obvious example is 1 Thessalonians 4:13–18.
- *Letter of recommendation* These were used to commend a particular person who was often the carrier of the letter; 1 Corinthians 16:3 and 2 Corinthians 3:1–2 refer to such letters.

No New Testament letter, with the possible exception of Romans, conforms strictly to any one letter type. But, as complex letters, they contain elements drawn from the above letter types. Even Romans has a clear paraenetic section.

Rhetoric

The epistolary analysis above provides us with the form and type of the letter but is unable to analyze the letter in terms of the flow of the argument. Classic rhetoric was concerned with the art of persuasion and the means of argumentation. Elementary exercises in rhetoric were taught at the secondary stage of education in the Greco-Roman world and formal rhetorical training took place at the tertiary stage. Whether Paul had such formal training is debatable; nevertheless his letters demonstrate a good knowledge of rhetorical technique and the study of at least his more complex letters from the perspective of rhetorical criticism serves to highlight the flow of his argument.

Rhetorical analysis of a sustained argument, based on the classical rhetorical works, divides the argument into the following sections:

- Introduction (*exordium*) Here the attention of the audience is gained and the speaker attempts to obtain the goodwill or sympathy of the audience.
- Narration (*narratio*) Here the speaker provides some background information.
- Proposition (*propositio*) This is the statement of the main thesis of the argument.
- Proof (*probatio*) In this section the main proposition is backed up with a series of proofs. These are often broken down into: confirmation (*confirmatio*); elaboration (*exornatio*); comparison (*comparatio*); and exhortation (*exhortatio*). The paraenetic section of Paul's letters, from a rhetorical point of view, serves as the exhortation section of the argument.
- Refutation (*refutatio*) Here opposing arguments are put forward and refuted. This section often contains a digression examining motives.
- Conclusion (*peroratio*) In the concluding section the argument is summarized and the speaker seeks to evoke a response in

the audience to take appropriate action or make an appropriate judgement.

This approach has been particularly fruitful in breaking down the arguments in complex letters such as Romans and 1 and 2 Corinthians. Here, for example, is Witherington's analysis of the rhetorical structure of Romans.

Romans

Expanded epistolary opening: addresser and addressee **1:1–7a**
Epistolary greeting **1:7b**
Exordium/epistolary wish-prayer **1:8–10**
Narratio **1:11–15**
Propositio **1:16–17**
Probatio
   Argument I: The bankruptcy of pagan religious experience and God's judgement on it
      Part a: The unbearable likeness **1:18–32**
      Part b: A critique of a judgemental Gentile hypocrite **2:1–16**
   Argument II: Censoring a censorious Jewish teacher **2:17 – 3:20**
   Recapitulation and expansion of *propositio*/main thesis **3:21–31**
   Argument III: Abraham as the forefather of a universal religion, of those who obtain righteousness by grace through faith **4:1–25**
   Argument IV: The blessed consequences for all who have been set right by grace through faith **5:1–11**
   Argument V: Adam as forefather of universal sin, suffering, and death; Christ as origin of universal grace, salvation, and life **5:12–21**
   Argument VI: Shall sin, death, and the Law continue now that Christ has come?
      Part a: Shall we go on sinning so that grace may increase? **6:1–14**
      Part b: Shall we go on sinning since we are under grace, not Law? **6:15 – 7:6**
      Part c: Shall we say that the Law is sin? Retelling Adam's tale **7:7–13**
      Part d: Retelling the present human condition: life outside Christ **7:14–25**

Argument VII: Life in the Spirit now **8:1–17**

Argument VIII: Life in Christ in glory (concluding doxological praise) **8:18–39**

Refutatio:

Argument IX: If salvation is by grace through faith in Christ and the Law is obsolete, has God abandoned his first chosen people? Has the word of God failed? Does Israel have a future? (with concluding doxology) **9:1 – 11:36**

Argument X: Unifying praxis and religion for Gentiles and Jews in Christ: true worship and true love **12:1–21**

Argument XI: Unifying praxis and witness: submission to authorities, payment of debts **13:1–14**

Argument XII: Unifying praxis and discernment: acceptance, not judging of other believers (with concluding doxology) **14:1 – 15:13**

Peroratio (with recapitulation of **1:16–17**) **15:14–21**

Epistolary reference to travel plans (with concluding doxology) **15:22–33**

Concluding epistolary greetings and instructions **16:1–16**

Supplemental *peroratio* to Jewish Christians against divisions, reinforcing arguments X–XII (with concluding benediction) **16:17–20**

Concluding epistolary greetings from co-workers (possibly with concluding benediction in v. 24) **16:21–23**

Final benediction **16:25–27**[5]

Paul as an apocalyptic theologian

Although the above literary analysis of the form and type of Paul's letters and their rhetorical structure goes some way to understanding the structure of the individual letters, it is also important to analyze the coherent center of Paul's theology.

> May I never boast of anything except the cross of our Lord Jesus Christ, by which the world has been crucified to me, and I to the world. For neither circumcision nor uncircumcision is anything; but a new creation is everything! (Gal. 6:14–15)

> From now on, therefore, we regard no one according to the flesh; even though we once knew Christ according to the flesh, we know

him no longer in that way. So if anyone is in Christ, there is a new creation: everything old has passed away; see, everything has become new! (2 Cor 5:16–17, NRSV margin)

Paul's apocalyptic understanding of the life, death, and resurrection of Jesus means that everything has to be re-examined, not in the light of creation ordinances or the story of Israel, but in the light of the "radical, uncompromising newness"[6] thus brought about. As Beker, Martyn, Harink, and others have pointed out,[7] Paul's theology is thoroughly apocalyptic in the sense that "God has acted critically, decisively, and finally for Israel, all the peoples of the earth, and the entire cosmos, in the life, death, resurrection, and coming again of Jesus, in such a way that God's purposes for Israel, all humanity, and all creation is critically, decisively, and finally disclosed and effected in the history of Jesus Christ."[8]

Apocalyptic theology consistently emphasizes God's action in invading the cosmos, which has been enslaved by cosmic powers, in order to liberate and rectify the whole creation. This demands a fresh reading of the Old Testament: "Paul reads the Bible in light of a central conviction that he and his readers are those upon whom the ends of the ages have come. They are God's eschatological people who, in receiving the grace of God through Jesus Christ, become a living sign, a privileged clue to the meaning of God's word in Scripture. This hermeneutical conviction demands a fresh reading of Scripture."[9]

This fresh reading of Scripture is carried out through the lens of the cross, the scene of God's triumph over the cosmic powers (Col. 2:15). Scripture reading is cruciform in character and carried out in the light of Jesus' own kenosis (Phil. 2:5–8), understanding this primarily in terms of servanthood (John 13:12–17; Mark 10:42–45). It is the argument of this book that the church quickly lost this thoroughly Jewish, apocalyptic perspective as it became more Hellenized and eventually, with the rise of Christendom, the church fundamentally lost the ability to read Scripture this way as instead it aligned itself with the rich and powerful.

Paul's apocalyptic perspective pervades his letters and insists that God has invaded this world in Christ. For Paul there is a "before" – typically termed "this age" or "this world" (Rom. 12:2;

1 Cor. 2:6, 8; 3:18; 2 Cor. 4:4; Gal. 1:4) – and there is an "after" in which God in Christ has secured our deliverance from bondage to the Powers. Various Powers are named in Paul's letters: law, flesh, sin, world. His whole thought is geared to encouraging believers to embrace their inheritance in Christ and thus no longer live as those enslaved to cosmic powers. In this context a revised understanding of Paul's justification language is possible.

> For Paul justification . . . is the definitive, cosmic, apocalyptic act of the one God of Israel in Jesus Christ, whereby this God, through the death and resurrection of the Faithful One, conquers the powers which hold the nations in bondage and reconciles the world to himself, in order that he might create in Christ a new people, indeed, finally a whole new world, in which loyalty, obedience, and faithfulness to the one God of Israel is made possible among the nations in the power of the Holy Spirit. In this way God demonstrates his own justice, that is, his faithfulness to the promise which he made to Abraham to bless not only Israel but also the nations and so too the whole of creation. God's right-making faithfulness thus also calls forth and enables a corresponding right-making (justice) among the peoples of the earth; specifically it creates the theological-political space for a reconciliation between Israel and the nations, a reconciliation made concretely real and present in the baptism and table fellowship of Jews and Gentiles in the new community that hears and obeys the good news which Paul preaches.[10]

Paul and empire

Paul's apocalyptic theology has clear political implications, as the above quote suggests. If indeed the whole world is in bondage to the Powers and thus needs redemption through the liberating message of the gospel then, for Paul, the imperial claims to provide peace, security, and salvation for the world are demonstrably false. Increasingly Pauline scholars are recognizing that imperial reality defined the whole of life in the world of earliest Christianity.[11] Recent postcolonial studies have demonstrated the various "hybrid" strategies used by colonized peoples to negotiate the reality of empire. These include mimicry, deference, self-protective opposition, subtle coding, and resistance.[12] Paul regularly uses the language of imperial rhetoric to subvert imperial claims.

Crossan notes that Roman imperial theology was the "ideological glue that held Roman civilization together".[13] He argues that imperial ideology was promoted throughout the empire by the political elites as it was in their own interests to do so. From Augustus onwards the divinity of the emperor was a matter of imperial prerogative and imperial propaganda was everywhere: in poetry, on inscriptions, coins and images, and in statues, altars, and other structures.[14] Crossan tellingly concludes his chapter as follows:

> Before Jesus the Christ ever existed and even if he had never existed, these were the titles of Caesar the Augustus: Divine, Son of God, God and God from God; Lord, Redeemer, Liberator, and Savior of the World. When those titles were taken from him, the Roman emperor, and given to a Jewish peasant, it was a case of either low lampoon or high treason. Since the Roman authorities did not roll over in their togas laughing, we may presume that Pilate, acting for them, got it precisely correct. He publicly, officially, and legally executed Jesus for nonviolent revolution against their imperial power. (He recognized it was nonviolent by making no attempt to round up Jesus' followers.)
>
> We have seen that the program of Roman imperial theology incarnated in Caesar was the sequence of religion, war, victory, and peace or, more succinctly, peace through victory. What, then, was the counter-program of that other Son of God? For without such a credible counter-program, those titles transferred from Caesar to Christ would be simply an absurdly bad joke.
>
> From the nonviolence of Genesis 1 with Sabbath-equality as crown, from the covenantal heart of Torah where the land belongs to God, from the relentless criticism of injustice in the prophets and the psalms, from the eschatological faith in a transformed world here below, that alternative vision is this: religion, nonviolence, justice, and peace, or, more succinctly, peace through justice.
>
> These, therefore, are – now as then – the two great transcendental visions for global peace – peace through violent victory or peace through nonviolent justice.[15]

Wright, writing of Romans, notes the wealth of counter-imperial signals contained in the salutation alone. In the first six verses he announces that Jesus is Lord, proclaims the gospel (a word used in imperial rhetoric to announce the "good news" of the emperor's accession or his birthday) and summons the whole world to the "obedience of faith" which outstrips the loyalty demanded by Caesar.[16] Wright goes on to show how this counter-imperial rhetoric continues throughout Romans and argues that Romans 13:1–7 should be read in conjunction with Romans 13:11–14. This latter passage matches closely the counter-imperial passage in 1 Thessalonians 5:1–11 (which plays on the imperial slogan "peace and security"). In other words, in the light of consistent counter-imperial language throughout the letter, Paul is concerned here not to encourage the Roman Christians into any kind of violent civil disobedience, while still emphasizing the subordinate status of the imperial regime.[17]

Paul and community

Paul's letters were addressed to congregations. Even Philemon is also addressed to the church in his house (Phlm. 2) and the letters to Timothy and Titus all end with "grace be with you" in which the "you" is plural, indicating their communal nature. Furthermore, these letters would have been read out to the congregation as not all would be literate. So the letters involve a communal address and a hearing-in-community. Undoubtedly, the contents would then be discussed by the community. Unfortunately, today so much of our reading of these letters takes place at an individual level. Even if we hear the texts read out and expounded in a church service there is little or no opportunity to engage *as a congregation* with these texts. This is very different from their original reception.

The Anabaptist emphasis on congregational hermeneutics fits precisely with the community-intentional nature of the letters. These Pauline communities operated on the margins of society and were undoubtedly small. Many consisted of churches that met in homes and even when these house churches came together as "the whole church" in Corinth they were still able to be accommodated by one host, Gaius (Rom.

16:23 – written from Corinth). Although some, like Gaius, would have been wealthy enough to accommodate the whole church at Corinth, for example, the majority were powerless and of low status (1 Cor. 1:26). One of the major problems of our Christendom heritage is that it is difficult to think of Paul as a marginal figure in the church leadership of his day which was dominated by the Jerusalem leaders – for example, Paul is fighting (metaphorically!) for his apostolic life in 2 Corinthians. We also often fail to acknowledge that his churches were small. Yet the genius of Paul was to plant these small communities in key cities of the day to be beacons of light in society; 1 Thessalonians provides an example. Paul spends some time in the city working to earn a living while proclaiming the gospel (2:9). In this he demonstrates that even the clear teaching of Jesus has to be contextualized. Paul makes it clear in 1 Corinthians 9:14 that Jesus commanded that those who proclaim the gospel should get their living from the gospel. Yet Paul, in both Corinth and Thessalonica, feels free to disregard a command of Jesus. This is because what was appropriate for Jesus' disciples in Palestine was not necessarily appropriate for life in a Greco-Roman city where being paid for services would have meant Paul being regarded as a wandering philosopher.

Paul's own example alerts us to the fact that we cannot simply apply first-century texts to our different context. Appropriate obedient response requires some wrestling with, and reflection on, these texts. Paul makes it clear to the Thessalonian Christians that what he did do in his time with them was instruct them how to live in a way pleasing to God (1 Thess. 4:1). By teaching (4:2) and example the Thessalonians learned a way of life that was so countercultural that their reputation spread not only to the surrounding districts but "in every place" (1:6–10). Paul significantly describes them as imitators both of himself and Jesus (1:6). Also, significantly, he mentions that they turned from idolatry (1:9).

This communal outworking of the gospel, encapsulated by turning from idolatry to a lifestyle emulating Jesus, must be the goal of all Bible reading and I will say more on this in Chapter 14.

Hebrews

Hebrews should not be regarded as an epistle in genre. Although it does have an ending characteristic of letters with a closing benediction and final greetings, it lacks the opening salutation necessary for the letter form. It is best regarded as an extended sermon or homily as can be seen by the conversational style adopted (e.g. 2:5; 5:11; 6:9; 8:1; 9:5; 11:32). The opening four verses consist of one sentence in Greek and its polished rhetorical style has long been noted. In this opening the major emphases of the homily are introduced: Christology and soteriology. Hebrews is effectively constructed as a series of mini-sermons which, like any good sermon, consist of teaching based on specific texts followed by an exhortation. A good outline is provided in *Exploring the New Testament*, volume 2 (Table 12.1, p. 168).[18]

At the macro level, Hebrews contains the longest sustained argument in the New Testament and is based on the rabbinic tradition of arguing from the lesser to the greater.[19] In this case the argument is: "if the Levitical priesthood accomplished this, how much more does Jesus' priestly status accomplish?" In this Hebrews functions as midrash on both Exodus/Leviticus and Psalm 110. Jesus is only ever referred to as "priest" or "high priest" in Hebrews in the New Testament. By reflecting on both the role of the priest in the sacrificial system of Exodus/Leviticus and the royal imagery of the priesthood of Melchizedek in Psalm 110:2–4, the writer is able creatively to combine the death and resurrection of Jesus (e.g. Heb. 10:12–13).

It is important to note the exhortations in 6:4–8 and 10:26–31. These passages have featured prominently in debates about Calvinism. However, the crucial point being made is intensely pastoral. Immediately after the warning in chapter 6 the writer goes on to praise the love at work in the community and encourages the recipients to show the same diligence to the very end (6:9–12). In chapter 10 the writer goes on to remind the readers about previous abuse and persecution, which resulted in the loss of possessions (10:32–34). The sharpness of the earlier warnings is due to pastoral concern that the believers might fail in the light of impending persecution. The author writes in the context of imprisonment and torture (13:3) and warns the readers that they

Table 12.1 An outline of Hebrews

Hebrews	Outline	Texts used
1:1–4	INTRODUCTION: GOD HAS SPOKEN	
1:5–14	*Teaching*: Jesus superior to angels	Various (mostly psalms)
2:1–4	*Exhortation*: Take the message seriously	
2:5-18	*Teaching*: Jesus made lower than angels	Psalm 8
3:1–11	*Teaching*: Jesus faithful, superior to Moses	Psalm 95
3:12 – 4:13	*Exhortation*: Be faithful to him, enter his rest	
4:14–16	*Exhortation*: Let us approach him for mercy	
5:1–10	*Teaching*: He has shared our suffering	Psalm 110
5:11 – 6:3	*Exhortation*: Press on to maturity	
6:4–8	*Teaching*: The danger of turning back	
6:9–20	*Exhortation*: Hope in God's promises	
7:1–12	*Teaching*: Melchizedek, the royal priest	Genesis 14:18–20
7:13–28	*Teaching*: Jesus, priest like Melchizedek	Psalm 110
8:1 – 9:10	*Teaching*: The first covenant, provisional and inadequate	Jeremiah 31
9:11-28	*Teaching*: The new covenant and its sacrifice bring access to heaven	Exodus 24:5–8
10:1–10	*Teaching*: Christ offers himself for us . . .	Psalm 40
10:11–18	*Teaching*: . . . and thus brings full forgiveness	Jeremiah 31
10:19–25	*Exhortation*: Come to God with faith, hope, love	
10:26–31	*Teaching*: The danger of turning back	Deut. 2:35–36
10:32–39	*Exhortation*: Endure till the promised salvation comes	Habbakuk 2
11:1–40	*Teaching*: The faith of our ancestors	Various
12:1–13	*Exhortation*: Like Jesus, endure testing	Proverbs 3
12:14–29	*Exhortation*: Do not turn back from the living God	
13:1–17	*Exhortation*: Serve God in the true community	
13:18–25	CONCLUSION: PRAYER AND GREETINGS	

have not yet had to shed their blood (12:4). I take this, following the culmination of the faith list in chapter 11 with accounts of martyrdom, also to be a reference to martyrdom, rather than blood shed in an athletic contest such as a boxing match.[20] The teaching concerning the total superiority of Jesus is designed ultimately to provide encouragement to believing communities living in the context of imperial ideology where their allegiance to Jesus could easily lead to persecution. The well-known chapter on faith (11) is not without its problems. Apart from Rahab no women are named and the writer includes Jephthah as a hero of faith, a position many readers would not want to associate with.

The General Epistles (James – Jude)

These seven letters have traditionally been called "general" or "catholic" epistles as they appear to be written for general circulation rather than to a specific community, even though both 2 and 3 John have specific addressees. I will comment briefly on each of these letters.

James is interesting in that, compared with Paul, it offers an inner-canonical debate within the New Testament concerning the relationship between faith and works (2:14–26). This reminds us of the inner-canonical debates within the Wisdom literature in the Old Testament. James sits well with the Old Testament emphasis on justice and, like many other texts in the New Testament, builds on "the royal law" of loving neighbor as oneself (2:8–13). It warns against riches (1:9–11; 2:1–7; 5:1–6), promotes peace-making (3:18) and, like Paul, sees believers at war with the world system (4:4).

The letter of *1 Peter* encourages faithful discipleship, conforming to the example of Christ (2:21–23), in the midst of a hostile environment; 2:11 could easily be a Pauline text! This letter also operates within an apocalyptic framework (e.g. 1:5, 20; 2:12; 4:7). It calls believers to faithful living and inspires hope of ultimate salvation in a time of persecution. The letter also, notoriously, contains an example of the household code in which believers are urged to accept subordinate roles: everyone in relation to government, slaves in relation to masters, and wives in relation to husbands (2:13 – 3:7). Although many critics have seen the examples of the household code in the New Testament as an example of the early church conforming to the wider society and thus accepting hierarchical values, Yoder has argued for viewing these texts as examples of revolutionary subordination. He points out that, unlike the traditional household codes, the subordinates are addressed first as moral agents, capable of making decisions in their own right. Furthermore, the very need for such exhortation suggests that within the earliest Christian communities a vision was provided of a new kind of humanity in which such societal distinctions were no longer of value.[21]

The letter of 2 *Peter* focuses on the transformative effects of the divine power at work in believers leading them onwards to participation in the divine nature (1:4), or entrance into the eternal kingdom (1:11), or experience of the new heavens and earth (3:13). It warns against false teaching and is written in the context of concern over the delay of Christ's return (3:4).

Like Hebrews, 1 *John* is not a letter in form. It contains no salutation and no concluding greetings. It too should be regarded as a homily in written form (e.g. 2:1, 7, 12–14, 26; 5:13). In 3:13 we get a hint of the bifurcation we have found in Paul. But the bulk of the letter concerns internal strife arising from the departure of those the writer calls "antichrists". The specific issue at stake appears to be a denial of the full humanity of Jesus (4:2–3). Johnson has the intriguing suggestion that the three Johannine epistles were sent at the same time to the same destination, otherwise it is difficult to account for the appearance of 2 *and* 3 *John* in the canon. For Johnson, 3 John is a personal letter to Gaius, who offers hospitality to the writer's delegates (3 John 5–8). It serves as a letter of recommendation for the bearer of the three letters, Demetrius (3 John 12), and refers to the main letter, 1 John (3 John 9). This personal letter has to accompany the other letters because another local leader, Diotrephes (3 John 9), does not acknowledge the authority of the writer, refuses to welcome the writer's delegates and expels those who do (3 John 10). Then 2 John serves as a cover letter to the church, introducing 1 John. Finally, the specific issues, summarized in 2 John, are spelled out in detail in 1 John. In the context of internal strife the community is exhorted to pursue love and resist sin.[22]

Jude is also written in the context of false teaching which rejects moral authority and encourages sexual immorality (Jude 4, 7–8). It urges faithful believers to pay attention to their faith, pray in the Spirit, keep walking in love, and wait for Christ's return.

Revelation

Genre

Revelation is unusual in that it combines three genres, all of which must be taken seriously in its interpretation. All three genres are introduced in the first four verses:

- The very first word in the Greek is *apokalypsis* – Revelation is first and foremost an apocalypse. As such the present experience of the reader is opened up to divine transcendence. Vision, symbol, and word pictures combine to evoke an alternative reality:
  - The dragon will always wage war against the woman (12:1–6)
  - The dragon is the power behind the beast (13:1–2)
  - The beast demands our worship (idolatry – 13:4)
- But
  - God is on the throne (4:1–11)
  - The Lamb is at the center of unfolding history (5:1–14)
  - The church is called to faithful witness (11:1–3; 14:1–6; 19:10)
- But it is also *prophecy* (1:3; cf. 22:6–10, 18–19). Revelation is both saturated with allusions to prophecy in the Hebrew Scriptures but is also itself prophecy. As such it engages in the twofold task of prophetic energizing (bringing hope of a transformed future) and prophetic critique (criticizing the structures of this world and calling the church to faithful obedience).
- Finally, it is cast in the form of a *letter* (1:4; cf. 22:21). The letter form is often not taken seriously enough. The letters to the seven churches in chapters 2 and 3 effectively form seven separate introductions to the book.[23] The letter is thus meant to be read from seven perspectives, reflecting the state of the various churches addressed:

- *Loss of radical discipleship (Ephesus)* For readers in this position the call is to repent and the book offers both hope for a transformed future and criticism of compromise.
- *Persecution (Smyrna)* For readers in this position the book offers the hope of resurrection.
- *Idolatry (Pergamum)* For readers in this position the book starkly warns of the dangers of idolatry and points to God's ultimate victory over the Powers.
- *Esoteric knowledge (Thyatira)* For readers in this position the book offers a vision of the truth of the risen Jesus who is available to all the churches. This cuts across all claims to esoteric knowledge which, of course, characterized emerging Gnosticism in the early church.
- *Loss of witness (Sardis)* For readers in this position the book calls for a return to faithful obedience.
- *Marginalized but faithful (Philadelphia)* For readers in this position the book urges them to remain faithful and offers the vision of the new Jerusalem to give hope.
- *Wealthy and powerful (Laodicea)* For readers in this position the book is uncompromising and calls on such readers to pay attention to its message of judgement on the economic wealth of the nations. True wealth comes from faithful obedience.

Attention to the letter form enables us to see that Revelation is not just written for Christians who are marginalized and persecuted – these represent just two of the seven situations addressed. It is, therefore, as much a call to repentance as an offer of hope. Furthermore, after the letter salutation in 1:4–8 there is a vision of the risen Christ. Interestingly, aspects of this vision are applied to each of the seven churches. It is as though the book begins with "the measure of the full stature of Christ", which Ephesians 4:13 states as the eschatological goal of the church, and then addresses the extant church in its weakness. So, in simple terms, the overall message of the book is: "Here is Jesus in all his glory; here is the church in its weakness; are we as readers going to continue to accept the status quo or will we rise up and conquer, challenging all that opposes the rule of God until the reign of God comes in all its fullness?" Of course, the church is not called to do this in her own strength but is equipped by the risen Jesus himself to fulfil the task of faithful obedience.

Within Christendom, religious tradition has tended to speak the same language as the dominant modes of discourse. In this context apocalyptic language was marginalized, prophecy was simply equated with visions of the future (and so the concept of prophetic critique of the present system was lost), and the relevance of the letter form for interpreting Revelation was also lost.

Methods of interpretation

Four methods have dominated interpretation of the book.

Preterist

This is the prevailing scholarly position which seeks to interpret the book in its first-century historical context. The seven seals either represent specific Roman emperors from Tiberius to Titus or Domitian with the sixth seal coinciding with the fall of Jerusalem in AD 70, or they represent the results of war: conquest, slaughter, economic scarcity, pestilence, martyrdom, and the fall of empire. The unholy trinity of the dragon, the beast, and the false prophet represent Satan, Rome, and the Imperial Cult respectively and 666 refers to Nero. This view still acknowledges that there is a future element from John's perspective in the final chapters: 18 refers to the eventual fall of Rome; 19 to the Parousia; 20 to judgement and 21 – 22 to the final eschatological state.

Idealist

The book is a symbolic portrayal of the cosmic conflict between the kingdom of God and the forces of evil. As such it portrays this conflict using vivid imagery which is not to be taken literally or seen as fulfilled in specific historical events.

Historicist

The book covers the entire sweep of history from the incarnation to the Parousia and the end of the age.

Futurist

This is the prevailing popular view. Almost the entire book relates to the future and concerns the events immediately leading up to the Parousia and the end of the world.

The problem with the futurist position concerns how such visions of the distant future would inspire hope and speak to the specific situations of the book's original recipients. This is true, albeit to a lesser extent, of the historicist position. A combination of the preterist and idealist positions appears to make most sense. The book clearly refers to first-century events but uses symbolic language in a way which transcends those events. So, for example, undoubtedly 666 referred to Nero; but the very symbolism of the number (especially when contrasted with Jesus = 888)[24] epitomizes evil. Thus an idealist stance would recognize its original historical referent but also accept that there have been numerous incarnations of 666 in history.

Structure

The clearest structural markers are the repetition of the phrase "in the spirit" in 1:10; 4:2; 17:3 and 21:10. The last two set up a clear structural parallelism between Babylon the harlot and the new Jerusalem the bride. The first two form narrative bookends marking off the vision of the risen Christ and its relevance to the seven churches strengthening the analysis given above under "Genre." In the main section between 4:2 and 17:3 we have a series of three sevens with two intercalations. This gives an overall structure as follows:

- Prologue (1:1–8)
- Inaugural vision of Christ and its relevance to the seven churches (1:9 – 3:22)
- Inaugural vision of heaven (4:1 – 5:14)
- Seven seals – 4 + 1 + (1 + intercalation) + 1 (6:1 – 8:5)
- Seven trumpets – 4 + 1 + (1 + intercalation) + 1 (8:6 – 11:19)
- God's people in conflict with evil (12:1 – 15:4)
- Seven bowls – 4 + 3 (no intercalation)

- Babylon the harlot (17:1 – 19:10)
- Transition from Babylon to the New Jerusalem (19:11 – 21:8)
- The New Jerusalem the bride (21:9 – 22:9)
- Epilogue (22:6–21)[25]

Themes

Worship

The book exudes worship but is also set in a liturgical context. It is expected that the book will be read out aloud for maximum impact on its hearers (1:3).

The centrality of the Lamb

The victory that God wins is nonviolent for the Lion who has conquered is the Lamb who was slain (5:5–6). The war is won by the sacrificial death of both the Lamb (5:6–9) and his followers (7:14; 12:11). Final victory at the Parousia is achieved by the Word of God (19:13) which is the sword from his mouth (19:15 cf. Isa. 11:4; 49:2; Heb. 4:12). Those who worshiped the beast are "killed" by this sword; in other words they are overcome by the Word of God! (19:21)

The role of the Spirit

The Spirit is described as the spirit of vision (1:10; 4:2; 17:3; 21:10) and the spirit of prophecy (2:7, 11, 17, 29; 3:6, 13, 22; 14:13; 19:10; 22:17). Reference is also made to the seven spirits (1:4; 3:1; 4:5; 5:6) who are both linked to God (4:5) and to the Lamb (5:6). This apparent Trinitarian formulation is made explicit in 1:4–5.

Eschatological victory

The conquering Messiah (5:5–6) has a messianic "army" (7:2–14; 14:1–5). But their victory is established through testimony. The martyrs conquer by faithful witness (6:9; 12:11) exemplified by the two witnesses (11:1–14). The final victory over the Powers is dramatized (19:1 – 20:10).

Conversion of the nations

The nations are currently aligned with evil (11:2, 18; 14:8; 18:3, 23; 20:3), but they will eventually worship God (15:4; 21:24–26; 22:2). The book speaks of a "remnant" being destroyed but the rest worship God (11:13–15). Using different imagery, the conversion of the nations is viewed as harvesting the earth (14:14–16). In the new Jerusalem, God dwells with humanity (21:3–4) and the leaves of the tree of life are for the healing of the nations (22:2). The judgements of God outlined in the book are, therefore, ultimately to bring the nations in and imagery reminiscent of Isaiah 60 is used to convey the sense of universalism here.

Economic critique (17 – 18)

In a devastating critique of the alliance of military and economic interests, the powerful ancient symbol of Babylon is evoked. The seer anticipates a future where the military and economic might of Rome is finally judged. From an idealist interpretative perspective these chapters evoke prophetic critique of all empires from Rome to the present day.

The new Jerusalem

Imagery from the garden of Eden is used but the final chapter demonstrates the sweep of history contained within the covers of the Bible. The garden of Genesis becomes the garden-city of Revelation (22:1–2). In the new Jerusalem the history of both Israel and the church come to fruition as symbolized by the twelve tribes of Israel and twelve apostles (21:12–14). Significantly, and unlike Ezekiel's vision, the city is named as the new *Jerusalem*. One of the characteristics of this city is there is no sea (21:1). Sea is symbolic of the chaos of uncreation (cf. Isa. 57:20; Ps. 107:25–28; Ezek. 28:8; Isa. 27:1; Rev. 13:1) and there are clear links in Revelation to the flood narrative. In 4:3 the rainbow echoes Genesis 9:8–17, and Revelation 11:15–18 echoes Genesis 6:11–13, 17. In the city flows the river of the water of life (Rev. 22:1) and the tree of life (22:2), previously barred to humanity (Gen. 3:22–24) is now available for the healing of the nations (Rev. 22:2). The imagery hints at an ongoing healing process for the whole world.[26]

Intertextuality

Surprisingly, there are no explicit citations in Revelation. But the book teems with allusions to the Hebrew Scriptures. It is generally acknowledged that Revelation contains more references to the Hebrew Scriptures than any other New Testament book. More than half the references come from Isaiah, Ezekiel, Daniel, and Psalms (in that order), with Daniel providing the greatest number in proportion to its length. Clusters of allusions can be found particularly in these passages:

- Description of the risen Christ (1:12–20)
- God on the throne (4:1–11)
- Beast (13:1–8)

We can see this, for example, in Revelation 4:2–9:

- 4:2 (cf. Isa. 6:1; 2 Kgs. 22:19)
- 4:3–4 (cf. Ezek. 1:28)
- 4:5a (cf. Ezek. 1:13; Exod. 19:16)
- 4:5b (cf. Ezek. 1:13; Zech. 4:2, 6)
- 4:6a (cf. Ezek. 1:22)
- 4:6b (cf. Ezek. 1:5, 18)
- 4:7 (cf. Ezek. 1:10)
- 4:8a (cf. Isa. 6:2)
- 4:8b (cf. Isa. 6:3)
- 4:9 (cf. Isa. 6:1)

Revelation alludes to the Pentateuch, Judges, 1 & 2 Samuel, 1 & 2 Kings, Psalms, Proverbs, Song of Songs, Job, Daniel, and the Major and Minor Prophets. There is hardly a book in the Hebrew Scriptures that does not find its way into the last book of the bible. Revelation is thus a fitting end to the biblical canon, not only for its eschatological vision but also for its literary allusions.[27]

Part 3

Contemporary Applications

13

Reading the Bible for Spirituality

Introduction

In Part 2 I provided an overview of the whole Bible in order to see the big picture while also paying attention to a number of the smaller stories within that overall picture. In this chapter and the next I want to focus on particular ways of reading the Bible which are particularly relevant in our post-Christendom context: reading for spirituality and reading for mission. Spirituality is certainly a growth industry in post-Christendom society. A plethora of books can be found in any good book store under the generic title "spirituality" with many people claiming to be spiritual but not religious. These claimants, of course, would never regard the Bible as a resource for contemporary spirituality and this has to be recovered in the current context.

In fact, Bible reading as a matter of private devotion has been the subject of numerous popular books and articles over centuries. The practice of *lectio divina* (spiritual reading), for example, has been particularly promoted by the Benedictines who base this practice on the sixth-century *Rule of Benedict*. Its fourfold rhythm of *lectio, meditatio, oratio*, and *contemplatio* provides a particular methodology for appropriating Scripture as a means of union with God. First, a chosen biblical text is read slowly and attentively, several times over with the aim of hearing God speak through a particular word or phrase (*lectio*). Second, attention is focused on that word or phrase by reflecting deeply on it (*meditatio*). Third, conversation with God takes place around the meditation through prayer (*oratio*). Finally, all words having been spoken, one rests silently in the presence of God (*contemplatio*).

This practice involves disciplined training within a particular tradition of meditative reading.

Christendom did not see the need for this kind of transformative Bible study for ordinary people (laity) and so it became the preserve of the ordained (clergy) and especially the monasteries. However, the current interest in spirituality as the lived experience of ordinary people is a powerful context for a fresh reappraisal of the significance of the Bible for such spirituality.

Definition

Spirituality is a notoriously slippery term. Sandra Schneiders provides a definition which has been widely accepted in the academic study of spirituality: "the experience of conscious involvement in the project of life-integration through self-transcendence toward the ultimate value one perceives."[1] This definition suggests that spirituality involves conscious participation in a process of integration of the whole self in recognition of the human capacity for transcendence – the awareness that reality consists of more than can be seen and touched – and speaks of spirituality as a lived experience that is shaped into a way of life. Christian spirituality recognizes that such human fulfilment comes from obedient response to God as revealed in Jesus. Consequently, it is synonymous with discipleship and this discipleship involves following Jesus "wherever he goes" (Rev. 14:4). Furthermore, as a process of life-integration, spirituality is profoundly transformative.

Transformative Bible study

This approach to reading the Bible assumes that when we come to the text we hear the word of God addressed to us personally. A word that summons us to a response, even if that response is angry questioning! The goal is to come out of such an encounter with the text, changed and equipped for the ongoing journey of becoming more Christ-like. Reading the Bible in this mode recognizes Scripture's function as "useful for teaching, for reproof, for correction, and for training in right-eousness" (2 Tim. 3:16).

> Transformation involves the movement from egocentric control of one's life toward a life centered on commitment to the will of God, whatever that might entail and however costly it might turn out to be. It is exploring all the sealed and stale rooms of this God's house we call our selves, and offering all we find to the real owner for forgiveness, acceptance, and healing. It is unmasking our complicity in systems and structures of society which violate people's lives, and becoming ready agents of justice. It is discovering the unjust and violated parts of ourselves as well. It is a process, not an arriving; we are "transforming," not transformed. But all along the way there are flashes of insight, moments of exquisite beauty, experiences of forgiveness and of being healed, reconciliations and revelations that confirm the rightness of our quest and whet our appetites for more.[2]

Wink's approach involves a Bible study leader who prepares for the session with a number of questions focused on the passage. A combination of practical exercises and questions designed to engage both sides of the brain leads to transformative encounter with the text. This approach recognizes the need to read in communion as we need each other and the insights of others to effectively engage with the text. However, this work comes out of a specific context: the Guild for Psychological Studies, and consequently the specific questions and methods may be too geared to a particular Jungian approach that may not suit all readers.

Nevertheless, Wink's book raises profound questions for spiritual transformation and I would suggest that Bible study for spiritual growth and discipleship should be at the heart of any church's pastoral program. Groups should be large enough to gain a variety of perspectives but small enough to allow everyone to participate.

I am privileged to belong to Bristol Peace Church, a small group of currently six people, who meet every Sunday at 5.00 p.m. around an Anabaptist liturgy devised by a group of liturgists.[3] At the heart of the liturgy is Bible study and this is followed by a period of prayer informed by that Bible study; we then conclude with a meal together during which we break bread. As eating together is central to our ecclesiology, we are committed not to grow beyond a number that can fit round the meal table. Further growth would result in breaking into two groups. All of us take it in turns to facilitate the Bible study and the study itself consists of time spent in a close reading of the text followed by bringing questions to the text and addressing issues arising out of the text. At all times the questions range round the ways in which this text addresses us, informs the way we look at the world, and challenges us in our individual and corporate behavior. Nearly always one or more of us find aspects of the text problematic and so our sessions are, in a real sense, wrestling with the text. Invariably our reading together has an impact on our subsequent prayers and the conversation often continues round the meal table. There is no overarching methodology but there is a clear stance taken that we treat the relevant passage seriously and expect to be transformed by our conversations together with the text. We are not interested in coming away from our sessions just with more information about the Bible.

In summary, this approach involves:

• A close reading of the text in small groups.
• Asking in what ways the text is problematic for any of us and taking those problems seriously.
• Ascertaining what aspects of the way we look at the world are informed by this text.
• Discovering what challenges this text poses to our current way-of-being in the world.

The spirituality of Jesus

Another way to approach reading the Bible for spirituality is to examine the way the text portrays the spiritual life of some of its leading characters. David provides us with probably the richest characterization in the Old Testament, followed closely by Joseph. In the New Testament, Jesus, Paul, and to some extent Peter provide us with most data. As Paul clearly states that he follows Jesus (1 Cor. 11:1), I will focus on Jesus.

First and foremost Jesus' spirituality was charismatic. Luke is most explicit; only he records that Jesus was "full of the Holy Spirit" before being led by the Spirit into the wilderness (Luke 4:1), and only he records that Jesus emerged from his temptations "filled with the power of the Spirit" (Luke 4:14). Jesus' Nazareth manifesto begins with the announcement of the anointing of the Spirit from Isaiah 61:1 (Luke 4:18). Jesus' whole life is lived with this sense of the Spirit's presence. It is manifest in his birth (Luke 1:35), at his baptism (Luke 3:22), in his exorcisms (Matt. 12:28), his healings, and his proclamation (Luke 4:18–19).[4]

Second, Jesus' spirituality is focused on prayer. There are nine references to Jesus at prayer in Luke (3:21; 5:16; 6:12; 9:18, 28–29; 11:1; 22:39–46; 23:34, 46). Only Luke has Jesus praying at his baptism (3:21). The choice of his twelve disciples is preceded by a night of prayer (6:12), and prayer features significantly in the account of Peter acknowledging Jesus as Messiah (9:18–20), and the transfiguration (9:28–36). The Lord's Prayer is given in response to his disciples seeing Jesus at prayer (11:1–4) and the most specific account of Jesus praying is in Gethsemane (22:39–46). Luke also has Jesus praying twice on the cross – a prayer of forgiveness (23:34) and a prayer of final commitment into God's hands (23:46). Finally, Luke records Jesus' regular practice of withdrawing for prayer in the face of the demands of the crowds (5:15–16). This last text significantly suggests a rhythm of engagement with the crowds and subsequent withdrawal for prayer as the key to Jesus' ministry. This pattern of passionate engagement and solitary withdrawal must inform all who seek to follow Jesus' example.

Third, Jesus' spirituality involved passionate engagement. His healings and exorcisms were profound acts of compassion and social justice in restoring the marginalized to their rightful place in society. His teaching involved the subversion of the ideology of power and a critique of the religious establishment, as has already been demonstrated in previous chapters. His itinerant ministry throughout Galilee and Judea would have left behind in villages and towns communities of disciples profoundly affected by his teaching concerning the kingdom of God. Although Jesus was clearly an eschatological prophet proclaiming the arrival in the present of the yet-to-be-consummated kingdom of God, I am not convinced that he expected its imminent consummation. Matthew 16:18 and 18:15–20 speak of the church and, even if these words are the creation of Matthew rather than sayings of the historical Jesus, they reflect a context of ongoing communities of disciples which I suspect Jesus himself would have envisaged as a direct consequence of his ministry in Palestine.

Fourth, Jesus' spirituality did not consist of asceticism. He is regularly to be found eating and drinking, not just with his disciples, but with both those respected in society (e.g. Luke 14:1) and disreputables (e.g. Luke 5:30). Crossan notes that food is one of the principal ways in which social differentiation is marked. Jesus' practice of open table is profoundly egalitarian and subversive of social hierarchy. Commenting on the mission of Jesus' disciples in the Synoptic Gospels, he notes: "The missionaries do not carry a bag because they do not beg for alms or food or clothing or anything else. They share a miracle and a Kingdom, and they receive in return a table and a house. Here, I think, is the heart of the original Jesus movement, a shared egalitarianism of spiritual and material resources."[5]

Discipleship

As the early Anabaptists insisted, Christian spirituality consists of following Jesus as revealed in the Gospels. Spirituality thus involves a rhythm of passionate engagement and purposeful withdrawal, as suggested above. This purposeful, prayerful withdrawal is to equip us for the task of mission – to engage society with the radical claims of the gospel, as we shall see in the subsequent chapter. This spirituality is manifested in all areas of life: economics, politics, peace-making, aesthetics, and so on. It is not confined to the so-called "moral" sphere but Christian morality deeply informs Christian engagement with the whole of life. Holiness remains the call of God in the New Testament (1 Pet. 1:15–16). This godly holiness is revealed in Jesus and so cannot be equated with its usual connotations of the ascetic life.

It does consist, however, in a lifestyle that is subversive to the domination system. Jesus' call to his disciples to take up their cross daily and follow him is too quickly watered down in contemporary interpretation. Luke 9:23–26 follows immediately after Jesus announces his own suffering, rejection, and death. His call to take up the cross could only have been understood in one way in the Roman context of his day. It is a challenge to live life in such a way that disciples are a constant ("daily") threat to the domination system by living and announcing a way of life that is so radically different and challenging that it could get them executed. To carry one's cross meant execution by the state as a seditious criminal. Crucifixion was the most extreme form of Roman execution reserved for bringing mutinous troops under control, subjugating conquered peoples, wearing down cities under siege, executing dangerous and violent bandits, and for the extreme punishment of slaves.[6] This challenge recognizes the reality of the violent backlash of the authorities in the face of the radical, non-violent, domination-free lifestyle of the kingdom of God.

Reading biblical texts canonically

As well as focusing on specific biblical characters, another way to read the Bible for spirituality is to read canonically with a "spirituality" lens, concentrating on intertextual allusions.

Four texts

As an attempt to read the Bible for spirituality in this way I will focus on four texts: one from Torah (Exod. 34:1–9), one from the Former Prophets (1 Kgs. 19:11–18), one from the Gospels (Mark 9:2–8), and one from the Epistles (2 Cor. 3:12–18). As we shall see, there is clear intertextual interplay between them.

Moses and the glory of Yahweh (Exodus 34:1–9)

The narrative preceding this text is full of dramatic tension. Moses has been in the presence of Yahweh on Mount Sinai for forty days and nights (Exod. 24:18) during which he has received detailed instructions for the construction of the tabernacle, its furniture, and the priesthood (Exod. 25 – 31), and two stone tablets of the covenant "written with the finger of God" (Exod. 31:18) have been given to him. During his absence on the mountain Aaron has constructed a golden calf from jewelry donated by the people and this has become an object of worship. The Second Commandment in Exodus 20:4–6 specifically forbids idolatry (and our text echoes some of the language of Exod. 20:5–6) and the people have subsequently entered into covenant with Yahweh pledging obedience to the commandments (Exod. 24:7–8). The people disappear from the narrative from this point until the golden calf incident. So the people move from a pledge of covenantal obedience to breaking the covenant in the very next scene involving them. As a result Yahweh resolves to wipe them out and start again with Moses (Exod. 32:10). However, Moses intercedes and Yahweh changes his mind (Exod. 32:14). Instead, on descending from the mountain, Moses breaks the two stone tablets in anger, destroys the golden calf and summons the Levites to take vengeance on the people, as a result of which three thousand are slaughtered (Exod. 32:19–29). Yahweh now refuses to enter the promised land with the people (Exod. 33:1–3) but again Moses intercedes and exacts from Yahweh the promise of his presence with the people (Exod. 33:12–17). Finally, Moses asks to see Yahweh's glory but the narrative suggests that Yahweh's glory, as consuming fire, would destroy him. For Moses cannot see the face of Yahweh and live; instead he is permitted only to see Yahweh's back (Exod. 33:20, 23). Here is the paradox – Moses desperately requires Yahweh's presence but the presence of God in the midst is not a comfortable experience.

In our text Yahweh reveals himself first as "merciful . . . gracious, slow to anger, and abounding in steadfast love and faithfulness" and as one who forgives sin and then as one who punishes iniquity for a period. Punishment is admittedly limited ("third and fourth generation") compared to Yahweh's steadfast love ("thousandth generation") but nevertheless there is clearly paradox in the presence of Yahweh – both forgiveness and punishment. Spirituality that seeks the presence of God is revealed as profoundly conflictual – there is bountiful forgiveness but also the possibility of punishment. This is reflected in the preceding narrative; Yahweh desires to punish but Moses secures both Yahweh's forgiveness and presence among the people yet three thousand people perish. This encounter with the forgiving-punishing Yahweh is profoundly transformational for

Moses as the text concludes with Moses identifying himself with the sin of the people, something that the Moses of chapter 32 would never concede. Furthermore, although Moses is not permitted to see the face of Yahweh, this transformational encounter is reflected in the face of Moses (Exod. 34:29–35).

Elijah and the glory of Yahweh (1 Kings 19:11–18)

This text provides another perspective on the spirituality of presence. Elijah, who had experienced the presence of Yahweh as consuming fire in the victory over the prophets of Baal on Mount Carmel, now undertakes a journey to another mountain for a very different encounter with the presence of Yahweh. This journey is also an interior journey for Elijah, from the ecstatic heights of Carmel to suicidal despair in the wilderness (19:4). In exhausted despair Elijah rests, nourished twice by the angel of Yahweh. Then there is a further journey in which Elijah only has the nourishment of that second encounter to sustain him. Just as Moses spent forty days and nights in the presence of Yahweh on Sinai so Elijah spends forty days and nights journeying to Horeb (Sinai) in the absence of God (19:8). At Horeb Yahweh passes by Elijah just as he passed by Moses in our previous text (19:11; cf. Exod. 33:22; 34:6). There follows the stereotypical language of theophany – wind, earthquake, and fire (Exod. 19:18; Pss. 29; 97:2–4; Hab. 3:3–12).

However, the clear difference in this text, unlike others where this language is used, is that Yahweh is explicitly said not to be in the wind, earthquake or fire. Furthermore, as some commentators note, the language also describes phenomena associated with the weather god, Baal. Previously Yahweh had appeared as consuming fire in a contest with Baal but he is specifically not that here. The threefold reference to Yahweh's absence prepares the reader for Elijah's encounter with Yahweh in "a sound of sheer silence".[7] This threefold reference suggests Elijah was used to the concept of Yahweh manifesting himself in storm, earthquake, and fire but the long journey has brought him to a place where a new understanding of Yahweh's presence is available to him. Yahweh is now encountered in awesome, tangible silence. This interior journey into the darkness finally to encounter God at the still center of one's being is well documented in the literature of spirituality. The example of Elijah is, of course, fundamental for Carmelite spirituality, especially as exemplified by Theresa of Avila and St John of the Cross.

This encounter draws Elijah out of his cave and causes him to wrap his face (that word again!) in his mantle. The mantle becomes the symbol of his prophetic status as he subsequently demonstrates the choice of Elisha as his successor by throwing his mantle over him (1 Kgs. 19:19) and Elisha dramatically picks up this mantle after Elijah's ascension (2 Kgs. 2:13). But here it is used to hide the face of Elijah in the presence of Yahweh. Although Elijah's response to Yahweh's question is exactly the same before and after the theophany (19:10, 14), he has now encountered God in a completely different way in the midst of deep depression and this transforming encounter enables him to be freshly commissioned. Elijah here learns the discipline of silence and solitude.

The disciples and the glory of Jesus (Mark 9:2–8)

The reference to Moses and Elijah and a high mountain links this text with the previous two. Joel Marcus highlights the parallels between this pericope (passage) and both Exodus 24 and 34.[8] Moses, of course, comes down from his encounter with Yahweh in Exodus 34:29 somewhat "transfigured". Interestingly, the Lukan version speaks of the appearance of Jesus' face (that word again!) changing, paralleling Exodus 34:29–35. Despite the dramatic nature of this pericope, the narrative keeps returning to the perspective of the three disciples "transfigured before them" (v. 2), "there appeared to them" (v. 4), "[t]hen Peter said" (v. 5), "they were terrified (v. 6), "a cloud overshadowed them" (v. 7), "when they looked around" (v. 8). Jesus does and says nothing in this pericope.

Commentators rightly focus on the significance of the appearance of Elijah and Moses here and also rightly generally dismiss the idea that they stand for the Law and Prophets, especially as Elijah comes first in the Markan account (this is reversed by both Matthew and Luke). The reference to six days and the voice from the cloud clearly echoes Exodus 24:15–18 with the glory of the

Lord settling on Sinai. This intertextual allusion, together with the appearance of Elijah, suggests that the prime reason for their appearance in this pericope is precisely due to their respective encounters with Yahweh on Sinai. Here, however, it is not Jesus who is on the mountain to encounter Yahweh. As noted above, the narrative focus is on the disciples. They are here to have their theophany and this theophany turns out to be the transfigured Jesus. The voice does not proclaim the attributes of Yahweh as in Exodus, nor does it commission the disciples as in 1 Kings, rather it affirms the identity of the transfigured Jesus. Furthermore, as Marcus notes, a development in the interpretation of the Moses story in Hellenistic Judaism concerned the twin notion of translation and subsequent divinization. This could equally apply to Elijah who is explicitly translated in 2 Kings 2:11–12. As Sharyn Dowd states: "Thus, the Moses typology enables the evangelist to portray Jesus as the prophet-like Moses who proleptically enters into his kingship at the transfiguration and who, in the present experience of the Markan audience, shares the rule of the universe with his Father by virtue of his translation and divinization."[9]

Although this concept of divinization links Jesus with Moses and Elijah it is clear that the narrative seeks to distinguish Jesus from them. Their divinization is not the same as Jesus' own identity affirmed by the voice from the cloud. There is a widely held misconception of the notion of divinization or *theosis* that it implies some form of mystical absorption into the divine. However, the doctrine, properly articulated, concerns union with the divine which maintains distinction.[10] The notion of divinization specifically appears in 2 Peter 1:4. If the notion of divinization in this pericope is accepted it takes us a further step in the spirituality of presence.

Believers and the glory of the Lord (2 Corinthians 3:12–18)

If the idea of divinization in the transfiguration narrative is unconvincing it moves center-stage in this key Pauline text. In 2 Corinthians 3:18 we have *metamorphoō*, just as in Mark 9:2 (and nowhere else apart from Matt. 17:2 and Rom. 12:2). But now this transformation is applied to believers. The case for *theosis* is convincingly made by David Litwa,[11] who is now followed by Michael Gorman.[12] Paul, of course, here provides us with his reading of Exodus 34:29–35, a passage that relates Moses' transformation after he had come down from Sinai following the encounter with Yahweh described in our first text. Moses had asked to see the glory of Yahweh in Exodus 33:18 and that glory is subsequently reflected in Moses' shining face. Although glory is not explicitly mentioned in our next two texts it is implicit in the notion of Yahweh passing by in 1 Kings 19:11 (cf. Exod. 33:22) and in the dazzling nature of Jesus' clothes in Mark 9:3 (which reflects the idea of being clothed with garments of glory in 1 Enoch 62.15). Here Paul comments that believers, like Moses, see the glory of the Lord (as in a mirror) and are being transformed into the same image (glory), that is subsequently identified as Christ, the image of God (2 Cor. 4:4). What was a unique revelation to Moses now, through the Spirit, becomes the experience of all believers. Transformation is a present experience and a process "from one degree of glory to another". The goal of this transformation is to become the same image, that is, the image of God. Finally, Paul adds in 2 Corinthians 4:6 that "the light of the knowledge of the glory of God" is found "in the face of Jesus Christ". Although many commentators take this to refer to Paul's Damascus Road encounter with Christ, it is much more likely to provide a contrast once again with Moses. Moses, in asking to see God's glory, could not see God's face and live. But now believers do behold the glory of God in the face of Jesus and believers, unlike Moses and Elijah, have unveiled faces to reveal this glory to the world.

Conclusion

This journey through the selected texts has brought us as readers on a journey with respect to the spirituality of presence. We have moved from Moses' encounter with Yahweh as the awesome Other whose presence remains problematic – loving and merciful yet confronting sin, through Elijah's encounter with Yahweh as present in profound stillness, through to the disciples' own experience of theophany centered on the transfigured Jesus who is thus experienced as "God with us" and finally to the notion of believers' own transformation into the image of God – "us like God". The spirituality of presence moves from a relation of trembling submission to an awesome Other to the Spirit-inspired freedom of ever-increasing union with that Other. This transformation, although clearly the work of God (note the divine passive in 2 Cor. 3:18) has definite ethical dimensions. The disciples, during their experience of the transfigured Jesus, are summoned to listen to him. The only other use of *metamorphoō* in the New Testament is found in Romans 12:2. As Litwa rightly states:

> We immediately observe that the church's divinity, for Paul, is not an ontological state – let alone a mystical one - but consists (at least in this life) in a mode of being that is manifested in concrete ethical acts. This is why in Rom 12:2 Paul's exhortation to "be transformed" . . . is definitely a moral transformation: "so that you may discern what is the will of God."[13]

I also leave the final word to Litwa:

> Endowment with the Spirit is nothing less than an entirely new ethical existence, a new creation, a new and true humanity, even a divine humanity. How does this divine humanity express itself in the world? It expresses itself, through the Spirit, in joyful obedience to God's commands.
>
> This life of joyful obedience, far from being a merely human life, is itself the expression of the divine life; it is, I propose, the key part of the content of Paul's doctrine of *theosis*.[14]

14

Reading the Bible for Mission

Introduction

I remember the occasion as though it were yesterday. In 1986 I left practice as a chartered accountant to join the paid staff of a large charismatic "new church" in Bristol. As well as having some responsibility for the church's teaching program I was involved in assisting one of the congregations based in the city. I remember the main leader returning from a conference on evangelism completely enthused and geared up to get the whole congregation involved in street evangelism. I pleaded with him not to go this route, arguing (as I still would today) that such evangelism is culturally irrelevant in contemporary Britain. Nevertheless, he insisted that this should be the emphasis for the whole congregation and I duly did my turns on the street, trying to engage people, who clearly were not interested, in conversation about Jesus. This experience had a profoundly negative influence on me and I adopted a strong "anti-evangelism" stance for many years.

Although I still maintain that this kind of evangelism is irrelevant – in the week I am writing this I have just encountered a sole "evangelist" preaching in the open air in the city-center shopping mall and it was patently obvious how people were doing their best to avoid him – I now readily acknowledge that the Bible should be viewed as a missional text. However, engagement in mission is a far cry from what I have observed happens in much street evangelism. Evangelism has traditionally been geared to getting non-Christians to accept "Jesus as their personal Savior". Although personal commitment to Jesus is, of course, at the heart of being Christian, that commitment necessarily leads to love of neighbor and a passion for social justice. The dichotomy between evangelism and social action was always misconceived. True commitment to Jesus will be countercultural and thus subversive. In a post-Christendom context, in which the contents of the Bible and the central message of the gospel are relatively unknown, I suggest the church finds itself in many ways analogous to the earliest Christian communities as they sought to engage with the Greco-Roman world. As sociologists of religion specializing in new religious movements have reminded us, such movements grow primarily through a network of social relations and this is precisely how the early church grew.[1] Effective mission involves a combination of social networks and attractive, but challenging, lifestyle.

Alan and Eleanor Kreider have reminded us that mission is the mission of God and that the Bible is a prime resource.

> God's actions today are in keeping with the whole story of God, with the Bible's missional metanarrative which points towards God's reign of comprehensive reconciliation. As would-be participants in God's mission today, we will discern God's activity by asking how something that someone proposes as God's work fits in with God's *shalom*-making activity across the Bible. And we will evaluate our own collaboration by asking how our actions point towards the reconciliatory banquet and healing of creation which God has promised as the culmination of the story (Matt. 8.6–13).[2]

The Kreiders argue that the biblical mission of God is creation-wide:

> The goals of God's mission are huge. God's mission is to bring God's kingdom, God's redemptive reign. God's mission is creation-encompassing; it is to recreate creation, to bring new creation (Isa. 65:17; 66:22; Gal. 6:15). God's mission is to make all things new (Col. 1:20; Rev. 21:5) – humans with "hearts of flesh" in a right relationship to God (Ezek. 36:26), humans reconciled to their bitterest enemies (Isa. 19:23–24), and the whole creation restored as a place where justice is at home (2 Pet. 3:13). In all of these dimensions – humans with God, humans with other

humans, humans with creation – God's project is *shalom*, an all-comprehending wholeness (Col. 1:20). God's mission is peace.[3]

The Kreiders' work is essential reading for reflection on worship and mission in the post-Christendom context. In this chapter I want to focus on some specific ways in which the Bible can be a resource for mission beyond the overall story that it tells.

The Great Commission

Matthew 28:18–20 has been regarded as the great missionary text of the Bible since at least the Reformation. Matthew 28:18 echoes Daniel 7:14 in which "one like a son of man" is given authority so that all nations should serve him. In Matthew 10 the mission of the disciples was restricted to Israel but now their commission takes in "all nations". The imperative in verse 19 is "make disciples". This is far more than just conversion involving belief in Jesus. The sense here is: "as you go, make disciples of all nations by baptizing them and teaching them to obey everything that I have commanded you". The goal of mission is to make disciples and this involves baptism into a community in which believers together seek to obey the commands of Jesus. Community and praxis are at the heart of mission. Praxis, of course, involves all that has been said above: the restoration of right relationship between God, humanity, and the whole created order.

This text should remind us that Christianity is, through and through, mission-oriented. The goal is the reconciliation of all things to God *through Christ* (Col. 1:20). This is important in the context of inter-faith dialogue. Post-Christendom is essentially a multi-faith context in which people of all faiths and none are found in society. In Christendom, mission was initially conceived as to the unevangelized outsiders. In late Christendom the need for mission within became apparent. But conversion was conceived in terms of personal salvation with no critique of the prevailing social norms of Christendom.[4] In Post-Christendom, mission occurs in a multi-faith context in which Christians continue to make universalizing truth claims for Christ. But now these claims should be accompanied by a Christ-like respect and affirmation of the Other. Furthermore, if there is going to be clear respect for all faiths in such dialogue then the missional character of Judaism and Islam must also be acknowledged and respected. It will not do, however, to water such dialogue down into agreement based on the lowest common denominator. Of course, there will be values which we can all agree on, based on our common humanity but this is not the same as affirming that all religions teach basically the same thing. Furthermore, the fundamentally missional nature of the Abrahamic religions means that Christians cannot agree not to engage members of other faiths with the claims of the gospel. At the same time this also means we respect the rights of other faiths (including secular humanism) likewise to engage Christians with the claims of their vision for humanity and the created order.

If disciples of Jesus are to obey all that he commanded then at the heart of Jesus' commandments is love for humanity. This involves, as stated above, the uttermost respect for the Other, including the right to religious liberty.[5] Unfortunately, this sort of respect was missing in Christendom and is also lacking in crass attempts to evangelize without truly understanding other faith perspectives. Furthermore, as the example of Proverbs demonstrates, true wisdom can be found outside our own faith tradition.[6] So, true inter-faith dialogue proceeds on the basis of affirming common values, the commitment to learn from each other, and the right to respect clear difference.

Mission as drama

Brueggemann speaks of mission as a drama in three scenes which are endlessly reenacted. The first scene involves the conflict between powerful forces at work in the world. This fits well with Paul's apocalyptic theology as outlined in Chapter 12. The second scene involves the announcement of victory, and the third scene involves appropriation of the new reality in obedient living. The drama is continually repeated because there are always fresh conflicts requiring fresh proclamation in different contexts and thus continually reworked praxis.[7] Mission thus engages with contested spheres in society, articulates a distinctive

Christian vision in that context, and requires of Christians that they work out this distinctive vision in practice. I will engage with three specific texts below to highlight versions of this ongoing drama.

Leviticus 25; Deuteronomy 15:1–18 (economic sphere)

I did not mention the text from Leviticus in Chapter 7 due to its treatment here. This, of course, is the passage concerning the Year of Jubilee. This key provision structured wealth redistribution into Israelite society. For every fifty years property is returned to its original family regardless of whether families have prospered beyond this or conversely have become impoverished in the meantime. Furthermore, the Deuteronomy text adds a shorter cycle of seven years in which, in the seventh year, the land is to lie fallow, debts are cancelled, and slaves set free. Deuteronomy envisions the possibility of a credit squeeze close to the seventh year as people refuse to lend due to debts being cancelled shortly. However, such a credit squeeze is forbidden (Deut. 15:7–11). The text commands the Israelites to "[o]pen your hand to the poor and needy neighbour in your land" (Deut. 15:11). Between these two texts we see the regular provision for: leaving the soil fallow, remitting debts, releasing slaves, and the redistribution of wealth. Jubilee economics thus had profound implications for agricultural livelihood, credit provision, slavery, and capital.

If, as the Kreiders insist, the mission of God involves bringing *shalom* into all spheres, it has a clear economic dimension. In the drama of mission in the economic sphere this vision of Jubilee is highly contested. Mammon, the god of wealth, is very much alive and well today. "The messages are all telling the same story: a finite world can sustain infinite growth, economic growth is the driving force of history, consumer choice is what makes us human, and greed is normal. If we live in an empire, it is the empire of global consumerism."[8]

As I write the world is in the midst of a global recession fuelled by massive debt defaults and the partial collapse of the banking system as a result. Mammon demands sacrifice. In this contested sphere of global consumerism, the church announces the gospel message of Jubilee in which debts are cancelled;

people are liberated from the enslaving effects of consumerism, and wealth is redistributed. Jubilee was at the heart of the praxis of the earliest Christian community (Acts 2:44–45; 4:32–37). In the light of this announcement, believers are called to a different economic lifestyle. Instead of the economics of greed, an economics of "enough", a commitment to the poor both within and without the community, and a prophetic challenge to the prevailing mindset of the West. This is mission!

1 Samuel 17 (military sphere)

The story of David and Goliath is a favorite one in Sunday school but its implications for mission in the contemporary context are seldom explored. In 1 Samuel 8, as we have seen, the Israelites ask for a king "like other nations." Their first king, Saul, is ideally suited for this role as he came from a wealthy family and "stood head and shoulders above everyone else" (1 Sam. 9:1–2). In terms of the expectations of the people, wealth and physical appearance would make Saul the ideal candidate. But having a king like the nations is not going too well! The Philistines have a champion who towers above Saul in terms of physical stature (1 Sam. 17:4). He demands single-handed combat with a champion from Israel and the terms of the battle seem certain to bring Israel into servitude to the Philistines (17:9). The result is that Saul and all the Israelites are reduced to fear (17:11, 24). The text lingers over a description of Goliath's armory (17:5–7). Here is the epitome of technological and military might and Israel cannot compete on equal terms.

After eleven verses a new character is introduced into the situation. David is the youngest son of Jesse and three of Jesse's sons are serving in Saul's army. The oldest of these, Eliab, has already been described in 16:6–7. Samuel expects to anoint Eliab as king precisely because of his appearance and physical height, just like Saul (16:7). But we are told that Yahweh sees in ways that humans do not and looks on the heart rather than outward appearance (16:7), and David is anointed as Saul's replacement (16:12–13). David goes back and forth from Jesse to the Israelite army bringing provisions for his brothers and their commander (17:15–18). On this occasion David hears Goliath defying the

Israelite army (17:23). Up to this point everything has taken place in the Goliath narrative without any reference to God. Eventually, in verse 26, on the lips of David, God is mentioned. As a result David is introduced to Saul and volunteers to fight Goliath (17:31–32).

Saul, looking at outward appearance, argues that David's complete lack of experience in combat makes him unsuitable. This is a perfectly reasonable evaluation – after all, the fate of Israel depends on the outcome of this battle! David responds with the experience of combat he has had – rescuing the sheep in his care from lions and bears – and attributes his victories to Yahweh (17:37). This is the first point in the narrative that Yahweh is named and this reference to Yahweh evokes a positive response from Saul at last (17:37b). However, Saul expects David to fight military technology with military technology. He clothes him in his armor. The armor is not as impressive as Goliath's; the text does not dwell on the details (17:38–39). But David quickly disposes of the armor; it renders him immobile because he is not used to it (17:39). David has not won his battles to date using the weapons of military technology. Instead he chooses five stones, a pouch to put them in, and a sling (17:40). Unarmored, and equipped only with these, and his staff, David finally after forty verses confronts Goliath.

The Philistine comes to him equipped with the latest in military technology but David has simply "the name of the LORD of hosts, the God of the armies of Israel" (17:45). Crucially, David announces that "the LORD does not save by sword and spear; for the battle is the LORD's" (17:47). The narrative does not dwell long on the battle; it is far more interested in developing the dramatic tension to the moment of battle. In four verses the battle is described, Goliath is defeated, and David prevails against his technological might with just a sling and stone (17:50).

In our contemporary scene Mars, the god of war, is very much alive and well, as he has been through the centuries. The military requires increasingly sophisticated weaponry with which to wage war. In this particular military discourse the name of God is absent. It is a question of weighing up one's own military capability against those of the "enemy". Furthermore, within Christendom, the church has generally accepted this discourse! Thus

1 Samuel 17 is a significant resource for contemporary mission. There is a battle taking place, and it is deadly. Conventional wisdom states that military might is necessary for national security. As a result there are far too many human sacrifices to the god of war. But, into the military sphere, the church is called to proclaim the biblical vision of universal *shalom* (Ps. 96:10–13; Isa. 2:1–4; Mic. 4:1–4). This vision has to be appropriated in faithful, nonviolent discipleship. This requires communities of believers to be actively involved in reconciliation, modeling forgiveness, and peace-making (Matt. 5:9).[9] It requires narratives of nonviolent victories won to subvert the dominant narrative that only military might guarantees national security.[10] It requires fully trained peace-makers with the same dedication to duty as professional soldiers. This too is mission! Goliath is very real and must be taken seriously but then so too must the eschatological vision of universal *shalom*.[11]

Philippians 4:4–9 (moral sphere)

In Philippians 3:20, Paul has made clear that the believers in Philippi (a Roman colony) constitute a different colony with a different Savior and Lord than Caesar – Jesus. This different political body is to be characterized by joy, gentleness, and peace (Phil. 4:4–7). Rather than be anxious (echoing Matt. 6:25–34; Luke 12:22–34), believers are exhorted to pray and, in so doing, make their requests known to God. In the midst of competing claims for what is true, honorable, just, pure, pleasing, and commendable, believers are encouraged to seek out those that are morally excellent and praiseworthy (Phil. 4:8). This requires moral discernment and the cultivation of appropriate community values. Paul suggests these are achieved through the gift of the peace of God by prayer which is able to guard the hearts and minds of believers (4:7) and by imitating him (4:9).

In the contemporary Western scene, Dionysus (Bacchus), the god of hedonism, is also very much alive and well. Often seen today in the company of Aphrodite (Venus), the goddess of erotic love, this pair are celebrated daily in the media and their worship exacts a huge price in terms of relationships, health, monetary resources, and even life itself. These gods dictate what our society sees as true, noble, just, pure, beautiful, and commendable. They commend a particular kind of joyfulness/happiness. At the same time anxiety is endemic, fostered by what these gods falsely declare to be aesthetically beautiful and by what these gods prescribe as true happiness. In this contested sphere the church is called to announce an alternative vision. As fellow humans, believers too long to experience joy; but this rich enjoyment of life is understood as received as a gift from God. This gospel announcement is demonstrated in lived communities of discernment where notions of the "good life" are informed by prayer, reflection, and the imitation of Christ. This too is mission.

Summary

I have worked with a handful of texts above simply to provide a way of demonstrating how texts from a variety of genres can inform mission. This way of reading the Bible requires a grasp of the idols of our time and some of the ways in which they demand sacrifice. Above I have mentioned Mammon, Mars, Dionysus (Bacchus), and Aphrodite (Venus). Further examples include *Technē*, the goddess of art, technical skill, and craft. In contemporary society, *Technē* (technology) is found operating alongside both Mars and Aphrodite. The needs of war and pornography drive technological progress on the one hand and, on the other, *Technē* insists that if the technology is there then it must be used.

Hestia, the goddess of the family, insists on sacrifice for the good of the family and is not far away from the rhetoric of family values. Of course, there is much about family that Christians will want to affirm, but even family can be idolatrous. Texts such as Mark 3:31–35 and 10:28–31 come to mind.[12] Minerva, the goddess of medicine, again ably assisted by *Technē*, promotes doctors as the new priests of post-Christendom society. I leave readers to make further connections between the ancient gods and goddesses and contemporary culture.

Having identified the idols, this way of reading then requires discerning the gospel message in any particular text that requires annunciation in the contemporary context, and finally it requires reflection in community on what the appropriate lived response should be in the context of that annunciation of good news.[13]

Mission and *targum*

The *targumim* (plural of *targum*) were early Jewish Aramaic translations of the Hebrew biblical texts. In translating the texts the writers also engaged in extensive explanation updating these texts for their contemporary context. *Targumim* exist for every book in the Hebrew Bible apart from Ezra, Nehemiah, and Daniel. Eschewing the traditional vehicle of commentary, Walsh and Keesmaat propose an imaginative rereading of Colossians for our contemporary culture using the *targum* as a model.[14] Building on Wright's model of biblical interpretation as participating in an unfinished drama, they propose moving from the biblical text to the contemporary situation by means of dynamic analogy. This involves both deep immersion in the biblical text and an act of imagination to construe dynamic cultural equivalents to the issues addressed in the text. The notion of *dynamic* analogy underscores the fact that no such analogy can ever be final and that there will not be strict one-to-one correspondence.[15]

What is at stake for writers such as Walsh and Keesmaat, and Brueggemann, is that contemporary society has so captured the imagination of the church that it has become almost impossible to envision an alternative reality shaped by the gospel. However, in the climate of post-Christendom, if the church faces up to its marginal status, it may at last be able to see that the privileged position it occupied within Christendom came at the price of being numbed to the radical claims of the gospel. This is what Walsh has to say:

> One thing would be that we need to read the Scriptures as offering us a liberating and alternative worldview – by which I don't just mean a framework of thinking, but rather an alternative imagination, shaping us so deeply. If every time we read the Scriptures they seem to confirm us in what we already believe, we're probably misreading the Scriptures. If when we read the Scriptures we're never upset, we're probably misreading the Scriptures. All

Scripture is inspired by God and useful for teaching and correction and reproof, and we need that correction and reproof. We have to liberate the Scriptures from two bad kinds of readings. One is the individualism we've been talking about. We have to hear this as God's story and God's revelation for the shaping of all creation and a whole new humanity in creation. A second thing would be that we have to liberate the Scriptures from the shackles of dogma. Yes, the Scriptures are there to teach us certain kinds of things, but I think what we do is, we criticise the Catholics because they have a magisterium that functions as the interpretive rule upon the Scriptures. Evangelicals have a "magisterium". It may be justification by faith. It's usually rooted in a bad reading of Romans, and that's why we're presently doing a new book called Romans Disarmed, trying to offer an alternative reading of Romans. I think that the Scriptures are shackled when they become a text of systematic theology as opposed to a living narrative, the testimony of the living community and what God is doing in that community.[16]

In order to demonstrate the sort of imaginative reading required to rekindle the imagination of the church through immersion in the biblical text I offer a portion of Walsh and Keesmat's *targum* on Colossians 1:1–14.

We want you to know that thankfulness permeates our prayers for you. We continue to give thanks to God, the Father of our sovereign Messiah Jesus, as we hear the stories of struggling and daring discipleship that continues to characterize his followers. We have heard that your faith and trust in Jesus is proved true because it takes on the real flesh of love in your midst – a love that is manifest in your care for the poor, providing shelter for the homeless, food for the hungry and hospitality to the stranger. Such faith and love are inseparable: one cannot exist without the other. But neither is possible without hope. And here at the end of a century of such bloodshed, betrayal and broken promises, it is an amazing thing to be a community animated by hope. May that hope sustain you in a world addicted to violence.

But your hope is not the cheap buoyant optimism of global capitalism with its cybernetic computer gods and self-confident scientific discovery, all serving the predatory idolatry of economism. You know that these are gods with an insatiable desire for child sacrifice. That is why your hope is not the shallow optimism of the "Long Boom" of increased prosperity. Such optimism is but a cheap imitation of hope. Real hope – the kind of hope that gives you the audacity to resist the commodification of your lives and engenders the possibility of an alternative imagination – is no human achievement; it is a divine gift. This hope isn't extinguished by living in "the future of a shattered past," precisely because it is a hope rooted in the story of kept promises, even at the cost of death.

You didn't get this hope from cable television, and you didn't find it on the Net. This hope walked into your life, hollering itself hoarse out on the streets, in the classroom, down at the pub and in the public square, when you first heard the good news of whole life restoration in Christ. This gospel is the Word of Truth – it is the life-giving, creation-calling, covenant-making, always faithful servant Word that takes flesh in Jesus, who is the truth. So it is not surprising that the Word of truth is no detached set of objective verities committed to memory and reproduced on the test. No, this Word of truth is active, bearing fruit throughout the cultural wilderness of this terribly scorched earth. From the beginning blessing, "Be fruitful and multiply," God has always intended that creation be a place of fruitfulness. Now the Word of truth is producing the fruit of a radical discipleship, demonstrated in passion for justice, evocative art and drama, restorative stewardship of our ecological home, education for faithful living, integral evangelism, and liturgy that shapes an imagination alternative to the empire's.[17]

I am suggesting that, inspired by the example of Walsh and Keesmaat, Christian communities should reflect on dynamic analogies to issues raised in the biblical text. Some may be able to render their own *targumim*, but all should seek to appropriate the text in this way. For example, 1 Thessalonians 1:8–10 speaks of the word of the Lord going forth from the Thessalonian believers into the surrounding areas and that word included the knowledge that they had turned from idolatry. Successful contemporary mission will result in transformed community living that not only exposes the idols of our time but also visibly demonstrates to the surrounding communities that there is an attractive, alternative way to live.

15

Conclusion

Recovering the script

In Chapter 6 I critiqued the prevailing creation-fall-redemption-consummation rendering of the overall biblical script. I suggested there that the canonical shape from creation to new creation should be taken seriously but left open the question as to how to render the intervening story. I argued in Chapter 12 that Paul's apocalyptic perspective should continue to inform the way we read the Bible. Reading the Bible through the lens of apocalyptic theology recoverable in a post-Christendom context enables us to look again at the overarching narrative and the following points at least are relevant in recovering the script.

- The plight which requires God's decisive action in Christ is not simply individual human sin but the bondage of the whole cosmos to the powers. In the New Testament this is stated most clearly in Romans 8:18–22, with its reference to creation longing to be "set free from its bondage to decay", Galatians 1:4, which speaks of deliverance "from the present evil age", and Galatians 4:1–7, with its reference to being "enslaved to the elemental spirits [*stoicheia*] of the world". This is also expressed, in Johannine terminology, as "the whole world [*kosmos*] lies under the power of the evil one" (1 John 5:19).
- The key issue, in reading the Old Testament then, is whom do we serve – God or the Powers? Serving God and avoiding idolatry are, of course, the first two of the Ten Commandments (Exod. 20:3–6).

- Genesis 3 then becomes not an account of the "fall", but a mythic drama powerfully raising the question as to whether humanity will fulfil its calling in reliance on God (obedience) or disobey by grasping at power – seeking to become "like God" (Gen. 3:5; cf. Phil. 2:6–8; Heb. 5:7–8).

- There can thus be no straightforward appeal to "creation ordinances" based on Genesis 1 and 2. We can affirm the fundamental goodness of original creation as stated in Genesis 1. In this affirmation we resist all escapist theologies that look for salvation in some disembodied existence apart from creation. Nevertheless, "this age" now consists of creation distorted by the effects of evil. This makes natural theology exceedingly problematic, as Karl Barth consistently maintained. Although Barth may have gone too far in rejecting any notion of general revelation,[1] he was surely right to insist that natural theology – the view that humans can obtain true knowledge of God through human reason and without God's decisive intervention in Christ – is profoundly flawed. For Barth, natural theology "is a construct which obviously derives from an attempt to unite Yahweh with Baal, the triune God of Holy Scripture with the concept of being of Aristotelian and Stoic philosophy".[2] Instead of any appeal to creation ordinances, our starting point for Christian ethics and praxis is the "new creation" brought about in Christ (2 Cor. 5:17).

- However, the creation accounts do portray an original state of ecological harmony with humanity taking its place alongside the rest of creation. In this way they can illumine what it means to be a new creation. This ecological harmony is disrupted in Genesis 3 – between the serpent and other animals (3:14), the serpent and humanity (3:15), men and women (3:16), and humanity and the environment (3:17–19). The question of ecological harmony runs throughout the Bible. Not only is it a theme of the Prophets but it is a major feature of the Song of Songs and reaches its climax in Revelation 21 – 22. Significantly, Jesus is portrayed as "with the wild beasts" during his period of temptation in the wilderness (Mark 1:13) – he enacts in his person, and thus anticipates the eschatological fulfilment of, humanity in harmony with the environment.

- "In Christ" the Scriptures can be read anew beginning with Jesus as portrayed in the four canonical Gospels. The very fourfold nature of the gospel means that there is no overarching, definitive account. This invites a plurality of perspectives. On the other hand, the content of the fourfold gospel does provide us with means to evaluate claims about Jesus. It is not a case of "any Jesus will do". Furthermore, it is the Jesus of the Gospels, and not some reconstructed historical figure behind the Gospels, who is our starting point.[3]

- The Lukan Jesus highlights that all the Scriptures point to him (Luke 24:25–27). On the one hand this suggests that Jesus is the climax of the story of Israel in the Old Testament and, on the other, that this Jesus provides us with the key to interpreting the Old Testament. As stated above, Jesus interprets the Old Testament as enlightening humanity concerning love of God, love of neighbor, and practicing justice, mercy, and faithfulness. It does not imply some kind of allegorical reading of Jesus back into every Old Testament text. Furthermore, as outlined in Chapter 5 above, Jesus as prophet, pastor, and poet provides us with multiple lenses with which to read the Old Testament.

- The disruption in the harmony of creation results in God calling Israel to demonstrate to the nations what it means for the whole of life to live in relationship with him. The particularity of Israel's calling was always for the benefit of the whole world and the Prophets continually remind Israel of this.

- Israel's continuing inability to fulfil this calling results in the realization that there are cosmic Powers opposed to God's purposes and continually thwarting Israel's vocation.

- Jesus, as the climax of Israel's story, demonstrates what it means to be truly human and provides the paradigmatic example for all who follow. Nevertheless, obedience to God inevitably provokes the hostility of the Powers which results in Jesus' death. However, in the resurrection Jesus' obedience to God is vindicated and the power of the Powers is consequently broken.

- Now the church, consisting of both Jew and Gentile, is to proclaim to the whole world what it means to live in harmony. Significantly, the language of Exodus 19:5–6 is taken up again in 1 Peter 2:9. This is to be lived out until even the hostile Powers are completely reconciled to Christ. This requires costly obedience and constant attentiveness to the specificity of the biblical texts in each historical context in which the church finds herself.

• Finally, in the end, portrayed briefly in passages such as Romans 8:18–30; 1 Corinthians 15:20–28; Colossians 1:15–20; 2 Peter 3:8–13 and Revelation 21 – 22, all things are reconciled to God and God is all in all.

However, in returning at last to the question of the overall biblical metanarrative, the "little stories" highlighted in Part 2 must not be forgotten. Indeed, as I insist in the penultimate point above, it is the specificity of the biblical text that has always to be kept in mind as the church wrestles with what it means to be faithful to Jesus in the contemporary context.

Reading from the margins

The reality of post-Christendom is that the church is already moving to the margins of society. This should be embraced rather than resisted and, as I have tried to show in Part 1, the aspiration to return to a Christendom in which the church wields political and economic power is by no means desirable. There are a host of resources readily available from those who have read the Bible from the margins. This stance towards Scripture will always be mindful of the words of Jesus in Luke 22:24–27 – that the hermeneutics of power should be eschewed. This will result in Bible reading that is sensitive to the needs of the poor and marginalized in society. In particular, the prophetic denouncement of wealth in the teachings of Jesus and the poetic subversion of power in the parables of Jesus will have rich resonance.

Reading in community

Biblical interpretation has traditionally been the preserve of the trained biblical scholar and ordained ministers within

Christendom. There has, of course, always been a tradition of private, devotional reading usually uninformed by scholarship, particularly among Protestants. However, as I have argued in Chapter 13, Bible study for spiritual growth and discipleship should be at the heart of every church's pastoral program. This can never be achieved by individual reading but requires the insights, questions, and experiences of every member of the group. It is all too easy as individuals either to gloss over difficulties in the text and/or to avoid its challenging implications. Reading together enables differing perspectives gained from different experiences and contexts to emerge. In this context, gifts of biblical scholarship can be valued but remain in the service of the group as a whole.

In Christendom biblical teaching has primarily been done through the magisterium in Catholicism and through the sermon in Protestantism. How different our church services would be if worship were multivoiced and the traditional monological sermon were replaced by interactive, dialogical sermons and corporate Bible study![4] Transformative Bible study at the heart of Christian worship would invite the participation of all and the perspective of nonbelievers on the biblical text would be welcome. Genuine openness to one another, respectful listening, and the art of communicating clearly, without fear of being dismissed out of hand, are some of the virtues that would be inculcated through such a practice.

This approach to reading the Bible should also serve constantly to remind us that we are on a journey together. There can be no settled, definitive interpretation for there are always fresh contexts and fresh challenges. In addition, reading also takes place within the wider global community. Our brothers and sisters in very different situations from ours are themselves coming up with very different readings. We need those insightful gifts to challenge further our own inevitably contextualized readings.

As we read in community, seeking the help of the Spirit to be transformed by our encounter with the text, the three angles of vision provided by Jesus as prophet, poet, and pastor will constantly come into play. In this way the Bible will always be:

- *Prophetic* – energizing us with its eschatological vision of the *shalom* of God; that all-encompassing wholeness permeating the whole cosmos and healing creation of the alienating effects of the Powers.

- *Subversive* – reminding us that we are called to proclaim the gospel of the kingdom of God whose values are so alien to the domination system which holds sway over the world and from which we have been liberated in Jesus.

- *Sustaining* – providing us with nourishment for the journey and equipping us with all we need for the ongoing task of mission.

Bibliography

Adam, A. K. M. *Faithful Interpretation: Reading the Bible in a Postmodern World*. Minneapolis, MN: Fortress, 2006.

Adam, A. K. M., Stephen E. Fowl, Kevin J. Vanhoozer, and Francis Watson. *Reading Scripture with the Church: Toward a Hermeneutic for Theological Interpretation*. Grand Rapids, MI: Baker Academic, 2006.

Aune, David E. *The New Testament in Its Literary Environment*. Philadelphia, PA: Westminster, 1987.

Barth, Karl. *Church Dogmatics*. Vol. 2/1. London: T. & T. Clark, 2004.

Bartley, Jonathan. *Faith and Politics After Christendom: The Church as a Movement for Anarchy*. Milton Keynes: Paternoster, 2006.

Bauckham, Richard. *The Bible in Politics: How to Read the Bible Politically*. London: SPCK, 1989.

Bauckham, Richard. *The Climax of Prophecy*. Edinburgh: T. & T. Clark, 1993.

Bauckham, Richard. "Reading Scripture as a Coherent Story." In *The Art of Reading Scripture*, edited by Ellen F. Davis and Richard B. Hays, 38–53. Grand Rapids, MI/Cambridge, MA: Eerdmans, 2003.

Bauckham, Richard. *The Theology of the Book of Revelation*. Cambridge: Cambridge University Press, 1993.

Beker, J. Christiaan. *Paul the Apostle: The Triumph of God in Life and Thought*. Philadelphia, PA: Fortress, 1980.

Beker, J. Christiaan. *Paul's Apocalyptic Gospel: The Coming Triumph of God*. Philadelphia, PA: Fortress, 1982.

Berkouwer, G. C. *Studies in Dogmatics: The Work of Christ*. Grand Rapids, MI: Eerdmans, 1965.

Blenkinsopp, J. *The Pentateuch: An Introduction to the First Five Books of the Bible.*The Anchor Bible Reference Library 5. New York: Doubleday, 1992.

Boers, Arthur Paul, Barbara Nelson Gingerich, Eleanor Kreider, John Rempel, Mary H. Schertz, and Willard M. Swartley, eds. *Take Our Moments and Our Days: An Anabaptist Prayer Book: Ordinary Time.* Scottdale, PA: Herald, 2007.

Bondurant, J. V. *Conquest of Violence: The Gandhian Philosophy of Conflict.* Princeton, NJ: Princeton University Press, 1988.

Brueggemann, Walter. *Biblical Perspectives on Evangelism: Living in a Three-Storied Universe.* Nashville, TN: Abingdon, 1993.

Brueggemann, Walter. *Finally Comes the Poet: Daring Speech for Proclamation.* Minneapolis, MI: Fortress, 1989.

Brueggemann, Walter. "A Fourth-Generation Sellout." In *Inscribing the Text: Sermons and Prayers of Walter Brueggemann,* edited by Anna Carter Florence, 59–62. Minneapolis, MI: Fortress, 2004.

Brueggemann, Walter. *Genesis.* Interpretation: A Bible Commentary for Teaching and Preaching. Atlanta, GA: John Knox, 1982.

Brueggemann, Walter. *An Introduction to the Old Testament: The Canon and Christian Imagination.* Louisville, KY: Westminster John Knox, 2003.

Brueggemann, Walter. *The Message of the Psalms: A Theological Commentary.* Augsburg Old Testament Studies. Minneapolis, MI: Augsburg, 1984.

Brueggemann, Walter. *The Prophetic Imagination.* Minneapolis, MI: Fortress, 1978.

Brueggemann, Walter. "The Recovering God of Hosea." *Horizons in Biblical Theology* 30, no. 1 (2008): 5–20.

Brueggemann, Walter. *Redescribing Reality: What We Do when We Read the Bible.* London: SCM, 2009.

Brueggemann, Walter. *Texts Under Negotiation: The Bible and Postmodern Imagination.* Minneapolis, MI: Fortress, 1993.

Brueggemann, Walter. *Theology of the Old Testament: Testimony, Dispute, Advocacy.* Minneapolis, MI: Fortress, 1997.

Burridge, Richard A. *Four Gospels, One Jesus?* London: SPCK, 1994.

Burridge, Richard A. *What Are the Gospels?: A Comparison with Graeco-Roman Biography.* The Biblical Resource Series. Grand Rapids, MI/Cambridge, MA: Eerdmans/Dove, 2004.

Caputo, John D. *The Weakness of God: A Theology of the Event.* Indiana Series in the Philosophy of Religion. Bloomington, IN: Indiana University Press, 2006.

Cardenal, Ernesto, ed. *The Gospel in Solentiname.* 4 vols. Maryknoll, NY: Orbis, 1982.

Carter, Craig A. *Rethinking Christ and Culture: A Post-Christendom Perspective.* Grand Rapids, MI: Brazos, 2006.

Carter, W. *Review of Christ and Caesar: The Gospel and the Roman Empire in the Writings of Paul and Luke.* Last Updated Date 2009 [cited 5 August 2009]. Available from http://www.bookreviews.org.

Chadwick, H. *The Early Church.* Edited by O. Chadwick. 6 vols., The Pelican History of the Church 1. Harmondsworth: Penguin, 1967.

Cheney, M. "Joshua." In *The Books of the Bible,* edited by B. W. Anderson (ed.), 103–12. New York: Scribner's, 1989.

Clines, D. J. A. *The Theme of the Pentateuch.* Sheffield: JSOT Press, 1978.

Clines, David J. A. *Job 21–37.* Vol. 18A, Word Biblical Commentary. Nashville, TN: Thomas Nelson, 2006.

Collins, Yarbro. "Introduction." *Semeia* 36 (1986).

Cornwall, Judson and Stelman Smith. *The Exhaustive Dictionary of Bible Names.* North Brunswick, NJ: Bridge-Logos, 1998.

Creach, Jerome. *Joshua.* Interpretation: A Bible Commentary for Teaching and Preaching. Louisville, KY: Westminster John Knox, 2003.

Crossan, J. D. *The Historical Jesus: The Life of a Mediterranean Jewish Peasant.* Edinburgh: T. & T. Clark, 1993.

Crossan, J. D. "Roman Imperial Theology." In *In the Shadow of Empire: Reclaiming the Bible as a History of Faithful Resistance,* edited by R. A. Horsley, 59–73. Louisville, KY: Westminster John Knox, 2008.

Crossan, J. D. and J. L. Reed. *In Search of Paul: How Jesus' Apostle Opposed Rome's Empire with God's Kingdom.* London: SPCK, 2005.

Davis, Ellen F. and Richard B. Hays, eds. *The Art of Reading Scripture.* Grand Rapids, MI/Cambridge, MA: Eerdmans, 2003.

de la Torre, Miguel A. *Reading the Bible from the Margins.* Maryknoll, NY: Orbis, 2002.

Douglas, M. T. *Purity and Danger: An Analysis of the Concepts of Pollution and Taboo*. London: Routledge & Kegan Paul, 1966.

Dowd, Sharyn. *Reading Mark: A Literary and Theological Commentary on the Second Gospel*. Macon, GA: Smyth & Helwys, 2000.

Dungan, David L. *Constantine's Bible: Politics and the Making of the New Testament*. Minneapolis: Fortress, 2007.

Dunn, J. D. G. *Jesus and the Spirit*. London: SCM, 1975.

Dunn, J. D. G. *Unity and Diversity in the New Testament*. London: SCM, 1977.

Ekblad Jr, Bob. *Reading the Bible with the Damned*. Louisville, KY: Westminster John Knox, 2005.

Ellis, E. Earle. "How the New Testament Uses the Old." In *New Testament Interpretation: Essays on Principles and Methods*, edited by I. Howard Marshall, 199-219. Exeter: Paternoster, 1985.

Evans, Craig A. and James A. Sanders, eds. *Early Christian Interpretation of the Scriptures of Israel*. JSNTSup 148. Sheffield: Sheffield Academic Press, 1997.

Fee, Gordon D. and Douglas Stuart. *How to Read the Bible for All Its Worth*. London: Scripture Union, 1983.

Fitzmyer, Joseph A. *The Gospel According to Luke I–IX*. The Anchor Yale Bible. New Haven, CT: Yale University Press, 1970.

Fowl, Stephen E. *Engaging Scripture: A Model for Theological Interpretation*. Oxford: Blackwell, 1998.

France, R. *The Gospel of Mark: A Commentary on the Greek Text*. The New International Greek Testament Commentary. Grand Rapids, MI/Carlisle: Eerdmans/Paternoster, 2002.

Fretheim, Terence E. *Exodus*. Interpretation: A Bible Commentary for Teaching and Preaching. Louisville, KY: John Knox, 1991.

Goodacre, Mark. *The Synoptic Problem: A Way Through the Maze*. Vol. 80, The Biblical Seminar. London/New York: Sheffield Academic Press, 2001.

Gorman, Michael J. *Inhabiting the Cruciform God: Kenosis, Justification, and Theosis in Paul's Narrative Soteriology*. Grand Rapids/Cambridge: Eerdmans, 2009.

Goudzwaard, Bob. *Idols of Our Time*. Downers Grove, IL: IVP, 1984.

Gould, E. P. *A Critical and Exegetical Commentary on the Gospel According to St. Mark*. International Critical Commentary. Edinburgh: T. & T. Clark, 1983.

Green, Joel B. *The Gospel of Luke.* The New International Commentary on the New Testament. Grand Rapids, MI: Eerdmans, 1997.

Greer, Rowan A. "The Christian Bible and Its Interpretation." In *Early Biblical Interpretation,* edited by James L. Kugel and Rowan A. Greer, 107–208. Philadelphia, PA: Westminster, 1986.

Guelich, Robert A. *Mark 1–8:26.* Word Biblical Commentary 34A. Dallas, TX: Word, 1989.

Guttiérez, G. *On Job: God-Talk and the Suffering of the Innocent.* Maryknoll, NY: Orbis, 1987.

Hall, Christopher A. *Reading Scripture with the Church Fathers.* Downers Grove, IL: IVP, 1998.

Harink, Douglas. *Paul among the Postliberals: Pauline Theology beyond Christendom and Modernity.* Grand Rapids, MI: Brazos, 2003.

Hays, Richard B. *Echoes of Scripture in the Letters of Paul.* New Haven, CT/London: Yale University Press, 1989.

Herzog II, William R. *Parables as Subversive Speech: Jesus as Pedagogue of the Oppressed.* Louisville, KY: Westminster John Knox, 1994.

Hooker, M. D. *The Gospel According to St. Mark.* Black's New Testament Commentary. London: Continuum, 2001.

Horsley, R. A., ed. *In the Shadow of Empire: Reclaiming the Bible as a History of Faithful Resistance.* Louisville, KY: Westminster John Knox, 2008.

Horsley, R. A., ed. *Paul and Empire: Religion and Power in Roman Imperial Society.* Harrisburg, PA: Trinity, 1997.

Janzen, J. Gerald. *Job.* Interpretation: A Bible Commentary for Teaching and Preaching. Atlanta, GA: John Knox, 1985.

Johnson, Luke Timothy. *The Writings of the New Testament: An Interpretation.* Revised ed. London: SCM, 1999.

Joint Declaration on the Doctrine of Justification of the Lutheran World Federation and the Roman Catholic Church. Grand Rapids, MI: Eerdmans, 2000.

Kannengiesser, Charles. *Handbook of Patristic Exegesis: The Bible in Ancient Christianity.* Leiden: Brill, 2006.

Keil, Carl Friedrich and Franz Delitzsch. *Commentary on the Old Testament.* Peabody, MA: Hendrickson, 2002.

Kim, S. *Christ and Caesar: The Gospel and the Roman Empire in the Writings of Paul and Luke.* Grand Rapids, MI: Eerdmans, 2008.

Kreider, Alan and Eleanor Kreider. *Worship and Mission After Christendom*. Milton Keynes: Paternoster, 2009.

Kreider, Alan, Eleanor Kreider, and Paulus Widjaja. *A Culture of Peace: God's Vision for the Church*. Intercourse, PA: Good Books, 2005.

Ladd, George Eldon. *The Presence of the Future: The Eschatology of Biblical Realism*. Grand Rapids, MI: Eerdmans, 1974.

Lane, William L. *Hebrews 9–13*. Word Biblical Commentary 47B. Dallas, TX: Word, 1991.

Lincoln, Andrew T. *Truth on Trial: The Lawsuit Motif in the Fourth Gospel*. Peabody, MA: Hendrickson, 2000.

Lind, Millard C. *Yahweh Is a Warrior: The Theology of Warfare in Ancient Israel*. A Christian Peace Shelf Selection. Scottdale, PA: Herald, 1980.

Lind, Millard C. *Ezekiel*. Believers Church Bible Commentary. Scottdale, PA: Herald, 1996.

Litwa, M. David. "2 Corinthians 3:18 and Its Implications for Theosis." *Journal of Theological Interpretation* 2 (2008): 117–33.

Lombaard, Christo. "Genealogies and Spiritualities in Genesis 4:17–22, 4:25–26, 5:1–32." In *The Spirit that Moves: Orientation and Issues in Spirituality*, edited by Pieter G. R. de Villiers, Celia E. T. Kourie, and Christo Lombaard, in Vol. 8 of *Acta Theologica Supplementum*, 145–64. Bloemfontein: University of the Free State, 2006.

Longenecker, Richard N. *Biblical Exegesis in the Apostolic Period*. 2nd ed. Grand Rapids, MI: Eerdmans, 1999.

MacMullen, R. *Voting About God*. New Haven, CT: Yale University Press, 2006.

Marcus, Joel. *Mark 1–8*. The Anchor Yale Bible. New Haven, CT: Yale University Press, 2002.

Marcus, Joel. *The Way of the Lord: Christological Exegesis of the Old Testament in the Gospel of Mark*. Louisville, KY: Westminster John Knox, 1992.

Marshall, I. H., Stephen Travis, and Ian Paul. *The Letters and Revelation*. Vol. 2, Exploring the New Testament. London: SPCK, 2002.

Martyn, J. Louis. *Galatians: A New Translation with Introduction and Commentary*. The Anchor Bible 33A. New York: Doubleday, 1997.

Miles, J. *God: A Biography*. London/New York: Simon & Schuster, 1995.

Murray, Stuart. *Biblical Interpretation in the Anabaptist Tradition*. Kitchener, PA/Scottdale, PA: Pandora/Herald, 2000.

Murray, Stuart. *Post-Christendom: Church and Mission In a Strange New World*. Carlisle: Paternoster, 2004.

Myers, Ched. *Binding the Strong Man: A Political Reading of Mark's Story of Jesus*. Maryknoll, NY: Orbis, 1988.

Nelson, Richard D. *First and Second Kings*. Interpretation: A Bible Commentary for Teaching and Preaching. Atlanta, GA: John Knox Press, 1987.

Noth, M. *The Deuterononomistic History*. Sheffield: JSOT Press, 1991.

Oakman, Douglas E. *Jesus and the Peasants*. Eugene, OR: Cascade, 2008.

O'Collins, Gerald G. "Crucifixion." In vol. 1 of *The Anchor Bible Dictionary*, edited by David Noel Freedman, 6 vols., 1207–1210. New York: Doubleday, 1992.

O'Connor, K. M. *Lamentations and the Tears of the World*. Maryknoll, NY: Orbis, 2002.

Pietersen, Lloyd K. "Commentary: Ecclesiastes 1.2–11." *Third Way* 21.10 (1998): 22.

Pietersen, Lloyd K. *The Polemic of the Pastorals: A Sociological Examination of the Development of Pauline Christianity*. JSNTSup 264; London: T. & T. Clark International, 2004.

Rad, G. von. *The Problem of the Hexateuch and Other Essays*. New York: McGraw-Hill, 1966.

Roth, Wolfgang. "To Invert or Not to Invert: The Pharisaic Canon in the Gospels." In *Early Christian Interpretation of the Scriptures of Israel: Investigations and Proposals*, edited by Craig A. Evans and James A. Sanders, in Vol. 148 of *JSNTSup*, 59–78. Sheffield: Sheffield Academic Press, 1997.

Rowland, Christopher. "The Book of Revelation: Introduction, Commentary and Reflections." In *The New Interpreter's Bible*, 501–736. Nashville, TN: Abingdon, 2000.

Rowland, Christopher and Jonathan Roberts. *The Bible for Sinners*. London: SPCK, 2008.

Said, Edward. *Orientalism*. London/New York: Routledge/Pantheon, 1978.

Sarna, Nahum M. *Exodus*. The JPS Torah Commentary. Philadelphia, PA: Jewish Publication Society, 1991.

Satterthwaite, Philip and Gordon McConville. *Exploring the Old Testament: The Histories*. London: SPCK, 2007.

Schaff, Philip. *The Greek and Latin Creeds with Translations*. New York: Harper & Row, 1931.

Schaff, Philip, *The History of Creeds*. New York: Harper & Row, 1931.

Schneiders, Sandra M. "The Study of Christian Spirituality: Contours and Dynamics of a Discipline." In *Minding the Spirit: The Study of Christian Spirituality*, edited by Elizabeth A. Dreyer and Mark S. Burrows, 5–24. Baltimore, MD/London: The Johns Hopkins University Press, 2005.

Schubert, Paul. *The Form and Function of the Pauline Thanksgivings*. Berlin: Alfred Töpelmann, 1939.

Scott, J. C. *Weapons of the Weak: Everyday Forms of Peasant Resistance*. New Haven, CT: Yale University Press, 1985.

Simonetti, Manlio. *Biblical Interpretation in the Early Church: An Historical Introduction to Patristic Exegesis*. Translated by John A. Hughes. Edinburgh: T. & T. Clark, 1994.

Singleton, Alex. *Anglican Bishops are Promoting Ignorance*. Last Updated Date 2008 [cited 5 August 2008]. Available from http://blogs.telegraph.co.uk/alex_singleton/blog/2008/07/28/anglican_bishops_are_promoting_ignorance.

Stark, R. *The Rise of Christianity: A Sociologist Reconsiders History*. Princeton, NJ: Princeton University Press, 1996.

Stowers, Stanley K. *Letter Writing in Greco-Roman Antiquity*. Philadelphia, PA: Westminster, 1986.

Sugirtharajah, R. S. *Postcolonial Criticism and Biblical Interpretation*. Oxford: Oxford University Press, 2000.

Swartley, Willard M. *Essays on Biblical Interpretation: Anabaptist-Mennonite Perspectives*. Elkhart, IN: Institute of Mennonite Studies, 1984.

Talbert, Charles H. *Reading Acts: A Literary and Theological Commentary on the Acts of the Apostles*. Reading the New Testament. Macon, GA: Smyth & Helwys, 2005.

Tannehill, Robert C. *Luke*. Abingdon New Testament Commentaries. Nashville, TN: Abingdon, 1996.

Thigpen, Paul. "The Second Coming: How Many Views?," *Charisma & Christian Life*, (February 1989): 42.

Thompson, John Lee. *Reading the Bible with the Dead: What You Can Learn from the History of Exegesis that You Can't Learn from Exegesis Alone.* Grand Rapids, MI/Cambridge: Eerdmans, 2007.

Trible, Phyllis. *Texts of Terror.* London: SCM, 2002.

Walsh, Brian J. *Slipstream Podcast 7 – Brian Walsh and Sylvia Keesmaat.* Last Updated Date 2008 [cited 14 August 2009]. Available from http://www.eauk.org/slipstream/podcast/slipstream-podcast-7-brian-walsh-and-sylvia-keesmaat.cfm.

Walsh, Brian J. and Sylvia C. Keesmaat. *Colossians Remixed: Subverting the Empire.* Milton Keynes: Paternoster, 2005.

Walter, J. A. *A Long Way from Home: A Sociological Exploration of Contemporary Idolatry.* Carlisle: Paternoster, 1980.

Watson, Francis. *Paul and the Hermeneutics of Faith.* London: T. & T. Clark, 2004.

Wenham, Gordon. *Genesis 1–15.* Word Biblical Commentary; vol. 1. Dallas, TX: Word, 1987.

Wenham, Gordon. *The Pentateuch.* Exploring the Old Testament; vol. 1. London: SPCK, 2003.

Whitman, Walt. "Passage to India, 5:101–5." In *Leaves of Grass.* New York: Mentor Books, 1954.

Wiersbe, Warren W. *Be Available.* An Old Testament Study. Wheaton, IL: Victor Books, 1994.

Wink, Walter. *Engaging the Powers: Discernment and Resistance in a World of Domination.* Minneapolis: Fortress Press, 1992.

Wink, Walter. *Transforming Bible Study.* 2nd ed. Nashville, TN: Abingdon, 1989.

Wink, Walter. *Unmasking the Powers: The Invisible Forces that Determine Human Existence.* Philadelphia, PA: Fortress Press, 1986.

Witherington III, Ben. *The Acts of the Apostles: A Socio-Rhetorical Commentary.* Grand Rapids, MI/Carlisle: Eerdmans/Paternoster, 1998.

Witherington III, Ben. *The Gospel of Mark: A Socio-Rhetorical Commentary.* Grand Rapids, MI: Eerdmans, 2001.

Witherington III, Ben and Darlene Hyatt. *Paul's Letter to the Romans: A Socio-Rhetorical Commentary.* Grand Rapids, MI: Eerdmans, 2004.

Woodman, Simon. *The Book of Revelation.* London: SCM, 2008.

Wright, N. T. *Bringing the Church to the World*. Minneapolis, MI: Bethany House Publishers, 1992.

Wright, N. T. *Jesus and the Victory of God*. Vol. 2, Christian Origins and the Question of God. London: SPCK, 1996.

Wright, N. T. *Paul: In Fresh Perspective*. Minneapolis: Fortress, 2009.

Yarbro Collins, Adela. "Introduction." *Semeia* 36 (1986): 1–11.

Yoder, John Howard. *The Politics of Jesus: Vicit Agnus Noster*. Grand Rapids, MI: Eerdmans, 1972.

Young, Jeremy. *The Violence of God and the War on Terror*. London: Darton, Longman & Todd, 2007.

Endnotes

1 – Introduction

[1] http://www.facebook.com/pages/Todd-Bentley/50871761807 accessed on January 5, 2009 (this page is no longer available).

[2] All biblical quotations are taken from the New Revised Standard Version.

[3] See, for example, Hall, *Reading Scripture with the Church Fathers*; De La Torre, *Reading the Bible from the Margins*; Ekblad Jr, *Reading the Bible with the Damned*; Adam, *Faithful Interpretation: Reading the Bible in a Postmodern World*; Adam, et al., *Reading Scripture with the Church: Toward a Hermeneutic for Theological Interpretation*; Thompson, *Reading the Bible with the Dead: What You Can Learn from the History of Exegesis That You Can't Learn from Exegesis Alone*; Rowland and Roberts, *The Bible for Sinners*.

[4] This stark statement is, of course, too blunt and in reality needs considerable nuancing which is beyond the scope of a book of this size. Suffice it to say that a "post-Christendom" stance should recognize the way centuries of tradition have beneficially shaped the reading of Scripture while at the same time remaining critical of that inherited tradition.

[5] Carter, *Rethinking Christ and Culture: A Post-Christendom Perspective*, 14.

[6] Murray, *Post-Christendom: Church and Mission In a Strange New World*, 83–84.

[7] Stuart Murray adds that Jesus was also marginalized in Christendom readings of the Bible. See Murray, *Post-Christendom*, 118–24.

[8] See the discussion in Murray, *Post-Christendom*, 132–44.

[9] Murray, *Post-Christendom*, 20.

[10] Murray, *Post-Christendom*, 293–300.

2 – Reading the Bible Before Christendom

[1] Carter, *Rethinking Christ and Culture: A Post-Christendom Perspective*, 101.

[2] There is not scope in this work to consider in detail the complex question of how the New Testament uses the Jewish Scriptures but see, for example, Hays, *Echoes of Scripture in the Letters of Paul* and Evans and Sanders, eds., *Early Christian Interpretation of the Scriptures of Israel*.

[3] Bauckham, "Reading Scripture as a Coherent Story", 41.

[4] Roth, "To Invert or Not to Invert", 59–78.

[5] Watson, *Paul and the Hermeneutics of Faith*, 16.

[6] Longenecker, *Biblical Exegesis in the Apostolic Period*, 14–35.

[7] E.g. Rom. 3:10–18 which brings together Pss. 14:1–3; 5:9; 140:3; 10:7; Isa. 59:7–8 and Ps. 36:1.

[8] Ellis, "How the New Testament Uses the Old," in *New Testament Interpretation: Essays on Principles and Methods* (ed. Marshall; Exeter: Paternoster, 1985), 210.

[9] Once again it is beyond the scope of this work to examine the use of Scripture by the early church fathers in detail; what follows is a very succinct summary of a select number of authors. For further reference see Kannengiesser, *Handbook of Patristic Exegesis: The Bible in Ancient Christianity* and Simonetti, *Biblical Interpretation in the Early Church: An Historical Introduction to Patristic Exegesis*.

[10] Ign. *Phld.* 8.2.

[11] Ign. *Smyrn.* 7.2.

[12] Greer, "The Christian Bible and Its Interpretation", 114.

[13] Combining Gen. 14:14 and Gen. 17:23.

[14] In Greek the letters of the alphabet have numerical value; here I=10, H=8 and T=300. The Greek for Jesus, ΙΗΣΟΥΣ, was often abbreviated to ΙΗ.

[15] Kannengiesser, *Patristic Exegesis*, 485.

[16] Irenaeus, *Against Heresies* 5.20.2.

[17] Irenaeus, *Against Heresies* 2.27.2.

[18] Irenaeus, *Against Heresies* 3.1–5.

[19] Tertullian, *The Prescriptions Against the Heretics* 7.

[20] Irenaeus, *Against Heresies* 3.3.1.

[21] Irenaeus, *Against Heresies* 1.10.1.

[22] Irenaeus, *Against Heresies* 3.4.2.

[23] Tertullian, *The Prescription Against Heretics* 13.

[24] Tertullian, *On the Veiling of Virgins* 1.
[25] Irenaeus, *Against Heresies* 4.26.1.
[26] Hilary (bishop of Poitiers around 350), *Traité des Mystères*, I Pref., cited in Hall, *Reading Scripture*, 192.

3 – Christendom and the Bible

[1] Cited in Hall, *Reading Scripture*, 68.
[2] Chadwick, *The Early Church*, 160–1.
[3] According to Chadwick, *The Early Church*, 163, "Origen had commented with asperity that in great cities bishops were being cultivated socially by 'ladies of wealth and refinement.'"
[4] Chadwick, *The Early Church*, 163–4.
[5] Carter, *Rethinking Christ*, 79.
[6] Chadwick, *Early Church*, 124.
[7] For further details see Dungan, *Constantine's Bible: Politics and the Making of the New Testament*, 108–13.
[8] Schaff, *The Greek and Latin Creeds with Translations*, 29–30.
[9] Schaff, *The History of Creeds*, 29.
[10] Eusebius, *Life of Constantine* 1.44 (my emphasis).
[11] Eusebius, *Life of Constantine* 3.66 (my emphasis).
[12] Eusebius, *Ecclesiastical History* 3.3.3 (my emphasis).
[13] For further details see Dungan, *Constantine's Bible*, 69–93.
[14] Dionysius, bishop of Alexandria and a contemporary of Eusebius, argued strongly that Revelation was not written by the apostle John but by another John. Eusebius quotes his argument at length in *Ecclesiastical History* 7.24–25.
[15] Dungan, *Constantine's Bible*, 92–93 (his emphasis).
[16] Cyril of Jerusalem (ca. 350); the Synod of Laodicea (ca. 363); Gregory of Nazianzus (ca. 389).
[17] Dungan, *Constantine's Bible*, 122. Dungan overstates the position as it is clear that other canonical versions persisted for some time. Nevertheless, imperial sanction would have been the decisive step on the way to canonical closure in the way Dungan suggests.
[18] Simonetti, *Biblical Interpretation*, 53.
[19] This remains the prevailing interpretation in most contemporary commentaries.
[20] Singleton, *Anglican Bishops are Promoting Ignorance*.

[21] Tannehill, *Luke*, 277.

[22] Something like this alternative reading of the parable can be found in Herzog II, *Parables as Subversive Speech: Jesus as Pedagogue of the Oppressed*, 150–68 and Cardenal, ed., *The Gospel in Solentiname*, 4:38–48.

[23] See Chadwick, *Early Church*, 165–6.

[24] Dungan, *Constantine's Bible*, 120.

[25] Fowl, *Engaging Scripture: A Model for Theological Interpretation*, 5–6 gives three reasons as to why the canon cannot be reopened. First, sociologically there is very little chance of getting significant numbers of Christians to agree on any particular reformulation of the canon. Second, reconstructions as to how the list of authoritative books was fixed remain speculative and the scholarly consensus is consequently a shifting one. Third, theological convictions about God's providence in connection with the canon must come into play. Furthermore, Christians in the Persian Empire, beyond the scope of Christendom, reached very similar conclusions as to the contents of the canon (some rejecting the "dubious" books but none including books excluded in the West).

[26] See, for example, MacMullen, *Voting About God*. MacMullen highlights the painful ways in which agreement was reached at Nicea and elsewhere.

4 – The Bible and the Subversion of Christendom: The Anabaptists

[1] Murray, *Post-Christendom*, 318–39.

[2] I am indebted to Stuart Murray whose notes duly edited by me, from a Master's course on Anabaptist origins at Spurgeon's College and from a session on Anabaptist hermeneutics on the Advanced Workshop course, form almost the entirety of this chapter. As this chapter consists of course notes it contains many names with which readers will undoubtedly be unfamiliar. Rather than provide a detailed account of the various characters, suffice it to say that the names appearing represent well-known figures from the four main branches of sixteenth-century Anabaptism: the Swiss Brethren, South German/Austrian, North German/Dutch, and the communitarian Hutterites. For those interested in a more advanced discussion of

Anabaptist hermeneutics see Swartley, *Essays on Biblical Interpretation: Anabaptist-Mennonite Perspectives* and Murray, *Biblical Interpretation in the Anabaptist Tradition.*

[3] Münster is regularly cited by those critical of the Anabaptists. On February 23, 1534 the elections for city councillors in Münster fell to the Anabaptists. The next day Jan Matthijs, a baker influenced by the apocalyptic teachings of the Anabaptist Melchior Hoffman, entered the city claiming prophetic authority as the End Time Enoch and declaring that the city was to be the New Jerusalem. A coercive regime was established with city members forced either to adopt Anabaptism or to leave the city. Matthijs and his successor, Jan van Leiden, instituted city regulations along Old Testament lines, including polygamy. Those who resisted were put to death. Münster eventually fell to a military siege on June, 25 1535. This sixteen-month version of coercive Anabaptism came to be viewed as an aberration by the Anabaptists. Unfortunately, Münster has tended to be regarded as true Anabaptism within Christendom circles.

5 – Jesus as the Center of Biblical Interpretation

[1] Both of these can be found in the New Testament itself. For example, Matthew's repetitive insistence that Jesus is the fulfilment of *specific* Old Testament texts and Paul's use of allegory in 1 Cor. 10:4 and Gal. 4:21–31.

[2] Davis and Hays, eds., *The Art of Reading Scripture*, 2.

[3] I am not entering into the complex debate, which has a long and contested history, concerning the historical Jesus. Throughout this book I am using "Jesus" as shorthand for the character depicted in the four canonical Gospels. Each Gospel presents a different characterization or portrait of Jesus. So biblical scholars are right to speak of "the Matthean Jesus", "the Markan Jesus", "the Lukan Jesus" and "the Johannine Jesus". Jesus is thus a complex character common to four narratives. This Jesus is the only one we have access to and that access is through the point of view of each of the Gospel narrators. For more on this, see Chapter 11 below.

[4] See, for example, Berkouwer, *Studies in Dogmatics: The Work of Christ*, 58–87.

[5] See Wright, *Jesus and the Victory of God*, 166–8.

6 See Wright, *Victory*, 168–243.

7 See especially Wright, *Victory*, 244–319.

8 See Brueggemann, *The Prophetic Imagination*.

9 Josephus, *Jewish War* 2.8.2–14; *Antiquities* 18.1.2–6.

10 See the discussion in Wright, *Victory*, 406–12.

11 For a sustained argument that Jesus was continually tempted by the option of revolutionary violence against Rome, but steadfastly rejected it, see Yoder, *The Politics of Jesus: Vicit Agnus Noster*.

12 See especially Wink, *Engaging the Powers: Discernment and Resistance in a World of Domination*.

13 E.g. Matt. 6:12–15; 18:21–35.

14 E.g. Matt. 6:25–34; 11:28–30.

15 E.g. Matt. 9:10–13; 21:31–32.

16 E.g. Luke 8:1–3; John 4:1–42.

17 E.g. Matt 6:19–24; Mark 10:42–45.

18 Matt. 18:15–22.

19 See Wright, *Victory*, 268–74.

20 Brueggemann, *Imagination*.

21 Brueggemann, *Imagination*, 66–69.

22 E.g. Israel: Num. 23:21; Ps. 149:2; Isa. 43:15; the whole earth: Pss. 47; 95:3; 96:10; 97:1.

23 E.g. Isa. 24:23; Zeph. 3:15; Obad. 21; Zech. 14:9.

24 See Wright, *Victory*, 166.

25 See Chapter 8, "Texts of terror".

26 Myers, *Binding the Strong Man: A Political Reading of Mark's Story of Jesus*, 209.

27 This is at the heart of Paul's criticism of the Corinthians in 1 Cor. 11:17–22.

28 Whitman, "Passage to India, 5:101–5", 324.

29 Brueggemann, *Finally Comes the Poet: Daring Speech for Proclamation*, 6.

30 See especially Oakman, *Jesus and the Peasants*.

31 *War* 2.228–9.

32 See, for example, Cardenal, *Gospel in Solentiname*, De La Torre, *Bible from the Margins*, and Ekblad Jr, *Bible with the Damned*.

33 See, for example, France, *The Gospel of Mark: A Commentary on the Greek Text*; Gould, *A Critical and Exegetical Commentary on the Gospel According to St. Mark*; Guelich, *Mark 1–8:26*; Hooker, *The Gospel According to St. Mark*; Marcus, *Mark 1–8*.

[34] Crossan, *The Historical Jesus: The Life of a Mediterranean Jewish Peasant*, 278–9. See also Oakman, *Jesus and the Peasants*, 111–17. Crossan's interpretation is also followed in Witherington III, *The Gospel of Mark: A Socio-Rhetorical Commentary*.

[35] For further details see Fitzmyer, *The Gospel According to Luke I–IX*, 469–70.

[36] Green, *The Gospel of Luke*, 570.

[37] So Oakman, *Jesus and the Peasants*, 288–9.

[38] Herzog II, *Parables*, 242.

[39] Herzog II, *Parables*, 257.

[40] See especially Yoder, *The Politics of Jesus*, 64–77.

[41] See Scott, *Weapons of the Weak: Everyday Forms of Peasant Resistance*.

[42] For the view that Jesus actively encouraged nonviolent strategies of tax resistance in collusion with the toll collectors he spent time with, see Oakman, *Jesus and the Peasants*, 280–97.

6 – Reading the Whole Bible

[1] Once again, in a work of this nature, it is impossible to be comprehensive. I hope to provide suggestive ways of reading a selection of texts which readers, hopefully, can explore further. In addition, I am fully conscious that the Old Testament does not point unambiguously to Jesus, as the whole history of Jewish interpretation reminds us. Nevertheless, a properly *Christian* reading of Scripture must inevitably be christocentric.

[2] Originally delivered as the Laing Lecture 1989 and the Griffith Thomas Lecture 1989 and available online at http://www.ntwrightpage.com/Wright_Bible_Authoritative.htm.

[3] I work with this notion of five acts for the time being as this is how Wright frames the model but the five acts he chooses are problematic and I suggest why below.

[4] Harink, *Paul among the Postliberals: Pauline Theology beyond Christendom and Modernity*, 28 (his emphasis).

[5] See the *Joint Declaration on the Doctrine of Justification of the Lutheran World Federation and the Roman Catholic Church*, 12, which states that the justification of sinful human beings by God's grace through faith is the main way in which Paul describes the gift of salvation.

[6] Brueggemann, *Genesis*, 41.

[7] See, for example, the discussion in Harink, *Paul Among the Postliberals*, 65.

[8] See especially Brueggemann, *Theology of the Old Testament: Testimony, Dispute, Advocacy*.

[9] For an excellent example of how this can be approached see Bauckham, "Reading Scripture as a Coherent Story," 38–53.

[10] See Brueggemann, *Texts Under Negotiation: The Bible and Postmodern Imagination* (Minneapolis: Fortress, 1993), 58.

[11] Brueggemann, *Texts Under Negotiation*, 70.

[12] See Caputo, *The Weakness of God: A Theology of the Event* (Indiana Series in the Philosophy of Religion; Bloomington: Indiana University Press, 2006).

[13] Brueggemann, *Redescribing Reality: What We Do when We Read the Bible*, 116.

[14] Brueggemann, *Redescribing Reality*, 115, his emphasis.

[15] Brueggemann, *Redescribing Reality*, 116.

[16] See Brueggemann, *Texts Under Negotiation*, 64–69.

7 – Reading the Pentateuch

[1] See Wink, *Engaging the Powers*, 13–17.

[2] Wenham, *Genesis 1–15*, 2.

[3] See, for example, Job 38:8–11 (where "the sea" represents "chaotic energy threatening destruction" [Janzen, *Job*, 234]) and Jer. 4:23–28.

[4] Brueggemann, *An Introduction to the Old Testament: The Canon and Christian Imagination*, 34.

[5] See Clines, *The Theme of the Pentateuch*.

[6] G. Wenham, *The Pentateuch*, 153.

[7] Gen. 5:1 is slightly different: "this is the book of the generations of . . ." In the NRSV this is rendered "[t]his is the list of the descendants of . . ." The NRSV, apart from 2:4, translates "generations" as "descendants" and, in 37:2, renders the Hebrew phrase as "[t]his is the story of the family of . . ."

[8] Except for those who take great delight in finding spiritual significance in the meaning of every name recorded. See, for example, Cornwall and Smith, *The Exhaustive Dictionary of Bible Names*. I do not subscribe to this approach.

[9] See Lombaard, "Genealogies and Spiritualities in Genesis 4:17–22, 4:25–26, 5:1–32," 148.

[10] If, as Lombaard suggests, Gen. 4:22 refers to the origins of prostitution, then this genealogy also poses the question of Yahwistic religion's relationship to sexuality. See Lombaard, "Genealogies," 150–1.

[11] Wenham, *The Pentateuch*, 36. For further parallels see Wenham, *Genesis 1–15*, 256–8.

[12] See Brueggemann, "A Fourth-Generation Sellout," in *Inscribing the Text: Sermons and Prayers of Walter Brueggemann*, 59–62.

[13] Brueggemann, "A Fourth-Generation Sellout," 61–62.

[14] For further insightful analyses of contemporary idolatry see Goudzwaard, *Idols of Our Time* and Wright, *Bringing the Church to the World*, 149–88. Goudzwaard speaks of revolution, nation, material prosperity, and guaranteed security as the key forms of contemporary idolatry. Wright names Mars, Mammon, Aphrodite (Venus), Gaia, Bacchus (Dionysus), and idols of mysticism and of the mind.

[15] Sarna, *Exodus*, 112.

[16] See Fretheim, *Exodus*, 263–4.

[17] Fretheim, *Exodus*, 271.

[18] See Douglas, *Purity and Danger: An Analysis of the Concepts of Pollution and Taboo*.

[19] See Bauckham, *The Bible in Politics: How to Read the Bible Politically*, 12.

[20] Reprinted as Noth, *The Deuterononomistic History*.

8 – Reading the "Historical" Narratives (Joshua – Esther)

[1] Satterthwaite and McConville, *Exploring the Old Testament: The Histories*, 209.

[2] Cheney, "Joshua." *In The Books of the Bible*, edited by B. W. Anderson, 103–12, cited in Brueggemann, *Introduction*, 156.

[3] See Satterthwaite and McConville, *Histories*, 51.

[4] Lind, *Yahweh Is a Warrior: The Theology of Warfare in Ancient Israel*. Lind argues that there is a tension in the biblical account between this Yahweh as warrior motif, based on the exodus and regularly called upon by the prophetic tradition, and the subsequent monarchy which increasingly relied upon the technology of war for victory in battle rather than on Yahweh. However, even if Lind's thesis is granted, this still leaves the problem of the violence of Yahweh himself.

[5] See especially Young, *The Violence of God and the War on Terror*.

⁶ See, in particular, Brueggemann, "The Recovering God of Hosea," 5–20 and Brueggemann, *Redescribing Reality*, 104–17. I am suggesting that, for Godself, something along the lines advocated by Gandhi is necessary. Gandhi insisted that one could not practice nonviolence consistently until one had come to terms with one's own capacity for violence. He famously wrote "that where there is only a choice between cowardice and violence, I would advise violence". See Bondurant, *Conquest of Violence: The Gandhian Philosophy of Conflict*, 28.

⁷ So, Satterthwaite and McConville, *Histories*, 48.

⁸ See Creach, *Joshua*, 59–61.

⁹ Brueggemann, *Introduction*, 113–14 citing Blenkinsopp, *The Pentateuch: An Introduction to the First Five Books of the Bible* and von Rad, *The Problem of the Hexateuch and Other Essays*.

¹⁰ For close readings of these texts see Trible, *Texts of Terror*.

¹¹ The LXX adds "for she was dead" to 19:28.

¹² In my view, given the male perspective of this entire passage, gender specificity should be retained here.

¹³ Trible, *Texts of Terror*, 66.

¹⁴ See, for example, Wiersbe, *Be Available*, 97–100 and Keil and Delitzsch, *Commentary on the Old Testament*, 388–95.

¹⁵ Brueggemann, *Introduction*, 369.

¹⁶ See Brueggemann, *Introduction*, 343–9.

¹⁷ Brueggemann, *Introduction*, 348.

¹⁸ Brueggemann, *Introduction*, 348.

9 – Reading Wisdom Literature (Job – Song of Solomon)

¹ Brueggemann, *Introduction*, 295.

² Brueggemann, *Introduction*, 296.

³ See the discussion on Job 23:13–14 in Clines, *Job 21–37*, 599–600.

⁴ Brueggemann, *Introduction*, 298.

⁵ Janzen, *Job*, 254.

⁶ This is a very different translation from the NRSV's "therefore I despise myself, and repent in dust and ashes," which uses the traditional interpretation as the lens to translate the ambiguous Hebrew of 42:6. However, both Guttiérez, *On Job: God-Talk and the Suffering of the Innocent*, 86–7, cited in Brueggemann, *Introduction*, 299, and Janzen, *Job*, 254–9 powerfully argue for the reading I adopt.

7 Miles, *God: A Biography*, 429–30, cited in Brueggemann, *Introduction*, 300.
8 Brueggemann, *Introduction*, 301.
9 Brueggemann, *The Message of the Psalms: A Theological Commentary* (Augsburg Old Testament Studies; Minneapolis: Augsburg, 1984).
10 Pietersen, "Commentary: Ecclesiastes 1:2–11," 22.
11 Brueggemann, *Introduction*, 324–5.
12 This definition comes from a lecture on the Song of Solomon by John Rogerson I heard as a postgraduate at the University of Sheffield. I am unaware of it being in print.
13 Brueggemann, *Introduction*, 326.

10 – Reading the Prophets (Isaiah – Malachi)

1 Thigpen, "The Second Coming: How Many Views?" 42, my emphasis.
2 Ladd, *The Presence of the Future: The Eschatology of Biblical Realism* (Grand Rapids: Eerdmans, 1974), 64–65.
3 For these forms see Fee and Stuart, *How to Read the Bible for All Its Worth*, 158–61.
4 See Brueggemann, *Introduction*, 159–75.
5 Brueggemann, *Introduction*, 186.
6 O'Connor, *Lamentations and the Tears of the World*, 78–79 cited in Brueggemann, *Introduction*, 342.
7 See Lind, *Ezekiel*, 13.
8 See, for example, Murray, *Post-Christendom*, 298.
9 For a slightly different arrangement, but also emphasizing the significance of the "Song of the Sea" for Ezekiel, see Lind, *Ezekiel*, 18–19.
10 For further reflection on the relationship between the secular city and the holy sanctuary see Lind, *Ezekiel*, 360–62.
11 Collins, "Introduction", 7.
12 See Wink, *Unmasking the Powers: The Invisible Forces that Determine Human Existence* (Philadelphia: Fortress Press, 1986), 88–93.
13 See Brueggemann, *Introduction*, 259–61.

11 – Reading the Gospels and Acts

1 See the discussion in Burridge, *What Are the Gospels?: A Comparison with Graeco-Roman Biography*, 275–9.

² Burridge gives the example of a speech by the Caledonian chief, Calgacus, in *Agricola* 30–32. The chief apparently speaks perfect Latin and knows a great deal about Roman behavior that, historically, would not be possible. Yet this speech is "true" in the sense that it conveys accurately the sentiments of Roman opponents. See Burridge, *Four Gospels, One Jesus?*, 166–8. For a detailed discussion of truth and historicity in relation to John as ancient biography, see Lincoln, *Truth on Trial: The Lawsuit Motif in the Fourth Gospel*, 369–97.

³ Burridge, *Four Gospels*, 168.

⁴ See Burridge, *What Are the Gospels?*, 248–51.

⁵ Burridge, *What Are the Gospels?*, 249.

⁶ What follows consists of the results of my own close reading of the texts, teaching various undergraduate courses on the Gospels, together with what I have learned from commentaries, too numerous to mention, over the years.

⁷ For an accessible introduction to the Synoptic Problem see Goodacre, *The Synoptic Problem: A Way Through the Maze.*

⁸ Josephus, *War* 2.258–263.

⁹ Wink's memorable phrase in Wink, *Engaging the Powers.*

¹⁰ Lincoln, *Truth on Trial.*

¹¹ Lincoln, *Truth on Trial*, 23.

¹² Lincoln, *Truth on Trial*, 30. For this whole section see Lincoln, *Truth on Trial*, 29–33.

¹³ Talbert, *Reading Acts: A Literary and Theological Commentary on the Acts of the Apostles*, xvi.

¹⁴ However, there are still a number of commentators who regard Luke-Acts as ancient historiography. See, for example, Witherington III, *The Acts of the Apostles: A Socio-Rhetorical Commentary*, 2–24.

¹⁵ Talbert, *Reading Acts*, xxi–ii.

12 – Reading the Letters and Revelation

¹ Dunn summarises this position neatly: "The striking feature about the Pastorals at this point is that although they bear the name of Paul they contain only a few echoes of the powerful and characteristic expressions of Pauline thought," Dunn, *Unity and Diversity in the New Testament* (London: SCM, 1977), 196–7. For my view, including the possibility that the Pastorals may actually have been written by

Timothy, see Pietersen, *The Polemic of the Pastorals: A Sociological Examination of the Development of Pauline Christianity.*

2 The interplay between contingency and coherence forms the basis of Beker's important work on Paul: Beker, *Paul the Apostle: The Triumph of God in Life and Thought.*

3 See especially Schubert, *The Form and Function of the Pauline Thanksgivings* (Berlin: Alfred Töpelmann, 1939). Schubert's position has subsequently been refined but his basic hypothesis has not been refuted.

4 The data is summarized differently by Aune, *The New Testament in Its Literary Environment* and Stowers, *Letter Writing in Greco-Roman Antiquity.* The classification followed here is that of Stowers.

5 Witherington III and Hyatt, *Paul's Letter to the Romans: A Socio-Rhetorical Commentary*, 21–22. Witherington has done a whole series of socio-rhetorical commentaries and these should be consulted for examples of rhetorical analyses of some of Paul's other letters.

6 Martyn, *Galatians: A New Translation with Introduction and Commentary*, 565.

7 Beker, *Paul's Apocalyptic Gospel: The Coming Triumph of God*; Martyn, *Galatians*; Harink, *Paul among the Postliberals.*

8 Harink, *Paul among the Postliberals*, 68.

9 Hays, *Echoes of Scripture in the Letters of Paul*, 121.

10 Harink, *Paul among the Postliberals*, 43–44. Wright has argued against the view of the apocalyptic Paul articulated by Beker and Martyn, suggesting that any talk of God invading the world in Christ inevitably negates creation and covenant theology. See Wright, *Paul: In Fresh Perspective* (Minneapolis: Fortress, 2009), 50–58. However, as the quote above demonstrates, a nuanced understanding of Paul's apocalyptic theology both affirms creation and covenant but understands that something decisive had to happen to redeem creation and covenant from the distorting effects of the Powers.

11 See, for example, Crossan and Reed, *In Search of Paul: How Jesus' Apostle Opposed Rome's Empire with God's Kingdom*; Horsley, *Paul and Empire: Religion and Power in Roman Imperial Society*; Horsley, *In the Shadow of Empire: Reclaiming the Bible as a History of Faithful Resistance*; Wright, *Paul: In Fresh Perspective.* For a dissenting view, see Kim, *Christ and Caesar: The Gospel and the Roman Empire in the Writings of Paul and Luke* but this has been subject to a devastating critique by Carter, *Review of Christ and Caesar: The Gospel and the Roman Empire in the Writings of Paul and Luke.*

[12] See, for example, Said, *Orientalism;* Sugirtharajah, *Postcolonial Criticism and Biblical Interpretation.*

[13] Crossan, "Roman Imperial Theology", 59.

[14] See Crossan, "Roman Imperial Theology", 59–62.

[15] Crossan, "Roman Imperial Theology", 73.

[16] Wright, *Paul,* 76–77.

[17] Wright, *Paul,* 77–79.

[18] Marshall, Travis and Paul, *The Letters and Revelation,* 234. I have adapted their table slightly.

[19] See Johnson, *The Writings of the New Testament: An Interpretation,* 463–4.

[20] Commentators are divided on this issue. See, for example, the discussion in Lane, *Hebrews 9–13,* 417–19.

[21] See Yoder, *The Politics of Jesus,* 163–92.

[22] See Johnson, *Writings,* 561–69. I find this interpretation quite compelling, although it has not been accepted by any major commentator.

[23] See especially Bauckham, *The Theology of the Book of Revelation,* 12–17.

[24] In both Hebrew and Greek letters were used to refer to numbers. So every name had a numerical equivalent. The Greek letters for Jesus add up to 888.

[25] For further details see Bauckham, *The Climax of Prophecy,* 1–22.

[26] This outline of the main themes is indebted to Bauckham, *The Climax of Prophecy.*

[27] For further excellent insights into the book of Revelation see Rowland, "The Book of Revelation: Introduction, Commentary and Reflections," and Woodman, *The Book of Revelation.*

13 – Reading the Bible for Spirituality

[1] Schneiders, "The Study of Christian Spirituality: Contours and Dynamics of a Discipline," 5–6.

[2] Wink, *Transforming Bible Study,* 77–78.

[3] Boers, et al., *Take Our Moments and Our Days: An Anabaptist Prayer Book: Ordinary Time.*

[4] For the classic exposition on Jesus and the Spirit see Dunn, *Jesus and the Spirit.*

[5] Crossan, *Historical Jesus,* 341.

⁶ See O'Collins, "Crucifixion", 1207–1208.

⁷ *Contra* Nelson, *First and Second Kings*, 124, who insists that it "is a completely unwarranted assumption" that God's presence is indicated in the fourth event.

⁸ See Marcus, *The Way of the Lord: Christological Exegesis of the Old Testament in the Gospel of Mark*, 80–93.

⁹ Dowd, *Reading Mark: A Literary and Theological Commentary on the Second Gospel*, 91.

¹⁰ Litwa, "2 Corinthians 3:18 and Its Implications for Theosis", 125, n.28.

¹¹ Litwa, "Theosis", 117–33.

¹² Gorman, *Inhabiting the Cruciform God: Kenosis, Justification, and Theosis in Paul's Narrative Soteriology*.

¹³ Litwa, "Theosis", 129–30.

¹⁴ Litwa, "Theosis", 131–32.

14 – Reading the Bible for Mission

¹ See especially Stark, *The Rise of Christianity: A Sociologist Reconsiders History*.

² Kreider and Kreider, *Worship and Mission After Christendom*, ch.7.

³ Kreider and Kreider, *Worship and Mission*, 26.

⁴ See Murray, *Post-Christendom*, 217–50 for further details.

⁵ See Bartley, *Faith and Politics After Christendom: The Church as a Movement for Anarchy*, 206–208.

⁶ See page 118.

⁷ Brueggemann, *Biblical Perspectives on Evangelism: Living in a Three-Storied Universe*, 16–19.

⁸ Walsh and Keesmaat, *Colossians Remixed: Subverting the Empire*, 85.

⁹ See, for example, Kreider, et al., *A Culture of Peace: God's Vision for the Church*.

¹⁰ See the examples in Wink, *Engaging the Powers*, 231–57.

¹¹ I appreciate that in this particular narrative Goliath is finally killed by David but, in New Testament terms, "killing" takes place by the word of God (Rev. 19:21)! Jesus, of course, clearly advocates nonviolence (Matt. 5:43–48).

¹² For a penetrating critique of family as a contemporary idol see Walter, *A Long Way from Home: A Sociological Exploration of Contemporary Idolatry*.

¹³ I am conscious that the above exposition seems like demonizing these ancient gods. In pointing out their idolatrous nature I am arguing that they are to be resisted but this is not to say that money, enjoyment, erotic love, technology, family, medicine, etc. are demonic. Col. 1:15–20 announces the reconciliation of all things in Christ. Mars, of course, in being reconciled is also transformed (Isa. 2:4).

¹⁴ Walsh and Keesmaat, *Colossians Remixed*.

¹⁵ Walsh and Keesmaat, *Colossians Remixed*, 136–7.

¹⁶ Walsh, *Slipstream Podcast 7 – Brian Walsh and Sylvia Keesmaat*.

¹⁷ Walsh and Keesmaat, *Colossians Remixed*, 39.

15 – Conclusion

¹ See, for example Ps. 19:1–6; Rom. 1:19–23.

² Barth, *Church Dogmatics*, 84.

³ As Albert Schweitzer pointed out brilliantly in his *Quest of the Historical Jesus* (1906), the attempt to write a definitive "life of Jesus" is doomed to failure and the quest for the historical Jesus simply results in the reconstruction of a Jesus who is the mirror-image of the writer. The various portraits of Jesus, arising from the so-called "Third Quest", as sage, wandering Cynic, charismatic miracle-worker, eschatological prophet, preacher of social change, etc. continue to demonstrate the validity of Schweitzer's conclusions.

⁴ See Kreider and Kreider, *Worship and Mission*.